JOSEPH
LOWERY'S
beyond

dreamweaver®

New Riders

201 West 103rd Street Indianapolis, IN 46290
An imprint of Pearson Education
Boston • Indianapolis • London • Munich • New York • San Francisco

Joseph Lowery's Beyond Dreamweaver®

Copyright © 2003 by Joseph Lowery

International Standard Book Number: 0-7357-1277-8

Library of Congress Catalog Card Number: 2001099405

Printed in the United States of America

First edition: November 2002

06 05 04 03 02   7 6 5 4 3 2

Interpretation of the printing code: The rightmost double-digit number is the year of the book's printing; the rightmost single-digit number is the number of the book's printing. For example, the printing code 02-1 shows that the first printing of the book occurred in 2002.

Trademarks

Warning and Disclaimer

Publisher
David Dwyer

Associate Publisher
Stephanie Wall

Editor in Chief
Chris Nelson

Production Manager
Gina Kanouse

Senior Acquisitions Editor
Linda Anne Bump

Senior Marketing Manager
Tammy Detrich

Publicity Manager
Susan Nixon

Senior Development Editor
Jennifer Eberhardt

Senior Project Editor
Lori Lyons

Copy Editor
Karen A. Gill

Indexer
Chris Morris

Composition
Gloria Schurick

Manufacturing Coordinator
Jim Conway

Book/Cover Designer
Alan Clements

Media Developer
Jay Payne

For my daughter, Margot, as she goes Beyond…

Contents at a Glance

Table of Contents

Part II   Automations   77

Part III Extensions   161

About the Author

 Joseph Lowery's books on the web and web-building tools are international bestsellers, having sold more than 300,000 copies worldwide in nine different languages. He is the author of the *Dreamweaver MX Bible* and the *Fireworks MX Bible* series as well as *From FrontPage to Dreamweaver* from Que Publishing. As a programmer, Joseph contributed two extensions to the latest release of Fireworks MX and many extensions for Dreamweaver. He is also a consultant and trainer and has presented at Seybold in both Boston and San Francisco, Macromedia UCON in the U.S. and Europe, ThunderLizard's Web World, and Fawcette Publication's WebBuilder. As a partner in Deva Associates, Ltd., Joseph developed the Deva Tools for Dreamweaver set of navigational extensions.

About the Contributing Author

Joe Marini received his bachelor of science degree in computer engineering technology from the Rochester Institute of Technology in 1991. He has been developing software professionally for 15 years for companies such as Quark, mFactor, and Macromedia, and is a founding partner of his own company, Lepton Technologies. While at Macromedia, Marini was an original member of the Dreamweaver development team and represented the company at the W3C's DOM Working Group. Marini lives and works in San Francisco, California with his wife, Stacy, and dog, Milo.

About the Technical Reviewers

These reviewers contributed their considerable hands-on expertise to the entire development process for *Joseph Lowery's Beyond Dreamweaver*. As the book was being written, these dedicated professionals reviewed all the material for technical content, organization, and flow. Their feedback was critical to ensuring that *Joseph Lowery's Beyond Dreamweaver* fit our readers' need for the highest-quality technical information.

Lon Coley is an information technology professional who specializes in Internet solutions and the Internet in education. She has been active professionally within the Internet sector for five years, working with companies and colleges that want to understand and expand into the Internet in the modern working environment.

A firm believer that anyone can build a web site with the right tools and training, Lon often works with companies that want to develop their own web sites but think they need an expert to call on when they are struggling. She also assists companies that need professional guidance about new technologies and want to avoid common pitfalls when developing their existing sites.

An experienced teacher and trainer, Lon writes and develops dedicated customized training courses for both business and education. These courses cover the Macromedia and Microsoft product families and are always prepared with the individual client in mind. In this way, Lon can guarantee that the needs of the client are addressed and met in full. She has written or contributed to a variety of titles, including *How to Use Dreamweaver MX and Fireworks MX*, *Flash Site Workshop*, and *Special Edition Using Flash MX*.

You can contact Lon at `LonColey@ariadne-webdesign.co.uk` and learn more about Lon's activities at `http://www.ariadne-webdesign.co.uk`.

Stephen Jacobs is a tenured assistant professor of information technology with the B. Thomas Golisano College of Computing and Information Sciences at the Rochester Institute of Technology. He's been a technical editor for *Web Site Programming with Java* and *The Dreamweaver Bible*. He's been a contributing editor for *Videomaker*, *Television Business International*, *Television 2.0* magazines, and the CNET technology web site. He was an interface designer and content editor for the "Break It, Fix It, Ride It" mountain bike repair CD-ROM. He edits and publishes the consumer technology web site The Gadgetboy Gazette at `http://www.gadgetboy.com`.

Acknowledgments

This book, as my dad used to say, has been a long row to hoe. I'd like to express my gratitude to those who helped with the cultivation. First and foremost on that list is my agent, Laura Belt, who helped me shape the Beyond idea and give it form. I also want to extend my warmest appreciation to Steve Jacobs and Lon Coley, who toiled on this book as Technical Editors under the most arduous circumstances.

Joe Marini did a great job uncovering some of Dreamweaver's better buried secrets, and I really appreciate his expertise and skill. My good friend Massimo Foti also had a significant impact on the book as he has on the Dreamweaver community as a whole; a special thank you to him for introducing me to the talents of Edoardo Zubler—I hope we all get to work together in the near future.

Additional thank you's go out to Bob Regan, Paolo Brajnik, and Jason Taylor of UsableNet for their time and efforts in clarifying accessibility issues. Tim Kennedy, author of *SMIL: Adding Multimedia to the Web*, was likewise helpful in regard to that technology.

I owe a gaggle of folks at New Riders a thank you. Jeff Schultz, my original Acquisitions Editor, was also tremendously supportive and, occasionally, pretty funny. Added thanks to David Dwyer and Chris Nelson for listening to my notions and indulging my questions. Jennifer Eberhardt contributed much of the hands-on work in tending this little patch of promise; she, like the best gardeners, exhibits tremendous patience and judicious, but ruthless editing ability. Special thanks to Linda Bump for stepping in mid-project; I'm sure we'll have lots of opportunities to plant other seeds and see them through to daylight.

Finally, all the best to the wonderful Dreamweaver team. I can't thank you enough for providing the one seed from which this entire garden of productivity has grown.

Tell Us What You Think

As the reader of this book, you are the most important critic and commentator. We value your opinion and want to know what we're doing right, what we could do better, what areas you'd like to see us publish in, and any other words of wisdom you're willing to pass our way.

As the Editor on this book, I welcome your comments. You can fax, email, or write me directly to let me know what you did or didn't like about this book—as well as what we can do to make our books stronger. When you write, please be sure to include this book's title, ISBN, and author, as well as your name and phone or fax number. I will carefully review your comments and share them with the author and editors who worked on the book.

Please note that I cannot help you with technical problems related to the topic of this book, and that due to the high volume of email I receive, I might not be able to reply to every message.

Fax: 317-581-4663

Email: linda.bump@newriders.com

Mail: Linda Bump
                New Riders Publishing
                201 West 103rd Street
                Indianapolis, IN 46290 USA

Foreword

Dreamweaver is the result of a collective effort by many people. Leading the endeavor is a core of dedicated software engineers who, with great skill and passion, design and implement each new version. To honor them and their work, I offered the Dreamweaver engineers a chance to voice their thoughts on the past, present, and future of Dreamweaver. Here is what they—the ultimate weavers of dreams—had to say:

Heidi Bauer Williams

Team Lead, Site Setup, New Document Dialog, Tag Inspector, XML Support

For me, Dreamweaver MX is the most revolutionary release since Dreamweaver 1.0. For the first version, no one believed we could build a visual tool that was appealing to hand-coders, but we did it. For MX, we had the impossible task of making one product appeal to hand-coders, designers, application developers, scripters, and technology gurus alike, but we've done that, too.

With Dreamweaver MX, web teams are even more efficient and productive because every team member can use the same tool to get their work done. The number of features added to this release is astounding, but they all come together in one unified workspace for more power and flexibility than you can possibly imagine. But be warned—once you use it, you can never go back!

Winsha Chen

Insert Bar, Snippets, Image Placeholder

Dreamweaver MX is jam-packed with some amazing features, and the new workspace makes it a great environment for everyone: hand coders, designers, and web application developers. The clean workspace hides the complexity inside. Dreamweaver simplifies the process of creating HTML and web applications. As a team, we really try to understand the issues that users encounter in their daily work and then build the best darn product to help them create amazing web sites. There have been a countless number of nights where some engineer has worked extra hard to squeeze in that last feature or fix that bug users keep running into.

Robert Christensen

JavaScript Extension Development. Tag Editors, Server Behaviors

Every release since its inception, the Dreamweaver development team has been challenged to provide innovative features that offer timesaving solutions to complex problems for its customers. It is our hope that Dreamweaver MX release, which includes more than 100 new features, has answered this challenge and that we've succeeded in providing useful and usable features for all types of Dreamweaver users (from application developers hoping to work with web services to providing better CSS support for designers). Please keep those feature requests coming by sending an email to wish-dreamweaver@macromedia.com. We read every one!

George Comninos

Site Management, FTP, Mac OS X Port, Flash Integration

Combine all the great design-oriented features of the previous versions of Dreamweaver with all the web application development features of UltraDev, and throw in a whole slew of new features for every type of user, and you have Dreamweaver MX. I've been with this team for more than four years, and this has by far been the toughest release; but the end result is also the most complete web development solution available anywhere. With this release, I think we've addressed all areas ranging from a vastly improved workspace to becoming a true coding environment for the hand coders. A big thanks to all our customers, who in the end are the ones who really make Dreamweaver a success. And, of course, there will be a lot more to come, [so] please keep the feedback coming.

David Deming

Product Manager

There are a couple of things that I really wanted to accomplish with the Dreamweaver MX release: I wanted to give every web developer out there easy access to building web applications. Those skills have been locked away in ivory towers long enough. I wanted to open up that world to a new class of people. At the same time, I wanted to make Dreamweaver into a more integrated development environment. People love writing code by hand, whether HTML, JavaScript, what have you. When I hear of people using Dreamweaver MX almost entirely in Code view, I smile because no one would have thought of using Dreamweaver that way in the past! Finally, I wanted to regain that cutting-edge feel of the product. We took a few risks with forward-looking technologies that aren't really in mainstream use today (ASP.NET, Web Services, CSS2, and XHTML come to mind), but I think they're important for developers to learn and expand their skills. I want people to feel like Dreamweaver will grow with them. Basically, in the end, I wanted a tool that all sorts of web developers would be happy to sit in front of all day, every day, as they go about their job of building the Internet.

Randy Edmunds

Server Model Extensibility, Code Coloring Extensibility, Database Panel, Extension Manager

I am excited to see Dreamweaver grow from a web page tool to a web application development platform. Every new feature of Dreamweaver has extensibility built in from the start, so the user can tailor the product to fit most any need. I can't wait to see how our users will extend Dreamweaver further than the developers ever imagined. Thanks, Joe, for helping to make that happen.

Nick Halbakken

Quality Assurance Manager for Dreamweaver MX

One of the major challenges in building Dreamweaver, especially Dreamweaver MX, has been balancing the needs of the variety of users and user knowledge levels. Technologies like CSS and ASP are good examples of where this challenge comes up. We strive to build a tool that can allow someone who has little experience with these technologies to successfully use them to create and enhance web sites, while also providing convenience and power for a user who is very familiar with the technologies. We've put many hours of thought into this difficult problem, and will continue to make improvements, such as the optional MDI-style interface introduced with Dreamweaver MX.

Russ Helfand

ASP.NET, Runtime Code, ColdFusion Components, Code Trust, Parser/Formatter

During the year and a half it took to build Dreamweaver MX, I imagine nearly every engineer was touched by inspiration at least once. It may seem crazy, but that one moment, or just the potential for such a moment, is enough to keep you going when it is 3 a.m. and your eyes are burning and the screen has become a hideous blur of garbled characters and unintelligible icons. In that moment, when inspiration strikes, your vision seems so clear, your hands (that were shaking from caffeine) grow steady, and in a sudden rush you "understand." Some of those moments of inspiration led to the features you'll come to love in Dreamweaver MX. Sometimes they ended up as low-level algorithms or chunks of obscure architecture that few people will ever stop to notice but are essential to the Dreamweaver MX machine. It doesn't really matter. The feeling, in the end, is the same. The accolades and recognition, which may or may not follow, are immaterial, really. It is my sincere hope that Dreamweaver MX will be a vehicle to inspire others—that it unleashes your potential, your creativity, and your genius.

Noah Hoffman

Installers; Build Environment

I think the most amazing thing about being a part of the Dreamweaver team is the quality of people I work with. This is without a doubt, the most enthusiastic, fun, creative, and dedicated group of people. It's a team that cares about honoring everyone's input, fostering individuality and working together to design the best software we possibly can. There are people on this team with years of industry experience who say this is the best group they've ever worked with, and I can believe it. But the best thing is that people really love what we make. I'd like to think this is in part because the spirit of the team somehow comes through when people use the product.

Lori Hylan

JavaScript Engineering; Pop-Up Menus, Objects, Tag Editors, Commands

From an engineering point of view, this release cycle was our longest and toughest yet, and about halfway through I wondered if it was worth it: Did we have enough compelling features? Would people actually want to use this product? As a former web developer (and current maintainer of two personal sites), I was able to answer that question for myself when I made the switch from Dreamweaver 4 to Dreamweaver MX a few weeks later.

The new interface alone would make me upgrade.

That's just the shiny red paint on the new car, though. Under the hood are all kinds of features that make building and maintaining sites so much easier than it was last year (and don't even get me started on what it was like seven or eight years ago): better templates, better CSS support, a new Insert bar, better code editing, you name it… and I haven't even gotten to the web application building options. It's very gratifying to see the wide range of customers that Dreamweaver MX is serving, and serving well. I guess the hard work and sleep deprivation were worth it after all.

Narciso Jaramillo (nj)

Helped design the Dreamweaver MX Workspace; General UI Kibitzing

When we started working on Dreamweaver 1.0 in 1997, we wanted to create a tool for both designers and coders, but we knew coders weren't comfortable with visual web editing tools. Web application servers were just starting to enter wide use. Many people were still hacking CGI scripts and building database connectivity with ad-hoc tools, and the phrase *web services* hadn't yet been coined. CSS was gaining traction, but it didn't work well across browsers. DHTML and "push technology" looked like the next big things, and XML was still just a gleam in the W3C's eye.

A lot has changed since then! The Dreamweaver MX team took on the challenge of reinventing the product from the ground up and produced a truly revolutionary release, one that both reflects the changes in the web landscape and points the way forward to the future.

I didn't play a large role in this release of Dreamweaver, but I did see how hard the team worked getting MX out the door—on time, and with more features than anyone imagined. I'm especially impressed with the way the team worked together with the ColdFusion and HomeSite teams, which joined Macromedia just at the beginning of last year, to produce a truly integrated application development suite. Many kudos to the whole team, and all the teams that worked together to make MX a reality. Now they just need to get some sleep!

Sho Kuwamoto

VP of Product Development, Dreamweaver Products

I remember interviewing with the Dreamweaver team right as the project was first starting back in January 1997. I entered the interview a bit skeptical. Could a web authoring tool really be flexible enough to meet the needs of professionals? During the interview, I started getting more and more excited. One thing I remember saying was that "This tool should be like emacs. The top layer of the tool should be built in a language that people have access to so that they can customize it to do whatever they want." The person I was interviewing with agreed wholeheartedly, and we kept talking about this and that, getting more excited the whole time. Shortly after, I joined the team and never looked back.

So, as you (probably) know, we built Dreamweaver to be almost ludicrously extensible and customizable, and this has served us well. I'm continually surprised at all the things power users do with Dreamweaver.

With Dreamweaver MX, we put a great deal of emphasis on the power user. We vastly improved our support for standards, added powerful new features for hand coders, and beefed up the extensibility model (again). It's amazing how much effect this is having already. People who I had never imagined would use a visual tool are telling me that they've switched.

Given this renewed emphasis on power users, I'm especially glad that Joe is writing this book. If it's anything like his other books, I'll learn things that I myself didn't know about the tool!

David Lenoe

Quality Assurance Management

Our goal on the Dreamweaver team is to revolutionize web development, and I believe we've made a significant step in that direction with the Dreamweaver MX release. In the course of the development process, we also conducted some interesting sleep deprivation experiments, but that's another story. Since our focus is making you, the Dreamweaver user, productive and happy, please keep the feedback—be it good, bad, or ugly—coming! With your help, we'll make the next version even more amazing.

Josh Margulis

Tag Chooser and File Browser

My goal for this release was to improve the experience for hand coders and app developers. Hand coders had little help in previous releases to quickly put tags onto the page; this is no longer true with the addition of so many coder features in Dreamweaver MX. The Tag Chooser and Tag Editor dialogs let coders quickly find the sets of tags they want to use and the appropriate attributes they want to set. The File Browser was a much-needed feature; a lot of our customers like to get at files from other projects they've worked on, and now they can do this from within Dreamweaver.

I'm very proud of what the Dreamweaver team was able to accomplish in one release. The product is leaps and bounds better than Dreamweaver 4 and addresses problems for so many designers and developers.

Jeff Schang

CSS Rendering and User Interface, JavaScript Debugger; also reviewed Extensibility Interfaces for consistency

Dreamweaver has always been focused on helping web developers get their job done and not interfering with the code as much as possible. Dreamweaver MX puts a lot of emphasis on working with standards, such as CSS and XHTML. We look at what the people ahead of the curve are doing. A developer can use Dreamweaver to expand his skills without being forced to adopt a different way of working.

Introduction

Wherever I talk to Web developers, I hear the same stories. The work is there, but the budgets are tight and resources are laughable—if they exist at all. Bosses and clients need to squeeze out more productivity at a lower cost; their jobs—and the developer's future job opportunities—are at stake. Do more with less is the order of the day, and do it now. Traditional boundaries between designer and coder are being blurred, if not dissipated altogether, by the work pressure. Web site creation has moved well past vanilla HTML. New standards and technologies break like waves, and developers must master them on-the-fly or go under. I hear the same stories wherever I go.

Beyond Dreamweaver is my reply. The title is not meant to lessen Dreamweaver—I'm certainly not suggesting that the program should be left behind. Far from it; it's latest incarnation, Dreamweaver MX, has more reach and power than ever before. Rather, my goal with this book is to demonstrate how the professional web developer can go further with Dreamweaver than ever before.

In one sense, Dreamweaver is a roadmap into the uncharted territories of web development. You know there must be a way to integrate your content management system with Dreamweaver, but how exactly is it done? You're sure there is a faster, more efficient way to bring your site into Section 508 compliance, but what are the techniques? You've seen Dreamweaver extensions boost productivity generally, but what's the key to dissolving your specific production roadblocks? I wrote *Beyond Dreamweaver* to answer these questions, and more.

Beyond Dreamweaver is also a celebration: I love this program. I love how the Dreamweaver engineers anticipate user needs with entire open architectures rather than locked-down single features. I love pushing Dreamweaver to the absolute limit and then finding a way to work past the limitations. I love Dreamweaver because the program constantly surprises me with its flexibility, grace, and brute strength.

Beyond Dreamweaver's Content

Beyond Dreamweaver is a need-driven book. I've seen more and more companies moving toward content management systems and looking for ways to integrate their authoring tools. I've received numerous emails from web developers looking for guidance and techniques on Section 508 compliance. I've been approached at conferences with questions about all sorts of multimedia technology, including SMIL. The initial section of the book is devoted to these particular cries for help.

As you look over the book's table of contents, you might notice a pattern. There is a progression from the more specific—CMS and accessibility—to the more general—cross-product integration and broad-spectrum extensibility. I wanted to cover Dreamweaver as I see it: a multilayered tool that grows in scope the deeper you dig. In the middle layer, you'll find an emphasis on Dreamweaver power features, including templates and XML connectivity. Armed with in-depth knowledge of capabilities such as these, your efficiency and production level can soar.

The last part of the book reflects a deep love of mine: extensibility. It's true that I derive great personal enjoyment from building extensions—it's a left brain/right brain kind of thing—but I don't expect everyone to begin building Dreamweaver extensions. No, I'm more interested in exposing the possibilities of Dreamweaver extensibility to a wider audience. Think of it as a paradigm shift: Once you know something can be done—whether it is cross-communicating with Flash and Dreamweaver or adding whole new layers of authoring functionality with C-level extensions—you can make it happen.

Beyond Dreamweaver's Audience

To get the most out of this book, you need to have some web and some Dreamweaver experience under your belt. I don't spend any time explaining the history of the web or what a library item is; there are a tremendous number of books out there for that. If you're looking for a general reference—and Dreamweaver MX is such a big program that I think you really need one to really get the most out of the software—try my *Dreamweaver MX Bible* or New Rider's *Inside Dreamweaver MX*.

Beyond Dreamweaver is really for working web developers and designers who need to overcome challenges in their work and push their designs further. If you're working on a corporate web site and are looking for techniques to facilitate your workflow, you'll find a lot of material here. If your workgroup just got hit with an increase in production responsibility without an increase in resources, *Beyond Dreamweaver* can help automate your efforts. If you're working on your own and need to blow the competition out of the water—but stay under budget—*Beyond Dreamweaver* will give you the edge you need.

Beyond Dreamweaver's Code

Beyond Dreamweaver is a solution-oriented detailed book. In many cases, I dig deep through code to explain how a function or extension really works so that you can gather the maximum benefit. To smooth the learning curve, this book has a number of special, code-related features.

First, you'll notice that the code is commented from within and without. In addition to standard HTML and JavaScript comments, you'll find pointers or callouts to specific sections of the code to help emphasize key points easily overlooked in a block of code.

When code is discussed in a chapter, I typically break it down into meaningful chunks. Because I also wanted readers to be able to grasp the code as a whole, you'll find the complete listings for all the code being discussed. At the beginning of each discussion, you'll find a Note that contains a reference to the listing that reproduces the code, and that code listing will appear at the end of the discussion. These listings, along with a few Bonus Listings, will also appear on this book's web site at www.idest.com/beyond.

You'll find all manner of code here—HTML, JavaScript, XML, ASP, ColdFusion, Fireworks, JavaScript, and Flash .FLA—because the world of the web developer is a multilingual one.

Beyond Dreamweaver's Web Site

Numerous extensions and other files are referenced throughout the book. You'll find them all posted on the *Beyond Dreamweaver* web site: www.idest.com/beyond. I'll also post links to resources and new examples as they become available.

As always, if you have a comment, question, or complaint, let me hear about it: jlowery@idest.com.

I remember this quote from a bio of Isaac Newton I read in the 5th grade: "If I've seen further than others, it is because I have stood on the shoulders of giants." For me, Dreamweaver is a true giant with lots of room on those shoulders for all of us. Time for you to see what you can see—here, let me give you a hand…

Part I

Connections

Chapter 1

Incorporating Content Management Systems

For many in business, the phrase *content management system* (CMS) has almost a magical ring. Managers look to content management to get a handle on the vast amount of information that a company must output and utilize—simultaneously lowering costs and return on investment (ROI). Contributors—writers and editors—want a CMS that will simplify their workflow and let them concentrate on the content rather than the presentation of the material. Publishers, including Web designers and developers, need a system that allows them to focus on the look and feel of the site, regardless of the content.

As the flood of information continues to rise, more organizations are considering purchasing or developing a CMS. What is Dreamweaver's role in a content management system?

Although the degree of integration depends on the system used, Dreamweaver can significantly ease the burden of manager, contributor, and publisher. With many available content management systems, Dreamweaver becomes a flexible front end. For a custom Web-based CMS, Dreamweaver has the power to develop the necessary administrative tools. Dreamweaver is also capable of serving as an automated file generator, combining content and layout in an output page.

The quest for a content management system fully integrated into a company's workflow is often long, arduous, and expensive. Rather than provide a canned CMS that might prove inadequate in one area or another, the goal of this chapter is to demonstrate how Dreamweaver can be engineered to support your chosen CMS, whether commercial or developed.

Integrating with Existing Content Management Systems

A wide variety of commercial CMS programs are available—some standalone and some integrated into a larger e-business package. The way they work varies significantly from program to program. Although not all content management systems work with external authoring tools, those that do can benefit by integrating Dreamweaver into their workflow. Interwoven and Blue Martini—both leading commercial CMS providers—have implementations that integrate Dreamweaver. As you'll see in this chapter, Dreamweaver rises to the challenge gracefully.

To use an external editor, a CMS typically recognizes a proprietary set of markup tags, often, but not always, coded within a custom file type. Dreamweaver MX handles custom file types with ease and offers full support for third-party tags. You can enter custom tags directly into the code or visually in Design view in a number of ways, including drag-and-drop. After the custom tags are inserted, you can display them or hide them at will.

Setting Up Custom Pages

You can use two approaches to set up custom pages—one using Dreamweaver templates and the other using document types. The first method is the easiest to implement; it can be used both for standard templates in which certain areas of the page are locked and for fully editable pages, which include custom <meta> tags or comments. Following is the procedure for setting up custom pages by using a Dreamweaver template:

1. The administrator saves a blank, customized page as a Dreamweaver template in a particular site.

    If the page is to be completely editable, you don't need to add editable regions. Dreamweaver displays an alert noting the lack of such regions when the file is saved; in this instance, it is safe to ignore the alert.

2. To make a new page from the template, the designer makes a new page by choosing File > New and selecting the custom template from the Template tab.

3. For the page to be totally editable and free of template markup, clear the Update Page When Template Changes check box.

Although this technique is workable, it is less than ideal. The designer must remember where the template is located; templates are site specific, and it would be burdensome for the administrator to establish the custom page in every site on an ongoing basis. Moreover, the designer must keep an eye on the Update Page When Template Changes check box, especially if he is creating both standard templates and detached templates. This technique is perhaps best used for projects that are restricted to a small number of sites.

TIP: If a standard template is created by mistake, choose Modify > Templates > Detach from Template.

The second method of creating a new custom base page is more involved, but it's an overall pervasive solution. Although it might not be obvious, the list of documents shown in the New Document dialog box is extensible. You can add both static and dynamic custom pages—in regular or template format—to the dialog box. After these pages are integrated into Dreamweaver, the designer just chooses the custom document type from the list.

For a complete integration of a new document type, several areas must be addressed:

- A new document type XML file should be added to the Configuration folder.

- A prototype of the document should be saved in the New Documents folder.

- The documents extension(s) should be added to the Extensions.txt file.

- An editor for the document type should be assigned either on the system level or within Dreamweaver.

Adding a New Document Type

Several files found in Dreamweaver's Configuration/DocumentTypes folder control what appears in the New Document dialog box. The MMDocumentTypes.xml file describes the standard Dreamweaver documents shown in the dialog box. Although it's possible to customize this document, you shouldn't. Custom document types are best added by including a separate XML file following the same syntax as MMDocumentTypes.xml in the DocumentTypes folder.

The MMDocumentTypes.xml file consists of a series of <documenttype> tags, one for each kind of file. Here, for example, is the entry for a basic HTML page:

```
<documenttype id="HTML" internaltype="HTML" winfileextension=
"htm,html,shtml,shtm,stm,lasso,xhtml" macfileextension=
"html,htm,shtml,shtm,lasso,xhtml" file="Default.html">
    <title>
        <MMString:loadString id="mmdocumenttypes_0" />
    </title>
    <description>
        <MMString:loadString id="mmdocumenttypes_1" />
    </description>
</documenttype>
```

The attributes within the <documenttype> tag define how the entry will appear within the New Document dialog box:

- id—A unique identifier for the document type. If two or more document types have the same ID, the first one defined is used.

- internaltype—Determines what modes are available in Dreamweaver for the given document type. Valid values are HTML, HTML4, XHTML1, XML, Dynamic, DWTemplate, and DWExtension.

- dynamicid—If DWTemplate is declared as the internalType and the desired page is data driven, the dynamicid attribute must be defined. Accepted values for dynamicid correspond to the supported server models: ASP.NET C#, ASP.NET VB, ASP VBScript, ASP JavaScript, ColdFusion, JSP, and PHP MySQL (optional).

- winfileextension—The file extensions, given in a comma-separated list, for the Windows platform. Dreamweaver automatically saves new files of the document type using the first extension in the list.

- macfileextension—The file extensions, given in a comma-separated list, for the Macintosh platform.

- `file`—The file used as the prototype for the document type. By convention, the file is named `Default.fileExtension`, where *fileExtension* is the first entry in the `winfileextension` or `macfileextension` attributes, such as `Default.jwl`. All prototype files are stored in the Configuration/DocumentTypes/NewDocuments folder.

- `servermodel`—Used only in the case of dynamic document types, this attribute specifies which server model is to be used. The acceptable values are `ASP.NET C#`, `ASP.NET VB`, `ASP VBScript`, `ASP JavaScript`, `ColdFusion`, `JSP`, and `PHP MySQL`. If custom server models are developed, their names as noted in the implementation files can be used (optional).

- `previewfile`—The path to the file shown in the Preview area of the New Documents dialog box (optional).

Two tags are within the `<documenttype>` tag: `<title>` and `<description>`. Both contain text strings (or references to text strings) that are used in the New Documents dialog box display. The content in the `<title>` tag displays in the category-specific list, whereas the `<description>` appears in the Description area (see Figure 1.1).

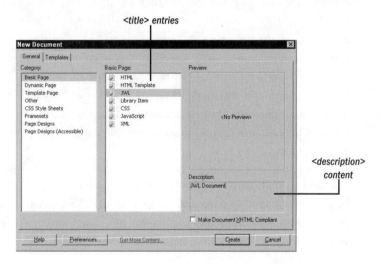

1.1

Information defined in the Document Type XML file is shown in the New Document dialog box.

Macromedia uses references to text entries within an external file (Configuration/Strings/documenttypes.xml) for localization purposes:

```
<title>
    <MMString:loadString id="mmdocumenttypes_0" />
</title>
<description>
    <MMString:loadString id="mmdocumenttypes_1" />
</description>
```

Custom document types can use plain text, like this:

```
<TITLE>
    JWL
</TITLE>
<description>
    JWL Document
</description>
```

As noted earlier, it's a better idea to define any custom document types in a separate XML file rather than to modify MMDocumentTypes.xml. To be most effective, the custom document type should be implemented at the administrator, not individual, user level. In that situation, if a new version of Dreamweaver were installed, any modified version of MMDocumentTypes.xml would be replaced. Moreover, there is no real need to alter the original file; Dreamweaver automatically reads any XML file stored in the DocumentTypes folder, incorporating the additions into the New Document dialog box.

The custom XML file must follow the structure of the MMDocumentTypes.xml file with an opening XML declaration identifying the Macromedia XML namespace, followed by a <documenttypes> tag, which encloses one or more <documenttype> tags:

```
<?xml version="1.0"?>
<documenttypes
xmlns:MMString="http://www.macromedia.com/schemes/data/string/">
    <documenttype id="JWL" internaltype="HTML"
winfileextension="jwl" macfileextension="jwl" file="Default.jwl">
        <title>
```

Pointer to prototype page

```
      JWL
    </title>
    <description>
      JWL Document
    </description>
  </documenttype>
</documenttypes>
```

Storing the Prototype

The page prototype—which could be either a static page or a Dreamweaver template—should include everything to be repeated in every file. Both code in the <head> (such as <meta> tags or other custom tags necessary to work with the CMS) and common elements in the <body> (such as a copyright line) should be included. When completed, save the file in the Configuration\DocumentTypes\NewDocuments folder. Although you're under no obligation to comply, the convention is to name the file Default combined with the needed file extension (Default.jwl).

Integrating the Document Extensions

The initial two steps—creating the document type XML file and storing the prototype—took care of making a new custom document. To open that document easily in Dreamweaver for editing, you need to perform two more steps. The first step allows custom extensions to appear in any of the Open or Select dialog boxes. To accomplish this, you need to modify the Extensions.txt file. This file is located in the root of the Configuration folder and can be edited directly in Dreamweaver.

When you open the Extension.txt file, you'll see a number of entries like this:

```
HTM,HTML,HTA,HTC:HTML Documents
SHTM,SHTML,STM,SSI,INC:Server-Side Includes
JS:JavaScript Documents
```

Custom entries follow this format of *extensions: description*. For example, if I wanted to insert an entry for the JWL documents that use the .jwl extension, I would include this line:

```
JWL:JWL Documents
```

The order of entries in the file is the same as the order in the dialog box. You can insert custom entries anywhere in the list.

Assigning the Editor

The final step to integrate a custom CMS file type into the Dreamweaver workflow is to make sure the file type is editable by Dreamweaver. You can accomplish this in two ways:

- Through the operating system. In Windows, this is done through the File Types tab of the Settings, Control Panels, Folder Options dialog box. On Macs, the best system I've found uses a freeware application called FileType. It's available at http://www.frederikseiffert.de/filetype/, and it works on both OS 9 and X.

- In Dreamweaver, add an Extension entry to the Files / Editor category of Preferences (see Figure 1.2). With the newly added extension selected, choose the Add button above the Editors list and navigate to the Dreamweaver executable.

1.2

Make Dreamweaver the primary editor for your custom file types through Preferences.

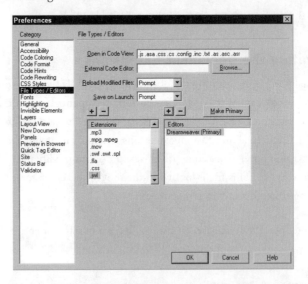

TIP: One file type can have more than one editor. Be sure to make Dreamweaver the primary editor if you want to be able to double-click on the file to open it. Otherwise, to open a custom file in the Site panel, right-click on the filename and choose Open With > Dreamweaver.

After you have completed either of these chores, double-click on any document with the custom extension in the Site panel to open that file in Dreamweaver for editing.

Adding CMS Tags Through Tag Libraries

Defining a page type has numerous benefits, including the ability to open and edit files with custom extensions. Perhaps the biggest plus, however, is defining custom tags to go with the custom page. As with page types, Dreamweaver has a multitiered support system that you can implement partially for quick coding of individual tags or completely for total integration. A key element of the Dreamweaver's tag extension layer is the Tag Library feature, where you can define custom tags with or without custom attributes and complete with formatting options.

In truth, you don't really need to do anything to use a custom tag in Dreamweaver. Nonstandard tags entered by hand are ignored, much as they would be in a browser. However, to my mind, the advantages to properly setting up custom code justify the time spent. Integrated code is easier to insert, modify, manipulate, and delete. Typographical errors are reduced to a minimum and flagged immediately. The learning curve for creating CMS-specific pages drops significantly.

Tag libraries represent one of the most far-reaching changes in Dreamweaver MX. Macromedia, in essence, placed all of the tag support within Dreamweaver in open source. Now you can modify any standard tag—HTML, ASP, ASP.NET, CFML, JSP, PHP, and more—to fit the standard coding of any organization, right down to the attribute level. More importantly, particularly when it comes to integrating into a CMS, you can create new tag libraries and link them to one or more page types. This means that for the new JLowery content management system (shipping two weeks after you read this*), I can define a JWL page type with a full complement of JWL tags and their attributes.

All tag library management is handled through the Tag Library Editor (see Figure 1.3). Let's walk through the setup of a whole new tag library, establishing a couple of custom tags with attributes.

*No, not reallly

1.3

To add several tags at one time in the Tag Library Editor, use a comma-separated list.

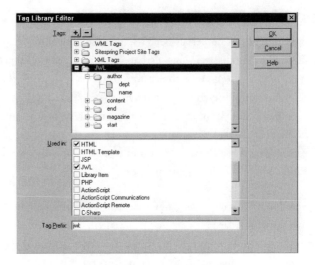

1. Choose Edit > Tag Libraries to open the Tag Library Editor.

   First, we'll establish the new tag library.

2. Select Add (+) and choose New Tag Library.

3. Enter a name for the tag library.

   The new tag library is added to the bottom of the list. I tend to use meaningful abbreviations wherever possible to identify tag libraries; in this case, I'll use JWL as the name of my tag library.

4. With the just-defined tag library still selected, choose the associated page types.

   Most CMS pages are a mix of HTML and custom tags. Be sure to select the HTML option as well as any special page types. In cases where data-driven pages are used, select the appropriate server model as well.

5. If all of the tags in the new tag library start with the same characters, such as jwl:, enter them in the Prefix field.

   Dreamweaver automatically prepends any prefix to the tags in the tag library. This simplifies the management of custom tags because they're easier to identify.

With a new tag library established, we're ready to insert the custom tags:

1. Continuing in the Tag Library Editor, make sure the new tag library is selected and select Add (+), New Tags.

   If you forget to select the desired tag library, you can choose it from the Tag Library drop-down list.

2. Enter the name for the new tag.

3. To enter multiple tags, use a comma-separated list.

4. If the tag(s) are not empty, select the Have Matching End Tags option.

   After clicking OK, you'll find the new tags under the selected tag library.

5. To control a new tag's formatting, select the tag and choose which aspect to modify:

   - **Line breaks**—Choose from No Line Breaks (default); Before and After Tag; Before, Inside and After; or After Tag Only.

   - **Contents**—Options are Not Formatted; Formatted But Not Indented (default); or Formatted and Indented.

   - **Case**—Choose from Default (default), Lowercase, Uppercase, or Mixed Case.

     The Default case is set in Preferences in the Code Format category or by selecting the Set Defaults link in the Tag Library Editor; only lowercase and uppercase options are offered in either place.

Tags can have one or more attributes. To add new attributes, follow these steps:

1. In the Tag Library Editor, select a tag you want to add attributes to and select Add (+), New Attributes.

2. Make sure that the proper tag library and tag are selected in the New Attributes dialog box and enter the name of the attribute.

   As with tags, you can create multiple attributes for a single tag by entering a comma-separated list of attributes rather than a single one.

3. To format a newly added attribute, select it and alter one or more of the following settings:

- **Case**—Again, you can choose from Default (default), Lowercase, Uppercase, or Mixed Case.

- **Type**—There are a wide range of attribute types: Text, Enumerated, Color, Directory, File Name, File Path, Flag, Font, Relative Path, and Style.

  Different attribute types display different controls in the Tag Inspector. For example, setting an attribute type to Color causes the color picker to appear when choosing a value in the Tag Inspector, as shown in Figure 1.4.

1.4

Custom attributes defined in the Tag Library Editor are much simpler to use properly; here, a color attribute is being applied via the Tag Inspector.

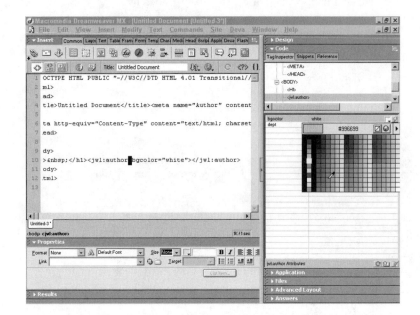

4. If you choose Enumerated as the attribute type, enter a comma-separated list of the accepted entries in the Values text area.

As you might suspect, to delete any tag library, tag, or attribute, simply select the unwanted item and choose the Remove (-) button. Changes made in the Tag Library Editor are immediate; there's no need to relaunch Dreamweaver.

After you define tags in the Tag Library Editor, open any page of the custom tag's document type and go into Code view. Type an opening angle bracket, and all of the defined tags for that tag library appear.

Customizing the Dreamweaver Workspace

Custom tag support is just the beginning when it comes to integrating Dreamweaver into a CMS workflow. Additional custom features include the following:

- **Toolbars**—Newly customizable in Dreamweaver MX, toolbars provide easy access to commonly used commands, such as Save File or Close.

- **Menus**—The entire menu structure—including main and context menus—is extensible, both to incorporate new CMS-specific commands and to limit certain Dreamweaver functionality.

- **Help files**—In the latest version, Dreamweaver switched from a browser-based to a system-specific help system: compiled Win Help files for Windows and Apple Help files for Macintosh. You can integrate custom help files under either operating system in Dreamweaver.

Dreamweaver can, in essence, be customized to such a degree that it functions as an extension of the CMS.

Modifying the Menus

The menus in Dreamweaver, like many other programs, are the primary interface for user interaction. Although you can accomplish an action in numerous other ways—selecting a toolbar button, dragging in an object—the same task is almost always accessible through the menus. Dreamweaver menus are completely customizable. CMS systems can integrate menu commands where users are likely to look as well as inserting a completely new, dedicated menu. Any element on the page or in the user interface that has a context menu can also be addressed. You could, for example, add a CMS-specific menu item to a context menu for a selected image.

The entire menu structure in Dreamweaver is controlled by a single XML file found in the Configuration/Menus folder, menus.xml. To customize the menus—beyond editing the shortcuts, which can be done by choosing Edit > Keyboard Shortcuts—you need to edit the menus.xml file. There are currently two ways to modify this file: by hand or by installing an extension. Either way, you need to understand the menus.xml structure before proceeding.

WARNING: Use extreme caution when editing the menus.xml file. Although Macromedia includes a backup file, menus.bak, in the same folder, I recommend that you store another copy of the menus.xml file in a separate location. Because of the structure of the menus.xml file, if an error occurs while you're modifying the file, the menus in Dreamweaver could be seriously damaged. Replacing the modified menus.xml with your backup restores full functionality.

The menus.xml file contains two main XML tag structures: <shortcutlist> and <menubar>. This discussion is concerned solely with the <menubar> construct. The <menubar> tag is used for both context and main menus. Each menu is identified with a unique ID attribute; the ID for the main menu, for example, is DWMainWindow, whereas the context menu for anchor tags is DWAnchorContext. Within each <menubar> tag is one or more <menu> tags. A menu tag corresponds to the drop-down menus, such as File, Edit, and View; context menu bars have only one <menu> tag. Within the <menu> tag is a series of <menuitem> tags, which are the individual menu selections. Submenus are created by nesting one <menu> tag within another.

Here's a typical <menubar> tag that defines the Search panel context menu:

```
<menubar name="" id="DWSearchTab">
    <menu name="" id="DWSearchTab_ContextMenu">
        <menuitem name="Open File"
enabled="dw.resultsPalette.canOpenInEditor();"
command="dw.resultsPalette.openInEditor()" domRequired="FALSE"
id="DWSearchTab_OpenInEditor"/>
        <menuitem name="_Find and Replace..."
domRequired="false" enabled="dw.getDocumentDOM() != null"
command="dw.showFindReplaceDialog()" id="DWSearchTab_Find_Replace"
/>
        <menuitem name="Clear Results"
enabled="dw.resultsPalette.canClear();"
command="dw.resultsPalette.clear()" domRequired="FALSE"
id="DWSearchTab_Clear"/>
    </menu>
</menubar>
```

To add a custom CMS menu item to an existing menu, you need to properly define the <menuitem> tag, which takes the following attributes:

- name—The label for the item as it appears in the menu.

- id—A unique identifier that typically includes a reference to the menu (DWSearchTab_Clear).

- enabled—An optional JavaScript statement that evaluates to either `true` or `false` and determines whether the menu item is available.

- command—A JavaScript command that executes when the menu item is chosen.

- file—A path to a JavaScript file that executes when the menu item is selected.

NOTE: The command and file attributes are mutually exclusive—only one may be included in any given `<menuitem>` tag. However, one or the other is required.

Let's look at the structure for a typical CMS-related `<menuitem>`. Our example, Mark JWL Index, is intended to wrap any selected text with a `<jwl:index>` tag. The menu item should be available only from the text context menu. The first attribute, `name`, is simple enough:

```
name = "Mark JWL Index"
```

Next, we'll add the identifying `id` attribute:

```
id="DWTextContext_JWL_Index"
```

Make sure that the `id` attribute is unique, or the menu structure could become corrupt. If you're not sure, do a search for the proposed ID value in the menus.xml file.

The third attribute, `enabled`, is somewhat more complex. Before we can apply the attribute, we need to make sure that text is selected, not some other item like an image. The Dreamweaver JavaScript API has all the power we need:

```
enabled = "dw.getDocumentDOM().getSelectedNode().nodeType ==
Node.TEXT_NODE"
```

Now we're ready to add the actual command attribute to execute the menu item:

```
command="dw.getDocumentDOM().wrapTag('<jwl:index>')
```

The completed `menuitem` tag looks like this:

```
<menuitem name = "Mark JWL Index" id="DWTextContext_JWL_Index"
enabled = "dw.getDocumentDOM().getSelectedNode().nodeType ==
Node.TEXT_NODE"
command="dw.getDocumentDOM().wrapTag('<jwl:index>') />
```

All you need to do now is locate the text context menu and insert the item. I generally use Dreamweaver's Find & Replace command to locate the proper menu. In this case, I'd search for `DWTextContext`, the `id` of the desired menu. Once found, it's merely a matter of adding the `<menuitem>` tag within the `<menu>` tag. You can even add `<separator />` tags on either side to isolate the custom command.

As noted earlier, entire menus can be added to the Dreamweaver main menu bar. To accomplish this, insert a complete `<menu>` tag with the needed `<menuitems>` after the Dreamweaver File menu (`id="DWMenu_File"`) and before the Dreamweaver Help menu (`id="DWMenu_Help"`). (You can add menus anywhere except before the File and after the Help menu.) Let's look at an example of a CMS `<menu>` tag with a submenu under one of the items, Utilities. To make the structure clear, I've only included the name attribute for the various `<menuitem>` tags:

```
<menu name="JWL CMS" id="DWMenu_JWL">
    <menuitem name="New Project..." />
    <menu name="Utilities" id="DWMenu_JWL_Utilities">
        menuitem name="Convert HTML Page to JWL..."  />
        <menuitem name="Convert JWL Page to HTML..."  />
    </menu>
    <menuitem name="Mark JWL Index" />
    <menuitem name="Add Keywords..." />
    <separator references="JWL_separator" />
    <menuitem name="JWL Help" />
    <menuitem name="JWL Online" />
    <menuitem name="About JWL" />
</menu>
```

Begin submenu ─────────────┘

As you can see, the menu item that opens the submenu is not another
<menuitem> tag, but the opening <menu> tag. You might also notice the ID
for the nested <menu> tag; although it is not required to refer to containing
elements in this way—DWMenu_JWL_Utilities—it makes it far easier to
see where a menu is located.

Inserting Customized Toolbars

Toolbars, like menus, are completely customizable in Dreamweaver. Toolbars
are great for providing shortcuts to often-used functionality without forcing
the user to memorize keystrokes.

Structurally, Dreamweaver toolbars are like Dreamweaver menus. Both are
defined by a central XML file; both allow individual items to be added to
existing elements; and both permit completely new elements to be added to
the system. Toolbars, however, do offer several key enhanced features over
menus:

- A variety of controls are available, including buttons, checkboxes,
  option buttons, menu buttons, drop-down lists, combo boxes, text
  fields, and color pickers.

- Greater interactivity with the user is allowed. Multiple images can
  be used to respond to mouse over, mouse out, selection, and
  deselection events.

- Reuse of toolbar items in multiple toolbars is possible.

The toolbars.xml file is found in Configuration/Toolbars. The file consists of
a series of <toolbar> tags, each containing a number of entries. Here's a
simplified version of the Standard toolbar definition, with only the id and
tooltip attributes:

```
<toolbar id="Standard_Toolbar" initiallyVisible="false"
label="Standard">
    <button id="DW_New" tooltip="New" />
    <button id="DW_Open" tooltip="Open" />
    <button id="DW_Save" tooltip="Save" />
    <button id="DW_SaveAll" tooltip="Save All" />
    <separator />
    <button id="DW_Cut" tooltip="Cut" />
```

continues

```
        <button id="DW_Copy" tooltip="Copy" />
        <button id="DW_Paste" tooltip="Paste" />
        <separator />
        <button id="DW_Undo" tooltip="Undo" />
        <button id="DW_Redo" tooltip="Redo" />
</toolbar>
```

Let's see how you would go about adding a toolbar item to an existing toolbar. In this example, you'll see how to add a type of text field, called an `editcontrol`, to a toolbar. The `editcontrol` allows the user to enter a text value. Then, when the user presses Enter (or Return) or selects another interface element, `editcontrol` executes a script. Our fictional `editcontrol` will be used to set a CMS start date tag for the given document and add it to the Standard toolbar.

The tag entry for each item on the toolbar is based on the item type. In our example, our toolbar item is an `<editcontrol>` tag. As with `<menuitem>` tags, all toolbar entries must have a unique ID attribute. For our example, that attribute is this:

```
id="JWL_SetStartDate"
```

Different item types have different attributes, but all require a ToolTip that shows the user what the toolbar item is:

```
tooltip="Start Date for JWL Content"
```

Special attributes for the `editcontrol` toolbar type include a `label`, which is positioned to the left of the text field, and a `width` value, given in pixels:

```
label="Start Date: "
width="150"
```

The `file` attribute is a path to an HTML file that is executed when the toolbar item is activated. Typically, this file is stored in the Toolbars folder in a custom directory:

```
file="Toolbars/JWL/StartDate.htm"
```

Here's the complete tag:

```
<editcontrol file="Toolbars/JWL/StartDate.htm"
id="JWL_SetStartDate" label="Start Date: " tooltip="Start Date for
JWL Content" width="150" />
```

When inserted as the last entry of the Standard toolbar definition, a text field appears, as shown in Figure 1.5.

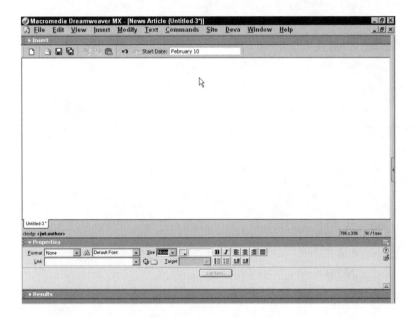

1.5

Editcontrol text fields are just one of the types of toolbar objects possible.

Incorporating Custom Help Files

Built-in help is an important aspect of any CMS system. Most content management systems are fairly complex, and users often need access to online documentation. Incorporating a custom help system within Dreamweaver makes it easier for designers and developers who are using a CMS to get answers as quickly as possible, without leaving the application they are working in.

TIP: A commercial extension, Deva Tools for Dreamweaver, is capable of outputting .chm files. Co-developed by me, Deva Tools is available at www.devahelp.com. Compiled help files also can be created by working with HTML Help Workshop, available from Microsoft at http://www.microsoft.com/downloads/release.asp?releaseid=33071. On the Macintosh side, a set of BBEdit extensions for creating Apple Help is available from http://www.powrtools.com/powrhelp/.

Dreamweaver MX now uses operating system style help files instead of Web-based help. Windows systems use a compiled help format in which the files use a .chm extension; Apple systems work with the Apple Help format. To incorporate custom help systems into Dreamweaver, you need to output your help files into these formats.

After the files are created, you need to modify three Dreamweaver files to integrate them into the Dreamweaver help system. The first file is the help.xml file found in the Dreamweaver/Help folder; note that this is one extensions folder that is not found within the Configuration folder. The standard help.xml file contains three entries: one for Using Dreamweaver, one for Extending Dreamweaver, and one for using ColdFusion:

```
<?xml version="1.0" ?>
<help-books>
    <book-id id="DW_Using" win-mapping="dwusing.chm" mac-
    mapping="Using Dreamweaver MX/book"/>
    <book-id id="DW_Extending" win-mapping="dwextend.chm" mac-
    mapping="Extending Dreamweaver MX/book"/>
    <book-id id="CF_Using" win-mapping="cfbooks.chm" mac-
    mapping="ColdFusion"/>
</help-books>
```

Modify the help.xml file to include a custom entry for your CMS help files, as in this example:

```
<book-id id="JWL_Using" win-mapping="jwlusing.chm" mac-
mapping="JWL/book"/>
```

The second file that needs modification is the menus.xml file. You need to add a <menuitem> tag to invoke the help systems, like this one:

```
<menuitem name="Using JWL in Dreamweaver" arguments="'JWLUsing'"
file="Menus/MM/CSHelp.htm" id="DWMenu_Help_JWLUsing" />
```

This <menuitem> passes an argument, in the example JWLUsing, to a file CSHelp.htm in the Menus/MM folder—which just happens to be the third file that you need to modify. The primary element within the CSHelp.htm file is the `receiveArguments()` function. This function is a series of `Else If` statements that display the proper help file given a particular argument. To incorporate a custom help system, an additional `Else If` statement is added, like this one:

```
else if (arguments[0] == 'JWLUsing'){
 helpDoc = "JWL_Using:index.htm";
}
```

Set to the index.htm, this function displays the opening page of the custom help file.

Working in Code with Snippets

Dreamweaver provides several ways to insert custom codes. One of the easiest methods uses snippets, introduced in Dreamweaver MX. Snippets are segments of code that are accessible from any site. A snippet can be inserted as a single block of code or wrapped around any selected content. Snippets are easily defined and straightforward to insert. You can even package snippets to be installed using the Extension Manager.

TIP: In a multiuser system, the administrator should install snippets or any extension intended to be used by all designers on the network.

Snippets are best used to insert CMS tags when no user-defined values for arguments are required. In other words, snippets are appropriate for `<meta>` or similar tags that identify a particular CMS page type and tags that identify content placement. For example:

```
<meta http-equiv="Creator" content="JWL Content Management System">
```

works well as a snippet. CMS tags that need a variety of values are better inserted with custom objects (covered later in the section "Adding a Custom Object").

If you're working with multiple custom snippets, it is best to create a folder to organize them. To add a new folder in the Snippets panel, do this:

1. Open the Snippets panel by choosing Window > Snippets or by clicking on the Snippets tab in the Code panel group.

TIP: If you have a large number of snippets, you can define subfolders as well. There's no real limit to the number of folders that can be nested within one another.

2. Select the folder you want to contain the new folder.

   To make a folder appear on the root, you must deselect all folders in the Snippets panel. This is a little trickier than it seems. First, open and select any single snippet. Then click the plus sign to collapse the snippet folder. Be sure to click the plus sign, not the snippet name.

3. Select the New Snippet Folder button at the bottom of the Snippet panel or choose New Folder from the Panel group menu.

As mentioned earlier, there are two types of snippets: code blocks and code wrapping. To define a new snippet, follow these steps:

1. Select the Add (+) button of the Snippets panel to display the Snippet dialog box, shown in Figure 1.6.

1.6

Any code that is selected before the Snippets dialog box is opened is copied to the Insert Block text area.

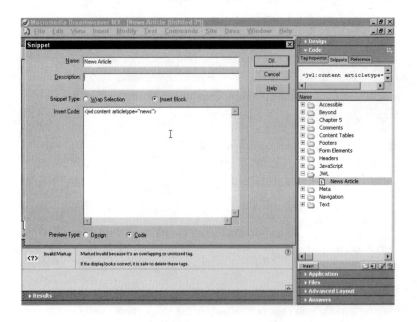

2. Enter a descriptive name for the snippet and a brief description, if desired, in the respective fields.

   The description appears to the right of the snippet name and should be concise if used at all. Long descriptions scroll offscreen and can be difficult to read.

3. Choose the Snippet type: Insert Block or Wrap Selection.

4. If you're creating an insert type snippet, enter the desired code in the Insert Block text area.

5. If you're creating a wrapping type snippet, enter the proper code in both the Insert Before and Insert After text areas.

6. Set the Preview Type to either Design or Code.

   Unless your snippet consists of a complete Web element, visible in Design view, choose Code as the Preview Type. Most CMS tags use the Code option.

TIP: If possible, it's more efficient to copy and paste your code into the snippet.

Inserting a snippet is even simpler than creating one:

- To place a block snippet on the page, drag it into place or position the cursor where you want the code block to appear. Then select Insert from the Snippet panel.

- To apply a wrapping snippet, first select the page section to be enclosed by the snippet. Then drag the snippet over the selection or, alternatively, choose Insert from the Snippet panel.

Adding a Custom Object

Snippets are great for what could be termed static tags: custom code that requires no user intervention. For CMS code with variable parameters, custom objects are the extension of choice. Objects are user friendly, and you can choose them directly from the Insert bar or from a menu.

The easiest way to understand objects is to look at a simple Macromedia-supplied example. Following is the entire code for the Copyright object, which inserts the code for a copyright character entity:

```
<HTML>
<HEAD>
<!-- Copyright 2000,2001 Macromedia, Inc. All rights reserved. -->

<title>Copyright</TITLE>

<SCRIPT SRC="characters.js"></SCRIPT>
<SCRIPT LANGUAGE="javascript">
```

continues

```
function isDOMRequired() {
    // Return false, indicating that this object is available in
        code view.
    return false;
}


function objectTag() {
    // Return the html tag that should be inserted
    checkEncoding();
    return "&copy;";
}
</SCRIPT>
</HEAD>
<BODY BGCOLOR="#FFFFFF">

</BODY>
</HTML>
```

Inserted on page

As you can see, an object file is a standard HTML page with one key function: `objectTag()`. Whatever is returned from the `objectTag()` function is what is written into the user's document at the cursor location. In this example, it is a simple character entity. More complex objects might return a much longer string of information culled from user input and concatenated with other code, but there is still just one string returned.

NOTE: To view the complete code, see Listing 1-1 at the end of this section.

The Copyright example shows how objects work on the most rudimentary level; for something like this, snippets could do the same job and are easier to set up. Objects really begin to shine when a parameter form is included in the HTML. Any standard HTML form element—text fields, option buttons, check boxes, drop-down lists—can be used in a parameter form. Each of the various form elements must be handled differently to extract the user input value. To see how it all works, let's look at an example that inserts a tag for the fictional JWL content management system (see Listing 1-1).

When designing objects, I always start with the interface. Most of the programming job consists of pulling values from form elements, and you need to have all the elements in place before you can begin. An object is completely enclosed in a form, as shown in Figure 1.7. To maintain a clean appearance, I generally use a table to structure the form. It's not necessary to add Execute or Cancel buttons—Dreamweaver does that for you for objects.

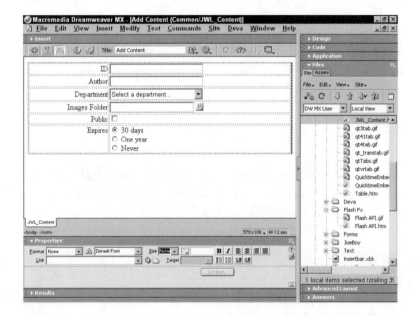

1.7

When you're creating a custom object, insert the form first, followed by the table and the form elements.

Make sure that all form elements have a unique, identifiable name. JavaScript requires the uniqueness; keeping the names understandable is good coding practice. Another good practice is to use the `findObject()` function whenever possible. Although it's not included in the JavaScript API—you have to insert it from the Snippet panel, under JavaScript, Readable MM Functions, Find Object—it's indispensable. The `findObject()` function, given an element's name, returns its object, which you can then manipulate and read. If, for example, I had a text field named `authorText`, I could get its value like this:

```
var theAuthor = findObject("authorText").value
```

After including the `findObject()` function—it is also available in Configuration/Shared/Macromedia/Scripts/CMN/UI.js—we're ready to launch right into the `objectTag()` function. The first lines of code put `findObject()` to work, setting up variables for all the form elements:

```
var theID = findObject("idText");
var theAuthor = findObject("authorText");
var theImageFolder = findObject("imagesFolderText");
```

```
var theDeptList = findObject("deptList");
var thePublicOption = findObject("publicCB");
var theExpiresChoice = findObject("expiresRB");
```

Text fields are the easiest of the form elements to work with and require little manipulation. When it comes time to write the return string, you can retrieve the user-entered value like this:

```
theAuthor.value
```

List objects, however, are a different story. First, you have to find which of the list items was selected, and then you have to get that item's value. To find the selected item, use code like this:

```
var theDeptListChoice = theDeptList.selectedIndex;
theDeptListChoice = theDeptList.options[theDeptListChoice].value
```

The first line gets the index of the selection, a zero-based number. If the first item in a list is selected, the index would be 0; if the second item is selected, the index would be 1, and so on. The second line returns the value of the selection, based on the index.

Checkboxes are either selected or not. After you determine the status of the `checked` property, you can set a value accordingly:

```
var thePublicValue = thePublicOption.checked ? "public" :
"private";
```

Using a conditional operator, the variable `thePublicValue` is set to `public` if the checkbox is selected and `private` if it is not.

Our final form element is the option button. You can select only one option button in a group. The task now is to figure out which one that is. Unfortunately, the only way to do this gracefully is to add a programming loop where every element is examined to see if it is checked. After you find the checked element, you can set the value to be returned accordingly. Here is one way to loop through a series of option buttons:

```
for (i = 0; i < theExpiresChoice.length; ++i) {
    if (theExpiresChoice[i].checked) {
        var theExpiresValue = theExpiresChoice[i].value;
        break;
    }
}
```

The final step in our object-programming example is to combine all the user values into one string and return it to the page. The surrounding tag elements are concatenated with the user values. Although you could format it in a single string, I broke it into sections to make it easier to read:

```
var theTag = '<jwl:content '
theTag += 'author="' + theAuthor.value + '" ';
theTag += 'id="' + theID.value + '" ';
theTag += 'imageurl="' + theImageFolder.value + '" ';
theTag += 'dept="' + theDeptListChoice + '" ';
theTag += 'display="' + thePublicValue + '" ';
theTag += 'expires="' + theExpiresValue + '" ';
theTag += '></jwl:content>';
return theTag;
```

When the HTML page is completed, the object is saved in one of the Object subfolders, such as Common or Script. You can also create your own subfolder to hold a collection of objects, if desired. Dreamweaver automatically uses a generic icon to represent your object on the Insert bar; if you'd like to use a custom icon, create a 16×16 pixel GIF image and store it in the same folder as your HTML file with the same base name. For example, an icon for the JWL_Content.htm object file would be called JWL_Content.gif. As noted earlier, Dreamweaver automatically renders the OK and Cancel buttons for the object, as shown in Figure 1.8.

1.8

When the object is selected from the Insert bar, the Custom Object dialog box is displayed, ready for user input.

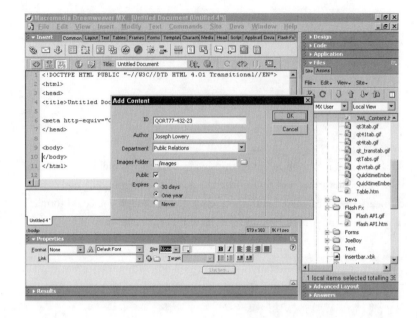

When the object is inserted into the page, the complete tag will look something like this:

```
<jwl:content author="Joseph Lowery" id="QORT77-432-23"
"imageurl="../images" dept="pr" display="public" expires="365" >
</jwl:content>
```

The tag is now ready to go to work. All the user needs to do is enter the content between the opening and closing tag. And with content management systems, adding content is the easiest part.

Listing 1-1 Add Content.htm (01_addcontent.htm)

```
<html>
<head>
<title>Add Content</title>
<meta http-equiv="Content-Type" content="text/html;
charset=iso-8859-1">
<script language='javascript'>
<!--
//*************** Primary Functions ********************
```

```
function commandButtons(){
    return new Array( 'OK', 'doCommand()', 'Cancel',
    'window.close()')
}


// Example: obj = findObj("image1");
function findObj(theObj, theDoc)
{
  var p, i, foundObj;

  if(!theDoc) theDoc = document;
  if( (p = theObj.indexOf("?")) > 0 && parent.frames.length)
  {
    theDoc = parent.frames[theObj.substring(p+1)].document;
    theObj = theObj.substring(0,p);
  }
  if(!(foundObj = theDoc[theObj]) && theDoc.all) foundObj =
  theDoc.all[theObj];
  for (i=0; !foundObj && i < theDoc.forms.length; i++)
    foundObj = theDoc.forms[i][theObj];
  for(i=0; !foundObj && theDoc.layers && i < theDoc.layers.length;
  i++)
    foundObj = findObj(theObj,theDoc.layers[i].document);
  if(!foundObj && document.getElementById) foundObj =
  document.getElementById(theObj);

  return foundObj;
}


function objectTag() {
    var theID = findObject("idText");
    var theAuthor = findObject("authorText");
    var theDeptList = findObject("deptList");
    var   theImageFolder = findObject("imagesFolderText");
    var   thePublicOption = findObject("publicCB");
    var theExpiresChoice = findObject("expiresRB");
```

continues

```
        var theDeptList = findObject("deptList");
        var theDeptListChoice = theDeptList.selectedIndex;
        theDeptListChoice = theDeptList.options
        [theDeptListChoice].value

        var thePublicValue = thePublicOption.checked ? "public" :
        "private";

        for (i = 0; i < theExpiresChoice.length; ++i) {
            if (theExpiresChoice[i].checked) {
            var theExpiresValue = theExpiresChoice[i].value;
            break;
          }
        }

        // Return the html tag that should be inserted
        return "&copy;";
    }


-->
</script>
<style type="text/css">
<!--
.inputBox {
   width: 200px;
}
.inputBoxIcon {
   width: 180px;
}
-->
</style>
</head>

<body>
<form name="form1" method="post" action="">
  <table width="100%"   border="0">
```

```
<tr>
  <td><div align="right">ID</div></td>
  <td><input name="idText" type="text" class="inputBox"
  id="idText"></td>
</tr>
<tr>
  <td><div align="right">Author</div></td>
  <td><input name="authorText" type="text" class="inputBox"
  id="authorText"></td>
</tr>
<tr>
  <td><div align="right">Department</div></td>
  <td><select name="deptList" class="inputBox" id="deptList">
      <option value="null" selected>Select a
      department...</option>
      <option value="hr">Human Resources</option>
      <option value="marketing">Marketing</option>
      <option value="pr">Public Relations</option>
      <option value="sales">Sales</option>
    </select></td>
</tr>
<tr>
  <td nowrap>
<div align="right">Images Folder</div></td>
  <td nowrap>
<input name="imagesfolderText" type="text" class="inputBoxIcon"
id="imagesfolderText">
      <img src="../Shared/MM/Images/folder.gif" width="16"
      height="16"></td>
</tr>
<tr>
  <td><div align="right">Public</div></td>
  <td><input name="publicCB" type="checkbox" id="publicCB"
  value="checkbox" onClick="showList()"></td>
</tr>
<tr>
  <td valign="top"> <div align="right">Expires</div></td>
```

```
                   <td><p>
                       <input name="expiresRB" type="radio" value="30" checked
                       onClick="showList()">
                       30 days<br>
                       <input name="expiresRB" type="radio" value="365"
                       onClick="showList()">
                       One year<br>
                       <input type="radio" name="expiresRB" value="0"
                       onClick="showList()">
                       Never<br>
                   </p></td>
             </tr>
           </table>
         </form>
       </body>
       </html>
```

✳ ───

Chapter 2

Meeting Accessibility Requirements

On June 21, 2001, Section 508 of the Federal Rehabilitation Act went into effect. As of that date, all Federal departments and agencies were mandated to make their web sites accessible in accordance with the specific regulations of Section 508. If you work on a Federal government web site, you already know this and are, in keeping with the law, creating accessible web sites. If you're not a developer for a U.S. government agency, you can skip this chapter, right?

Wrong. Section 508 has had a tremendous ripple effect across the entire web:

- State, city and municipal governments are following the Federal lead.

- Universities, colleges, and other educational institutions—many of which depend on Federal grants—are embracing accessibility standards rapidly.

- Companies that do business with any government—but especially with the Federal government—have a vested interest in complying.

- Businesses that are outside the government circle see an increased market available through accessible web sites.

Macromedia itself has significantly embraced the pursuit of accessibility standards, even to the point of establishing a product manager where there is no single product. The accessibility initiative has had a profound effect on Dreamweaver MX. In addition to the software becoming far more accessible for web developers who have disabilities, numerous features were added to make the crafting of accessible web sites workable and efficient. Moreover, Dreamweaver provides functionality to validate anything from the current page to an entire site for Section 508 compliance and more.

The goal in this chapter is to help you build Section 508-compliant web sites in Dreamweaver MX creatively and efficiently. To that end, you'll find a great deal of specific information about the various statutory requirements and, perhaps more importantly, how you can best implement those requirements. You'll also see how to use Dreamweaver to check your work—both for new pages and for existing sites.

Accessibility Overview

What do we mean when we say that a site is or is not accessible? The objective of Section 508 is to ensure full access to online information to any impaired individual who is working for the government or in the public sector, regardless of the disability. The disabilities in question—visual impairment, hearing impairment, and restricted locomotion, primarily—affect a wide range of people in the U.S. According to a 1997 study by the U.S. Census*, almost 1/5th of the population (19.7%) suffers from some disability. Moreover, disabilities are seen to rise with age: 35.7% of Americans age 55 to 64 years old have a disability, as do more than half (54.5%) of those over the age of 65. These figures do not include those who are suffering from temporary disabilities, such as a broken arm. However, these people are also helped by Section 508; an accessible web site is navigable both by folks who are able to use a mouse and by those who are not.

Befitting the numbers, an entire industry has risen to supply the disabled with assistive technology. Some such technology is built in to the browser, such as the ability to use arrows and other keys to navigate a site. Other technology, such as screen readers, is more special purpose and must be added on. A *screen reader* is a software component that reads the page out loud for a web visitor. One example is Window-Eyes from GW Micro.

*Source: http://www.census.gov/hhes/www/disable/sipp/disab97/ds97t1.html

Not only is the content read, but the navigation links and image `alt` text are read also. In addition to screen readers, accessible web pages must be able to handle touch screens, head pointers, and other mouse-less input devices. One key way that accessibility standards are implemented is by including HTML markup that is readable by an assistive device and ignored by a standard browser.

Although this chapter is specifically concerned with U.S. guidelines covered in Section 508, accessibility is a worldwide concern. The U.S. regulations are based on the World Wide Web Consortium's (W3C) Web Content Accessibility Guidelines, Priority 1. (Priority 1 is deemed most important on three checkpoint levels.) Many other countries, including Germany, France, and Australia, have followed the same set of checkpoints. Some countries, including the United Kingdom (with the Guidelines for U.K. Government Web Sites) and Canada (with the Common Look and Feel Standard) have adopted stricter standards, based on Priority 1 and Priority 2 checkpoints. You can find a complete list of checkpoints at `http://www.w3.org/TR/WCAG/checkpoint-list.html`. Implementing the Section 508 guidelines takes your site well down the road to compliance over much of the globe.

Understanding Federal Accessibility Requirements

In all, 16 different specific guidelines make up Section 508 as they pertain to web-based intranet and Internet information and applications. The guidelines cover everything from commonplace images to timed tests for online learning. The letter designations (a) through (n) are referenced in Dreamweaver validation reports, as discussed later in this chapter. The following table gives a quick overview of all the sections and the HTML elements that are most affected:

Guideline	Area	HTML Elements Affected
1194.22(a)	Non-text elements	`<img>` tags; `alt`, `longdesc` attributes
1194.22(b)	Multimedia presentations	Flash, QuickTime, Real and Windows Media Player movies
1194.22(c)	Color	`<img>` and `<font>` tags; color attributes
1194.22(d)	Style sheets	Cascading Style Sheets, code layout
1194.22(e)	Server-side image maps	`<map>` and `<a>` tags

continues

NOTE: For the full text of these guidelines, visit the "Guide to the Section 508 Standards for Electronic and Information Technology" at http://www.access-board.gov/sec508/guide/index.htm.

1194.22(f)	Client-side image maps	`<map>` tags
1194.22(g)	Table—Simple headers	`<table>`, `<th>`, and `<td>` tags
1194.22(h)	Table—Complex headers	`<table>`, `<th>`, and `<td>` tags
1194.22(i)	Frames	`<frameset>` and `<frame>` tags; name attribute
1194.22(j)	Screen flicker	`<script>` tags
1194.22(k)	Text-only page	Page layout
1194.22(l)	Scripted pages	`<script>` tags, data-driven pages
1194.22(m)	Applets and plug-ins	`<embed>`, `<object>`, and `<applet>` tags
1194.22(n)	Forms	`<input>` and `<label>` tags; `accesskey` attributes
1194.22(o)	Navigation links	`<a>` and named anchor tags
1194.22(p)	Timed responses	`<form>` and `<input>` tags

Setting Accessibility Preferences in Dreamweaver

So, you've heard about all the new accessibility features that are built into Dreamweaver MX, and you start to work right away. You insert an image and examine the code, but nothing seems different. The `alt` attribute should have been automatically added, and there's no `longdesc` attribute in sight. What gives?

The accessibility features in Dreamweaver MX are implemented as an additional optional layer on the existing user interface and must be enabled in Preferences. Choose Edit > Preferences and then select the Accessibility category. In this category, shown in Figure 2.1, select any or all of the five options to display the associated accessibility dialog boxes. Additional accessibility dialog boxes are available for the following:

- Form objects—Text fields, text areas, radio buttons, and check boxes

- Frames—Framesets, frames, and no-frames content

- Media—Flash movies, Flash buttons, Flash text, Shockwave movies, Applets, QuickTime movies, ActiveX controls, and plug-ins

- Images—JPEGs, GIFs, and PNGs

- Tables—Structured data tables, not tables for layout

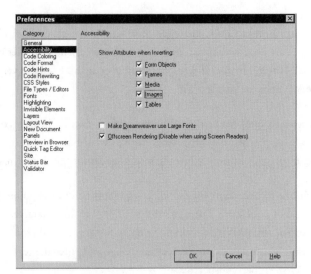

2.1

Choose whatever accessibility options you need through Preferences.

In almost all cases, if an option is selected, a secondary dialog box containing the accessibility options appears after the standard Dreamweaver interface. Only the form input objects are somewhat different. Because the input objects do not normally use a dialog box—all parameters are set through the Property Inspector—only the accessibility dialog box appears.

The Guidelines

The following sections present interpretations of the standards. If you have a legal question regarding compliance, consult with the enforcing agency. This is especially true for countries other than the U.S. where standards are not mandatory but are expected.

Note that the bold text is the same wording as the actual guideline.

1194.22(a): Text Tags

A text equivalent for every non-text element shall be provided (e.g., via "alt", "longdesc", or in element content).

(http://www.access-board.gov/sec508/guide/1194.22.htm#(a))

Perhaps because images are so prevalent on the web, the text equivalent for every non-text element guideline is one of the more time-consuming—but vital—ones to follow. When a screen reader or text-only browser encounters a graphic on the page, it merely says "Image" unless the image has one or more recognized attributes to assist the reader. The situation is especially bad when sliced images are used without accessibility attributes; then the reader can be heard to say, "Image. Image. Image." over and over again. It's not a very user-friendly experience, to say the least.

TIP: Many screen readers, when encountering an image that serves as a link, read the alt text in a different voice, making it redundant to specify that the graphic is a link to another page. Rather than entering the alt value as "link to site search page," just use "site search" and your meaning will still be clear.

Three basic techniques can be used to address this problem. The primary tool for making images accessible is the `<img>` tag's alt attribute. Any text assigned to the alt attribute is substituted by the screen reader for the term "Image."

The text in the alt attribute is best when it is short and to the point—informative, but not chatty. The alt value is limited to 256 characters, but in most situations, you'll want to restrict the entry further. To add an alt value to an existing image on the page, select the image and enter the text into the Alt field of the Property inspector.

For images that require a more in-depth description, you can use two alternatives jointly or separately. First, another attribute to the `<img>` tag—longdesc, which stands for long description—is readable by most of the newer screen readers. The longdesc attribute is a link to another HTML page that contains nothing more than the text description. The screen reader opens—and reads—the longdesc page, but standard browsers ignore the attribute. Here's an example of the code for an `<img>` tag with both longdesc and alt attributes:

NOTE: The accessibility options for images appear after you insert a graphic through the Image object, through the Insert Image menu option, or when using the Assets panel. The additional dialog box does not appear if you drag a graphics file onto your page from the Files panel or from the desktop.

```
<img src="/images/clarke.jpg" alt="Arthur C. Clarke on the set of
2001:A Space Odyssey" longdesc="/images/clarke.htm">
```

You can enter both alt and longdesc attributes when a graphic is inserted and the Image accessibility option has been selected. After the user chooses a graphic from the standard Select File dialog box, the Image Tag Accessibility Attributes dialog box appears (see Figure 2.2). For the alt attribute, enter the desired text in the Alternative Text field. To use the longdesc attribute, select the folder icon to locate a file or data source or enter the path directly into the Long Description field.

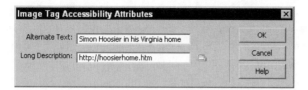

2.2

Use the `alt` and `longdesc` attributes together to provide two levels of information.

Although the `longdesc` attribute solves many problems for the present technology, it is not supported by many older screen readers that are still in operation. There is, however, a recognized convention that can supplement the attribute that places an uppercase D to the right of the image and links the letter directly to the `longdesc` HTML file, as shown in Figure 2.3. You must enter this technique—referred to as the D or Descriptive link—manually in Dreamweaver.

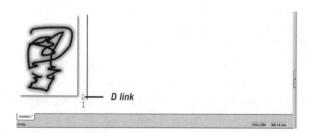

D link

2.3

The D link is intended to add `longdesc` functionality to older screen readers.

Automating LongDesc Conversions

If you are tasked with adding D links to pages where `longdesc` attributes are already in place, you can use Dreamweaver's Find and Replace feature to automate the process. Here are the steps for doing that:

1. Choose Edit > Find and Replace.

2. Select the Use Regular Expressions option.

3. In the Find and Replace dialog box, set the desired scope of the operation by selecting an option from the Find In list.

4. Set the Search For list to Specific Tag and enter (or choose) `img` in the Tag field.

5. Set a single set of conditions to the following:

```
With Attribute longdesc = (.*)
```

With this regular expression, you're looking for any <img> tag with a longdesc attribute and value. The parentheses in the regular expression also serve to group and remember the longdesc value.

6. Set the Add Action to this:

```
Add After <a href="$1">D</a>
```

The $1 code is a regular expression that inserts the remembered longdesc value.

7. Choose Replace or Replace All to effect the operation.

NOTE: Because this is a somewhat complex Find and Replace operation, you might want to save the query. Unfortunately, Dreamweaver MX has a bug that prevents the Add Action portion of a query from being loaded. You'll need to enter the <a href="$1">D</a> code each time you run the query.

As with all Find and Replace procedures—especially those that involve regular expressions—it's best to run a number of test cases when modifying an entire site and to always keep a backup available.

One particular type of graphic—used in sliced images—deserves special mention. Called a *spacer* or *shim*, these transparent GIF images keep the table of images from breaking apart. When a screen reader encounters these spacers, it notes that they are images unless an empty alt attribute is included. In Dreamweaver, you have two ways to enter an empty alt attribute:

- In code view, enter alt="" into the <img> tag.

- In Design view, select the image and in the Alt field, choose <empty> from the drop-down list.

1194.22(b): Multimedia Presentations

Equivalent alternatives for any multimedia presentation shall be synchronized with the presentation.

http://www.access-board.gov/sec508/guide/1194.22.htm#(b)

The multimedia alternatives guideline basically mandates that any multimedia presentation—such as a Flash or QuickTime movie—must provide some method of conveying the information for the impaired. This method could be internal to the movie, such as a closed captioning option that displays subtitles. It's also possible to embed content in an external layer on the page. However, unless the content is extremely limited, it is probably more difficult to synchronize the multimedia presentation and the external content than to provide a solution within the multimedia presentation.

To add an external layer that is visible only to screen readers, put the layer on top of the multimedia movie. All active content, including Flash and other movies that use plug-ins or ActiveX controls, rise to the top of a page. With a layer drawn out on top of the movie, the content layer is hidden from regular view but is accessible by the screen reader. Placement of the layer's `<div>` tag is key to working properly with the assistive technology; it's best to put the `<div>` tag just before the `<object>` tag that holds the Flash or other movie.

TIP: If you're trying to synchronize a Flash movie with HTML content, use Flash's `LoadVars` object, as described in Chapter 8, "Making Flash Connections."

The latest version of the Macromedia Flash Player has made great strides in accessibility with its built-in support for the Microsoft Active Accessibility (MSAA) protocol. MSAA serves as a bridge to communicate between the Flash Player and screen readers, such as GW Micro's Window-Eyes and other assistive technologies.

1194.22(c): Color

Web pages shall be designed so that all information conveyed with color is also available without color, for example from context or markup.

http://www.access-board.gov/sec508/guide/1194.22.htm#(c)

To comply with 1194.22(c), you must make sure that your designs do not rely on color alone to impart information. In an extreme example, let's say your client wanted to highlight the company color (red) and sponsored a contest in which a user who selected the bouncing red ball from amidst a bunch of bouncing green balls would be eligible for a prize. Without another way to designate the red ball—such as an `alt` attribute—your site would not pass Section 508 regulations.

Color blindness—the inability to distinguish between certain colors—is more widespread than generally believed. About 7% of men—approximately 10 million in the U.S.—suffer from the most common form of color blindness and have difficulty telling red from green.* Additionally, saturation of color can be a problem. Text or graphics in two different colors with the same

*Source: http://www.hhmi.org/senses/b130.html

saturation can be seen as a single mass by the color blind. However, this guideline is intended to assist more than just those who experience color blindness; anyone who has a visual impairment or who is restricted to using a text-only browser benefits from the color guideline.

1194.22(d): Readability

Documents shall be organized so they are readable without requiring an associated style sheet.

http://www.access-board.gov/sec508/guide/1194.22.htm#(d)

This guideline governing style sheets has become important with the increasing use of CSS for layout purposes. Basically, this guideline requires backward compatibility with non-CSS capable browsers—considered by many to be a best practice in web design. One key problem lies with the absolute positioning ability of <div> tags: layers and poor planning. With a CSS-proficient browser, it is possible to insert the layers anywhere on the page and have the content render properly. Here's a simple example with three areas of content: headline, mainbody, and footer:

```
<style type="text/css">
#footer {
      position:absolute;
      left:76px;
      top:382px;
      width:556px;
      height:51px;
      font-family: Verdana, Arial, Helvetica, sans-serif;
      font-size: 10px;
}
#headline {
      position:absolute;
      left:76px;
      top:23px;
      width:556px;
      height:67px;
      font-family: Verdana, Arial, Helvetica, sans-serif;
      font-size: 24px;
```

```
}
#mainbody {
      position:absolute;
      left:76px;
      top:101px;
      width:556px;
      height:272px;
      font-family: Verdana, Arial, Helvetica, sans-serif;
      font-size: 12px;}
</style>

<div id="footer">Next issue: Warts!</div>
<div id="headline">In this issue: Fungus!</div>
<div id="mainbody">Ever wonder where fungus comes from?...</div>
```

When this page is viewed in a CSS-enabled browser, it renders as the designer intended, as shown in Figure 2.4.

2.4

Absolute CSS positioning lays a trap for the unsuspecting designer.

However, the same page, viewed without CSS capability, reads like this:

```
Next Issue: Warts!
In this issue: Fungus!
Ever wonder where fungus comes from?...
```

In addition to placing the code in the same order as it is intended to be read (a process called *linearization*), you need to be sure that the page is still legible if the CSS style sheet is not executed. Pages most often become unreadable under these circumstances when the page contains a combination of both CSS styles and presentation markup in HTML.

Let's say, for example, that a legacy page containing mostly HTML presentation markup—where the <body> tag specifies a black background and white text—has been upgraded to CSS. Unfortunately, when the designer inserted the CSS code specifying the same color combination (white text on a black background), the bgcolor="black" attribute was left in the <body> tag. Should the CSS be unable to load, the user would see the default text color (black) on a black background. If the page's presentation had been completely separated from its content in a CSS, the browser's default settings would have taken over and the page would be legible.

1194.22(e): Server-Side Image Maps

Redundant text links shall be provided for each active region of a server-side image map.

```
http://www.access-board.gov/sec508/guide/1194.22.htm#(e)
```

Two guidelines pertain to image maps: one for server-side maps and one for client-side maps. The first image map guideline, although geared specifically toward the server-side variety, is also a good idea when you're working with client-side image maps. Essentially, the guideline requests that for every linking region of a server-side image map, there must be a corresponding text link. If, for example, your page uses a server-side image map of the five New York boroughs, the page should also contain five text links connecting to the same files.

By default, Dreamweaver creates client-side image maps, so this guideline really only applies to legacy pages. In truth, server-side image maps are not used much any more, partially because of their lack of browser support but mostly because client-side image maps are far easier to create and maintain.

1194.22(f): Client-Side Image Maps

Client-side image maps shall be provided instead of server-side image maps except where the regions cannot be defined with an available geometric shape.

```
http://www.access-board.gov/sec508/guide/1194.22.htm#(f)
```

The W3C, in their Web Content Accessibility Guidelines, Priority 1 checkpoints—which formed the basis for the Section 508 guidelines—throw their considerable weight behind client-side image maps. The instances where a hotspot cannot be defined with any of the available client-side shapes (rectangle, oval, and polygon) are few and far between.

When you're working with image maps, keep in mind that a hotspot falls into the category of a non-text element as covered under 1194.22(a). In short, the `alt` attribute must be completed for image map regions just as for standard graphics. Typically, `alt` is defined for both the basic image and the hotspots drawn on top of the image.

1194.22(g): Data Tables (Simple Tables)

Row and column headers shall be identified for data tables.

```
http://www.access-board.gov/sec508/guide/1194.22.htm#(g)
```

Although tables have long been subverted into performing layout chores, they really are intended to hold structured data. Structured data almost always has series of cells that act as the headings for the table. The headings can be in a row, in a column, or both. Standard data in a table cell is placed in a `<td>` tag. If a cell is designated to be a header cell, a `<th>` tag is used. Browsers generally render the unstyled `<td>` tag as bold and centered.

For existing tables, convert a `<td>` cell to a `<th>` by selecting that cell and then choosing the Header option in the Property inspector; the same technique can be applied to an entire row or column. For new tables—with the proper accessibility preference selected—Dreamweaver sets the header cells at creation time. After the standard table dialog box is completed, the Accessibility Options for Tables dialog box appears (see Figure 2.5). Choose the desired option from the Header drop-down list: Row, Column, or Both.

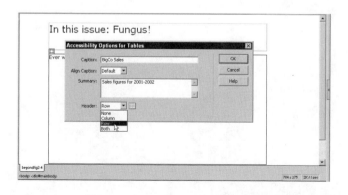

2.5

The Accessibility Options for Tables dialog box permits you to choose whether the headers are in the first row, the first column, or both.

The Accessibility Options for Tables dialog box contains other options as well, including Caption and Summary, which are helpful but not required under Section 508. (Summaries for tables are a Priority 3 checkpoint.) I find captions to be useful in tables, although not all browsers support the `<caption>` tag.

This guideline—like all legal regulations—is open to interpretation. Dreamweaver takes a somewhat relaxed view and depends exclusively on the row and column headers that are being identified by `<th>` tags. Other experts in the field are more rigid and believe additional markup is necessary. The goal of the added attributes is to associate each table cell explicitly with a specific header. A standard that renders like this:

Sales Region	Representative	YTD Sales
Northeast	Franklin Simons	$2,234,000
Southwest	Alicia Norway	$2,560,000

is coded like this in Dreamweaver:

```
<table width="75%"  border="1">
    <tr>
      <th>Sales Region</th>
      <th>Representative</th>
      <th>YTD Sales</th>
    </tr>
    <tr>
      <td>Northeast</td>
      <td>Franklin Simons</td>
      <td>$2,234,000</td>
    </tr>
    <tr>
      <td>Southwest</td>
      <td>Alicia Norway </td>
      <td>$2,560,000</td>
    </tr>
  </table>
```

To specify the relationship between headers and individual cells, use `id` attributes in the `<th>` cells and `headers` attributes in the `<td>` cells, like this:

```
<table width="75%"  border="1">
    <tr>
      <th id="Sales Region">Sales Region</th>
      <th id="Representative">Representative</th>
      <th id="YTD Sales">YTD Sales</th>
    </tr>
    <tr>
      <td headers="Sales Region">Northeast</td>
      <td headers="Representative">Franklin Simons</td>
      <td headers="YTD Sales">$2,234,000</td>
    </tr>
    <tr>
      <td headers="Sales Region">Southwest</td>
      <td headers="Representative">Alicia Norway </td>
      <td headers="YTD Sales">$2,560,000</td>
    </tr>
  </table>
```

Identifies a specific header cell

Ties cell to a header

Such cell-by-cell designations are helpful for those users who require assistive technologies.

1194.22(h): Data Tables (Complex Tables)

Markup shall be used to associate data cells and header cells for data tables that have two or more logical levels of row or column headers.

http://www.access-board.gov/sec508/guide/1194.22.htm#(g)

Complex tables take the markup concepts covered in the previous section a step further. Consider the following table.

	Northeast	Southeast	West	Totals
2001				
In-Store Sales	$3.50M	$4.20M	$6.00M	$13.70M
Online Sales	$2.20M	$3.10M	$3.90M	$9.20M
Subtotal	$5.70M	$7.30M	$9.90M	$22.90M
2002				
In-Store Sales	$4.50M	$3.20M	$4.00M	$11.70M
Online Sales	$3.20M	$2.10M	$4.90M	$10.20M
Subtotal	$7.70M	$5.30M	$8.90M	$21.90M
Totals	$13.40M	$12.60M	$18.80M	$44.80M

Without additional guidance, a screen reader that encounters this table would read many of the cells in one long indecipherable string. Not only must headers and header-related cells be identified, but so must the category or axis. The example table contains four different axes: regions, sale_types, years, and totals. The header cells take an additional attribute to assign the particular axis. Here is how the top row of regions is coded:

```
<tr>
  <td> </td>
  <th id="Northeast" axis="regions">Northeast</th>
  <th id="Southeast" axis="regions">Southeast</th>
  <th id="West" axis="regions">West</th>
  <th id="Subtotals" axis="regions">Totals</th>
</tr>
```

After an axis is identified, the headers attribute for a particular <td> cell incorporates all the axes that are relevant to that cell, like this:

```
<td headers="2001 Northeast in-store">$3.50M</td>
```

Axes should be included in a readable fashion. For example, the cell that holds the grand total for the two years of sales is written like this:

```
<td headers="2001 2002 Totals">$47.80M</td>
```

Here's the code for the entire table:

```
<table width="514" border="1">
  <tr>
    <td> </td>
    <th id="Northeast" axis="regions">Northeast</th>
    <th id="Southeast" axis="regions">Southeast</th>
    <th id="West" axis="regions">West</th>
    <th id="Subtotals" axis="regions">Totals</th>
  </tr>
  <tr>
    <th id="2001" axis="year">2001</th>
    <td> </td>
    <td> </td>
    <td> </td>
    <td> </td>
  </tr>
  <tr>
    <th id="in-store" axis="sales_types">In Store Sales</th>
    <td headers="2001 Northeast in-store">$3.50M</td>
    <td headers="2001 Southeast in-store">$4.20M</td>
    <td headers="2001 West in-store">$6.00M</td>
    <td headers="2001 Subtotals in-store">$13.70M</td>
  </tr>
  <tr>
    <th id="online" axis="sales_types">Online Sales</th>
    <td headers="2001 Northeast online">$2.20M</td>
    <td headers="2001 Southeast online">$3.10M</td>
    <td headers="2001 West online">$3.90M</td>
    <td headers="2001 Subtotals online">$9.20M</td>
  </tr>
  <tr>
```

continues

```
    <th>Subtotal</th>
    <td headers="2001 Northeast">$5.70M</td>
    <td headers="2001 Southeast">$7.30M</td>
    <td headers="2001 West">$9.90M</td>
    <td headers="2001 Subtotals">$22.90M</td>
  </tr>
  <tr>
    <th id="2002" axis="year">2002</th>
    <td> </td>
    <td> </td>
    <td> </td>
    <td> </td>
  </tr>
  <tr>
    <th id="in-store" axis="sales_types">In Store Sales</th>
    <td headers="2002 Northeast in-store">$4.50M</td>
    <td headers="2002 Southeast in-store">$3.20M</td>
    <td headers="2002 West in-store">$4.00M</td>
    <td headers="2002 Subtotals in-store">$11.70M</td>
  </tr>
  <tr>
    <th id="online" axis="sales_types">Online Sales</th>
    <td headers="2002 Northeast online">$3.20M</td>
    <td headers="2002 Southeast online">$2.10M</td>
    <td headers="2002 West online">$4.90M</td>
    <td headers="2002 Subtotals online">$10.20M</td>
  </tr>
  <tr>
    <th>Subtotal</th>
    <td headers="2002 Northeast">$7.70M</td>
    <td headers="2002 Southeast">$5.30M</td>
    <td headers="2002 West">$8.90M</td>
    <td headers="2002 Subtotals">$21.90M</td>
  </tr>
  <tr>
    <th id="totals" axis="totals">Totals</th>
```

```
    <td headers="2001 2002 Northeast totals">$13.40M</td>
    <td headers="2001 2002 Southeast totals">$12.60M</td>
    <td headers="2001 2002 West totals">$18.80M</td>
    <td headers="2001 2002 Totals">$44.80M</td>
  </tr>
</table>
```

As you can see, a great deal of detailed work goes into a table like this. At this point, all of the additional `headers`, `id` and `axis` attributes must be coded by hand.

1194.22(i): Frames

Frames shall be titled with text that facilitates frame identification and navigation.

```
http://www.access-board.gov/sec508/guide/1194.22.htm#(i)
```

This guideline reflects good coding standards and, to me, common sense: Give your frames meaningful titles. But why are frame titles important from an accessibility viewpoint? Although the standard browser does not give an indication of the names, text-only browsers, upon encountering a frameset, display a list of frame names if no `title` attribute is found. Would you find it easier to choose from a list that contains these items:

```
lframe
bframe
mframe
```

Or these items:

```
banner
menu
content
```

As the guideline suggests, the best course is to give the frames meaningful, functional titles. To add a title or change the title of an existing frameset in Dreamweaver, you need to alter the code of the frameset. The original frameset looks something like this:

```
<frameset cols="*,80" frameborder="NO" border="0" frame-
spacing="0">
  <frame src="mainstory.htm" name="mainFrame">
  <frame src="nav.htm" name="rightFrame" scrolling="NO" noresize>
</frameset>
```

The title attribute is added to each of the `<frame>` tags:

Added title attributes

Added title attributes

```
<frameset cols="*,80" frameborder="NO" border="0" frame-
spacing="0">
  <frame src="mainstory.htm" name="mainFrame" title="content">
  <frame src="nav.htm" name="rightFrame" scrolling="NO" noresize
title="menu">
</frameset>
```

New framesets can give a proper title to each frame at creation, if you have the Frames Accessibility option enabled. When a Frame object is inserted, either from the Insert bar or from the Insert, Frames menu, Dreamweaver displays the Frame Tag Accessibility Attributes dialog box, shown in Figure 2.6. To title the frames, choose the frame name from the drop-down list and enter the desired title in the bottom frames.

2.6

Cycle through the frames in the frameset by choosing the items listed in the Frame list.

NOTE: The Frame Tag Accessibility Attributes dialog box does not appear if you build your frameset by Alt-dragging (Option-dragging on the Mac) the frame border.

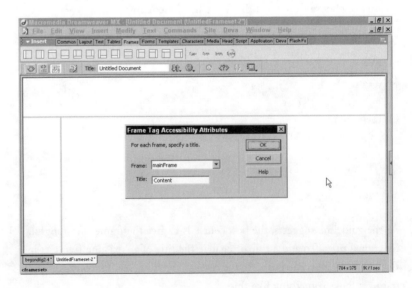

1194.22(j): Flicker Rate

Pages shall be designed to avoid causing the screen to flicker with a frequency greater than 2 Hz and lower than 55 Hz.

`http://www.access-board.gov/sec508/guide/1194.22.htm#(j)`

If you've ever opened a page with an attention-grabbing, quickly flickering graphic or area, you know they can be tremendously annoying—but did you also know they can be dangerous? People who suffer from a disease called photosensitive epilepsy are prone to seizures when they encounter these rapidly blinking, strobe-like effects.

To my mind, these types of effects should never be used; you're not much of a designer if you have to rely on them to get attention. However, if the client or boss insists on the flickering effect, to comply with this guideline, you need to warn visitors that selecting a particular link triggers a screen flicker and give them an alternative effect-less route to the same page.

1194.22(k): Text-Only Alternative

A text-only page, with equivalent information or functionality, shall be provided to make a web site comply with the provisions of this part, when compliance cannot be accomplished in any other way. The content of the text-only page shall be updated whenever the primary page changes.

`http://www.access-board.gov/sec508/guide/1194.22.htm#(k)`

I've termed this the "worst-case scenario" guideline. When all else fails, if the content in your page cannot be conveyed to screen readers and other assistive technologies, you need to create a parallel text-only page. Naturally, a link from the main page to the text-only page should be available. Although creating a text-only page is not too great a task—indeed, at first glance, many developers might see this as the easiest road to travel—maintaining that page is an ongoing chore.

Should you need to create text-only pages, I strongly suggest that you use server-side technology to do so. To change this worst-case scenario into the best of both worlds, the original page and its text-only equivalent should be constructed from the same data source. Using this technique, when the content is changed for one, it automatically is updated for the other—and the maintenance chore disappears.

1194.22(l): Scripts

When pages utilize scripting languages to display content, or to create interface elements, the information provided by the script shall be identified with functional text that can be read by assistive technology.

http://www.access-board.gov/sec508/guide/1194.22.htm#(l)

JavaScript programming has added a great deal of interactivity to the web. Unfortunately, many developers use JavaScript effects exclusively without providing a non-JavaScript alternative. For example, a rollover button that exposes a secondary menu is quite common; both Dreamweaver MX and Fireworks MX include such pop-up menu functionality. When a screen reader comes across such a navigation element, it has no way of seeing the secondary menus. A similar problem occurs when the JavaScript function document.write() is used. The document.write() function allows coders to construct a portion of their page on the fly; for example, a script detects the time of day and displays different content depending on whether it is morning, afternoon, or evening. If the content is significant—not just "Good Morning"—the scripting languages guideline requires an alternative method of providing the content.

Aside from a text-only page link, one highly recommended alternative is server-side scripting. Unlike JavaScript, which is client-side scripting, server-side scripting preprocesses the page—detecting the time, as in the previous example, and inserting the desired content—before delivering the HTML-only page to the browser.

1194.22(m): Applets and Plug-Ins

When a web page requires that an applet, plug-in, or other application be present on the client system to interpret page content, the page must provide a link to a plug-in or applet that complies with §1194.22(a) through (l).

http://www.access-board.gov/sec508/guide/1194.22.htm#(m)

Here, again, is a solid coding practice established as a legal regulation. If key content is contained in a Flash movie, plug-in, applet, or ActiveX control, make sure that users can get the required application if they don't already have it. Most multimedia applications that use the <object> or <embed> tag, such as Flash movies, have attributes that are designed to contain a link to a player. To play it safe, many developers provide another link, often using a logo provided by the application developer for that very purpose.

1194.22(n): Electronic Forms

When electronic forms are designed to be completed on-line, the form shall allow people using assistive technology to access the information, field elements, and functionality required for completion and submission of the form, including all directions and cues.

http://www.access-board.gov/sec508/guide/1194.22.htm#(n)

Online forms are difficult enough for people who don't have disabilities, and they present special challenges to those who are using assistive devices. Three accessibility elements can be used with forms:

- **Labels**—Specifically associates a text label with a particular form element, such as a check box or radio button.

- **Access Key**—Sets a keystroke that, when used in combination with the Alt key, focuses on the associated form element.

- **Tab Order**—Presets the sequence in which the form elements are tabbed through, regardless of their position on the page.

You can add all three elements through the Input Tag Accessibility Attributes dialog box, show in Figure 2.7. This dialog box appears when any input form element—text field, text area, list/menu, option button, check box, image field, file field, or button—is inserted, assuming that the Form Objects accessibility option has been selected in Preferences.

2.7

The Input Tag Accessibility
Attributes dialog box
contains options for labels,
access keys, and tab order
for almost all form
elements.

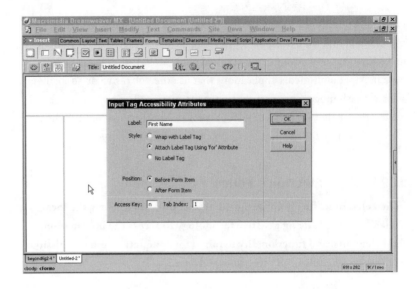

Labels play a key role in making forms accessible. With standard form layouts, it is not always easy to tell which text description belongs to which form element. Labels solve that problem in one of two ways: implicitly or explicitly. The implicit method simply wraps the associated form element with the <label> tag:

```
<label>First Name:
    <input type="text" name="firstnameText">
</label>
```

This example places the label to the left of the text field. You can easily place it to the right by moving the actual text after the <input> tag:

```
<label>
    <input type="text" name="firstnameText">First Name
</label>
```

The second, explicit method of using the <label> tag is coded like this:

```
<label for="firstnameText">First Name:</label>
<input type="text" name="firstnameText">
```

As with the previous method, the label can appear after the text field. With the explicit method, the entire `<label>` tag pair is moved. In fact, that's the key advantage for the explicit over the implicit technique. I prefer to use tables to align almost all of my forms, with the labels in one column and the form elements in another; such a layout technique is only possible with the explicit method. For example:

```
<tr>
  <td><label for="firstnameText">First Name:</label></td>
  <td><input type="text" name="firstnameText"></td>
</tr>
<tr>
  <td><label for="lastnameText">Last Name:</label></td>
  <td><input type="text" name="lastnameText"></td>
</tr>
```

The Dreamweaver accessibility dialog box for input objects also provides an easy method for setting keyboard shortcuts for form elements. The `accesskey` attribute allows the designer to assign a keystroke which, when combined with the Alt or Cmd key, brings focus to the associated form element. If, for example, you were to assign the "c" key to a credit card text field like this:

```
<input type="text" name="creditcardText" accesskey="c">
```

then when the PC user selects Alt+c (or the Mac user selects Cmd+c), the cursor would jump to the Address text field. All form elements on the page should be given a unique `accesskey` value to avoid conflict.

The typical non-mouse method for navigating a form is to tab through the various input fields. Browsers interpret tab order according to the placement of the form elements, left-to-right, top-to-bottom. Although this is acceptable in many situations, it's certainly not applicable for all forms. To control the tabbing sequence, use the `tabindex` attribute. The `tabindex` attribute is a number between 0 and 32,767; the tabbing order follows the numbers from lowest to highest. For example, to explicitly set the tabbing order for three text fields, the code would look like this:

TIP: In addition to labels making it easier for assistive technologies to identify form elements, they also provide a larger selectable region. In supporting browsers, such as Internet Explorer 5 and later, you can click on either the label or the form element to select it, just as you can with most non-web applications. Anyone who has spent a little too much time trying to select the right option button will certainly appreciate this feature.

TIP: Although it's probably best not to assign any of the letters used by the browser menus, such as F for File or E for Edit, you can do this if you need to. The `accesskey` attribute is given priority over the menu key.

```
<tr>
    <td>City:<input type="text" name="cityText" tabindex="1"></td>
    <td>State:<input type="text" name="stateText"
    tabindex="2"></td>
    <td>Zip:<input type="text" name="zipText" tabindex="3"></td>
</tr>
```

> **NOTE:** If you intend to use the `tabindex` attribute, be sure to assign `tabindex` values to all form elements on a given page; failure to do so will result in an unexpected and undesired tabbing order.

The `tabindex` values need only be positive integers. You can start with any value, and the numbers don't have to be sequential; for three elements in a row, you could just as well set their `tabindex` values to 143, 436, and 999.

1194.22(o): Navigation Links

A method shall be provided that permits users to skip repetitive navigation links.

```
http://www.access-board.gov/sec508/guide/1194.22.htm#(o)
```

When you're browsing a site, your eye tends to focus on the content and skips over the navigation elements on each page. Screen readers don't have that luxury. Every time a page loads, if a navigation bar is located on the top, that's the first thing the screen reader starts to announce. Anyone who is using such a screen reader must listen to the link selections each time before he arrives at some content. If you can understand how tedious and annoying this behavior would be, you can understand the reason behind the repetitive navigation links guideline.

To skip navigation links, use a link to a named anchor at the top of the page where the named anchor is placed right before the content starts. The link to a named anchor can either be visible, like this:

```
<a href="#content">Skip Navigation</a>
```

or you can use a transparent GIF. If the link is at the top of the page, the screen reader encounters it first and gives the user the option to jump past the navigation elements.

1194.22(p): Time Delays

When a timed response is required, the user shall be alerted and given sufficient time to indicate more time is required.

http://www.access-board.gov/sec508/guide/1194.22.htm#(p)

The thrust of the final guideline is to make sure that users who have cognitive disabilities are given the opportunity to complete any online testing for which a response within a certain time limit is needed. This guideline has two separate parts:

- The web page must clearly state that the question is to be answered in a specific amount of time.

- Users should also have a way to reset the timer if they require additional time to complete the question.

Scanning Pages and Sites for 508 Violations

Integrating accessibility aspects into your web pages as you build them is obviously the most efficient way to construct new Section 508 compliant sites. But how do you bring legacy pages into compliance? Dreamweaver provides a useful tool for checking individual pages or entire sites against the Section 508 guidelines. By running the Accessibility report, you not only can validate legacy pages, but you also can make sure you haven't overlooked any requirements in new pages.

To check a page or pages for accessibility compliance, do this:

1. Choose Window > Results > Site Reports, and then select Reports (the green arrow).

    The Reports dialog box, as shown in Figure 2.8, is displayed.

2.8

Run an accessibility report for the current document, the whole site, selected individual files, or a selected folder.

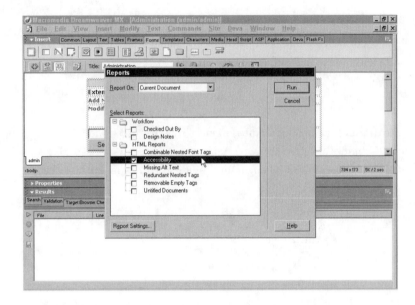

2. From the Reports dialog box, check the Accessibility option.

3. Choose the scope of the report from the Report On drop-down list.

4. To alter or verify the current settings, choose Report Settings (see Figure 2.9).

2.9

Restrict the Accessibility report by deselecting unneeded rules.

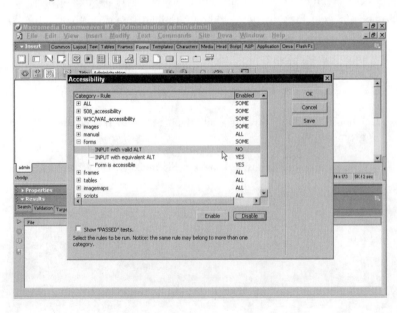

By default, all of the possible guidelines—from Section 508 and W3C/WAI Accessibility—are enabled. Expand the regulation by clicking on its plus sign to see any of the specific guidelines. If you don't want to check for a particular rule, clear that rule's check box. To include a list of items that were properly handled, select the Passed Test option.

5. From the Reports dialog box, select Run.

As Dreamweaver inspects each page requested, suspected problems found are listed in the Results panel. Blatant errors are noted with a red X, whereas issues that require a closer look are flagged with a question mark. If you opted to show passed tests, a check mark appears next to those items.

As with all Dreamweaver reports, the accessibility report directs you to the exact code in question. Simply double-click the entry to open the document (if necessary) and go directly to the line of code that contains the problem.

After the report has been run, you can save the results in an XML format by choosing the Save icon. You can then import the XML data into a data source or combine it with an XSL document to produce a formatted report.

Chapter 3

Streaming Multimedia Layout Using SMIL

Imagine that you're playing Charades at a party. The category is "Web technologies that combine animation, text, video, music, and images." Your teammate looks at the answer, moves to the center of the room, turns to you and grins. She keeps grinning. Do you think she's crazy? Do you guess Flash? Or do you just say, "SMIL?"

SMIL, short for Synchronized Multimedia Integration Language, is one of the Web's best-kept secrets. SMIL is a product of the W3C and a markup language in the increasingly long line of XML lineage. Currently in its second major version, SMIL is, as the acronym reveals, all about media integration. With SMIL, you can—as our Charades player indicated—combine the full complement of modern multimedia: Flash animation, MP3 music, streaming video, and plain old text. Best of all, you can synchronize all of these diverse elements into a cohesive, interactive presentation. SMIL 2.0's main playback mechanism is the RealOne player from Real, Inc., whereas Apple's QuickTime player has been SMIL 1.0 savvy since version 5.

But Dreamweaver is an HTML editor, you say. What does it have to do with SMIL? Starting with the MX version, Dreamweaver is far more than an HTML editor—it's an integrated design environment for all manner of code, including SMIL. This chapter has two main goals, one obvious and the other more subversive. The upfront objective is to detail how Dreamweaver can be used to script SMIL files, both manually and—with a little help from Dreamweaver's extensibility layer—visually. The subliminal purpose is to demonstrate how Dreamweaver can be used to code almost any structured language and to expose the built-in tools and techniques that makes a new language setup straightforward and manageable.

SMIL: A Coder's Overview

So what, exactly, does SMIL do, and how does it do it? Essentially, SMIL allows for the simultaneous or sequential interactive playback of various multimedia elements in a controlled layout. As noted earlier, SMIL is an XML-based language, and all SMIL documents start with an XML declaration:

```
<smil xmlns="http://www.w3.org/2001/SMIL20/Language">
```

This declares a SMIL 2.0 document, while just

```
<smil>
```

is sufficient for a SMIL 1.0 file.

Like HTML, SMIL files are divided into <head> and <body> regions. Unlike HTML, the <head> area is completely optional. If you just want to play back a video while showing a separate image, the entire SMIL page would look like this:

```
<smil>
    <body>
        <par>
            <video src="video/tour.rm" />
            <audio src="audio/narration.rm" />
        </par>
    </body>
</smil>
```

Indicates parallel playback ——————

SMIL presentations take on many forms when played; one example—coded in Dreamweaver—is shown in Figure 3.1.

3.1

By using only SMIL 1.0 tags, this presentation can be played in either the QuickTime or Real players.

The <head> region is used for <meta> tags and to establish the layout of the SMIL presentation. The <meta> tags work the same way that they do in HTM; the layout mechanism is something else. To specify a specific area in a SMIL presentation, a <region> tag is set within a <layout> and given a unique identifier, which is referenced by the media component. The following example establishes a video playback region, which is then referenced by the <video> tag:

```
<smil>
    <head>
        <layout>
            <region id="vid" height="320" width="240">
        </layout>
    </head>
    <body>
        <par>
            <video src="video/tour.rm" region="vid" />                    Specifies layout area
            <audio src="audio/narration.rm" />
```

continues

```
        </par>
      </body>
   </smil>
```

If you think about it, the SMIL layout structure is really not so different from a strict CSS implementation of an HTML page. In both instances, the layout areas are defined in the <head>. Within HTML pages, the <style> tag contains the CSS declarations, whereas in SMIL pages, the definitions—the <region> tags—are found in the <layout> tag. And, in both cases, the <body> tag contains the actual elements (usually <div> tags in HTML and <img>, <video>, or other media tags in SMIL) that refer to the previously defined layout areas. Besides width and height, <region> tags can also be absolutely positioned with left and top attributes and can include a z-index, much like <div> tags in HTML.

The overall size of the presentation is controlled by another tag in the <layout> section: <root-layout>. With <root-layout>, the height, width, and background color can be specified:

```
<root-layout width="500" height="500" backgroundColor="black">
```

The <root-layout> tag is a SMIL 1.0 implementation and somewhat limited; only one such tag can be defined in a presentation. If you're writing to SMIL 2.0 spec, you have a bit more flexibility by using the <topLayout> tag. Multiple <topLayout> tags are permitted and, besides dimension and color attributes, also include parameters that allow them to open and close as the media within them is played. You could, for example, have a video with streaming text presentation in the regions of one <topLayout> tag close when finished and allow a Flash animation with synchronized audio to begin playing.

SMIL offers two basic approaches to media playback over time: parallel and sequential. Media that is grouped in a <par> tag pair is played all at the same time, or in parallel; media within <seq> tags is played one after another, or sequentially. To play a video followed by an animation, the SMIL code would look this:

```
<seq>
    <img src="images/slide01.rm" />
    <img src="images/slide02.rm" />
    <img src="images/slide03.rm" />
    <img src="images/slide04.rm" />
</seq>
```

The <seq> tags are extremely useful for slideshow presentations. On the other hand, to display several media elements simultaneously, use code like this:

```
<par>
    <audio src="audio/narration.rm" />
    <video src="video/tour.rm" />
    <img src="images/poster.jpg" />
</par>
```

These essential timing tags are not exclusive—you can nest one inside the other. In this example, an ongoing slideshow takes place at the same time as the audio and video presentation:

```
<par>
    <audio src="audio/narration.rm" />
    <video src="video/tour.rm" />
    <seq>
        <img src="images/slide01.rm" />
        <img src="images/slide02.rm" />
        <img src="images/slide03.rm" />
        <img src="images/slide04.rm" />
    </seq>
</par>
```

These are the core elements of SMIL, but there is much more. Further exploration uncovers synchronization tags, transition elements, animation methods, and interactive modules, among others. You can find the entire SMIL specification, as well as many resources, at www.w3.org/AudioVideo/.

NOTE: A full discussion of SMIL is beyond the scope of this book, but if you're interested, be sure to check out *SMIL: Editing Multimedia for the Web* by Tim Kennedy and Mary Slowinski.

Making SMIL Available in Dreamweaver

Before you can truly code SMIL files in Dreamweaver, you have to do a little prep work. It's true that you can basically use Dreamweaver as a text editor to code in SMIL with any preamble, but you would be wasting Dreamweaver's potential—and you might as well use a text editor at that point.

Some of the techniques necessary for setting up for a new technology were covered in Chapter 1, "Incorporating Content Management Systems," but there are enough differences to warrant a step-by-step procedural. The core remains the same, though; you still need to do the following:

- Establish a new document type.

- Set Dreamweaver as the editor for SMIL documents.

- Build the SMIL tag library.

Following through on these three steps will turn Dreamweaver into a decent SMIL hand-coding tool.

Setting Up a SMIL Page Type

To review, new document types are defined by these methods:

- Placing an XML definition in Dreamweaver's Configuration/DocumentTypes folder

- Saving a prototype of the page in the NewDocuments subfolder

When working just in code, as we will be with the SMIL files, set the `internaltype` attribute of `<documenttype>` tag to other. This ensures that Dreamweaver opens only in Code view; Design view and the split Code and Design view are not available options. If you set the attribute to XML, Dreamweaver inserts an XML declaration at the top of each new page. Listing 3-1 shows how the document type definition would look with the `internaltype` attribute properly set. (As mentioned earlier, you should store the document type file in the Configuration/DocumentTypes folder alongside the MMDocumentTypes.xml file. I named my definition file `SMIL.xml`.)

Listing 3-1   **SMIL.xml** (03_SMIL.xml)

```
<?xml version="1.0"?>
<documenttypes>
    <documenttype id="SMIL" internaltype="XML" winfileextension="smil"
    macfileextension="smil" file="Default.smil">
        <title>
            SMIL
        </title>
        <description>
            SMIL Document
        </description>
    </documenttype>
</documenttypes>
```

After you have defined the document type, you need to create and save the prototype file. If you like, you can save a totally blank file called Default.smil in the NewDocuments folder, and that will do the trick. That does mean, however, that you must enter all the code for the page over and over again. When a document type has a set structure, it makes far more sense to provide a basic template for the file, much like the basic HTML page that Dreamweaver creates.

There are no guidelines as to what the basic SMIL page looks like, but Listing 3-2 shows what I suggest:

NOTE: Both .smil and .smi are generally accepted extensions for SMIL files. However, Real has suggested that developers would be better served by using .smil. Because Real is the 800-pound gorilla in this particular arena, I think it is best to follow Real's suggestion.

Listing 3-2   **Default.smil** (03_Default.smil)

```
<smil>
    <head>
        <layout>

        </layout>
    </head>

    <body>

    </body>
</smil>
```

My SMIL prototype is lean, but it's user-friendly. All the key elements are in place, ready to be used. I even have tabs added in the empty lines between the `<layout>` and `<body>` tag pairs to maintain my whitespace structure. You can make any alterations that are necessary. For instance, if you're only working with SMIL 2.0, you should change the opening `<smil>` tag to the following:

```
<smil xmlns="http://www.w3.org/2001/SMIL20/Language">
```

You also might want to add comments (SMIL uses HTML style comments) or meta tags to identify your organization or your authorship.

After you have stored both the document types XML file and the prototype SMIL file, close Dreamweaver and relaunch it. Choose File > New and, under the Other category, you should see your SMIL document type. Now we're ready to move on to the next stage of our preparation and define the SMIL tag set.

Establishing a SMIL Tag Library

NOTE: If you're unfamiliar with the Tag Library Editor, you might want to read through Chapter 1 where it is discussed in detail.

The SMIL tag set is an impressive one. SMIL 2.0 is composed of 10 inter-related modules with 36 separate tags and more than 100 attributes. Although you could enter each of the tags and their attributes by hand into Dreamweaver's Tag Library Editor as shown in Chapter 1, you'd be crazy to do it that way. Not only is the manual approach a mind-numbingly tedious process, it's also—thankfully—completely unnecessary.

Dreamweaver MX includes the capability to import Document Type Definition (DTD) schemas to produce tag libraries. With just one operation, you can make all the SMIL tags and attributes available within Dreamweaver. Here's how it's done:

1. Before you can import the SMIL DTD, you'll need to get a copy from the W3C site. At this writing, you can find all of the modules in one handy file at `http://www.w3.org/2001/SMIL20/DTD.zip`. Extract the compressed files to their own folder.

2. Choose Edit > Tag Libraries to open the Tag Library Editor.

3. Select the Add (+) button and choose DTDSchema > Import XML or DTD Schema File.

4. Locate the SMIL20.dtd file in the Open File dialog box.

 The rest of the process is automatic and pretty immediate. A new tag library, SMIL20.dtd, is created with all the tags and attributes in place, as shown in Figure 3.2.

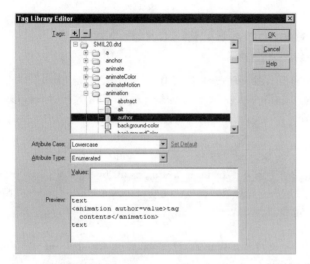

3.2

Adding the SMIL tag set by importing its DTD includes all 10 SMIL 2.0 modules.

5. Expand the SMIL tree to modify any tag or attribute's formatting.

 Keep in mind that as an XML file type, all tags must be lowercase; attributes use lower- or mixed-case.

6. With the SMIL tag library entry selected, choose the SMIL document type from the Used In list and deselect any other entries, such as HTML.

There's no need to relaunch Dreamweaver to use the newly defined tag library. Just choose File > New and select SMIL from the Other category and begin coding. To see the code hints in action, place your cursor between the `<layout>` tag pair and enter the opening angle bracket. All the SMIL tags should appear in the drop-down code Hints menu, as shown in Figure 3.3.

TIP: You might notice that all of the attributes are set to the Enumerated type. This is a consequence of the DTD import. Although you could change the type of the numerous attributes to something more suited, such as changing the `backgroundcolor` attribute to a color type, it is really not necessary. The attribute types are useful only when you're working with the Tag Inspector. That panel is inactive when you're working exclusively in Code view.

3.3

When the code hints appear, begin typing the tag, and the menu selection moves to the closest match. When you find the tag you want, press Enter (Return) to insert it.

```
1   <smil>
2       <head>
3           <layout>
4               <reg
5           </layout|    <> img
6       </head>          <> layout
7                        <> meta
8       <body>           <> metadata
9                        <> par
10      </body>          <> param
11  </smil>              <> prefetch
12                       <> priorityClass
                         <> ref
                         <> region
```

Constructing a SMIL Layout within Dreamweaver

When I first started investigating SMIL, I saw an immediate parallel between SMIL regions and Dreamweaver layers. Both are used for layout purposes and both have similar attributes: id, top, left, width, height, z-index, and background color. Dreamweaver layers have the major benefit of being extremely easy to draw out and position. With regions, you either have to figure out the pixel measurements by hand or play a protracted guessing game—or both. Wouldn't it be nice if you could draw your SMIL layout using Dreamweaver layers and then convert them to regions?

With the help of Dreamweaver's extensibility power, now you can. To facilitate the conversion, I created an extension called Convert Divs to Regions, shown as Bonus Listing 3-A (03_ConvertDivs2Regions.mxp), on this book's Web site. Here's how it works:

1. Open a blank HTML page.

2. Use Dreamweaver's Draw Layer tool to drag out a layer.

3. Give the layer the same name you want the region to have.

4. Re-size and position the layer to match the placement and dimensions of the region.

   For precise positioning, use the Left, Top, Width and Height values of the Property inspector.

5. If necessary, adjust the z-index property on the Property inspector.

6. Choose a background color for the layer from the Bg Color color picker.

7. Repeat steps 2–6 for every region needed until all layers are drawn and positioned properly. Save the file.

8. Open a new or previously saved SMIL document.

9. Choose Commands > Convert Divs to Regions and select the just saved layer layout file (see Figure 3.4).

3.4

The Convert Divs to Regions extension turns Dreamweaver into a SMIL layout tool.

When Convert Divs to Regions executes, all of the parameters from each of the `<div>` tags is added to a newly created `<region>` tag in the SMIL `<layout>` area. For example, the following tags

```
<div id="videoregion" style="position:absolute; left:50px;
top:50px; width:550px; height:247px; z-index:1; background-color:
#990000; layer-background-color: #990000; border: 1px none
#000000;"></div>
<div id="textregion" style="position:absolute; left:50px;
top:300px; width:550px; height:60px; z-index:2; background-color:
#000000; layer-background-color: #000000; border: 1px none
#000000;"></div>
```

are converted to these tags

```
<region id="videoregion" left="50px" top="50px" width="550px"
height="247px" z-index="1" backgroundColor=" #990000" />
<region id="textregion" left="50px" top="300px" width="550px"
height="60px" z-index="2" backgroundColor=" #000000" />
```

It is my hope that this utility will make coding SMIL pages within Dreamweaver easier.

Part II

Automations

Chapter 4

XML Transference from Data to Layout

The speed at which XML was adopted across the business sector was stunning. My first indication of the XML phenomenon came when I was teaching a seminar on maximizing the potential of Dreamweaver 3 at the Seybold conference in Boston. Trying to gauge the audience's level of expertise, I asked how many people had used Dreamweaver before. All but two or three raised their hands. When I asked how many people were familiar with Cascading Style Sheets, only about 1/3 responded. "How many people here use XML in their business?," I asked next. Three-quarters of the audience—an audience of Web developers, mind you—shot up their hands. Clearly, XML was a technology about to explode.

Dreamweaver has long maintained—since version 3, in fact—a strong XML connection. Importing and exporting of the well-formed XML file is only a menu option away. Of course, Dreamweaver assumes you know how to format the XML file properly for importing and how to make the most of exported data. Don't worry if you don't know how to do these things; those topics are part of what will be covered in this chapter.

The standard Dreamweaver XML features are powerful ones, but really only serve as a foundation for what is possible. In this chapter, you'll see how to automate the production of Web pages from XML data. We'll also explore techniques for structuring XML data as content, ready for import into a

Dreamweaver template. Finally, we'll look at how to extract the content from a document derived from a template and how to store the information in a data source.

A Brief Introduction to XML

XML, short for Extensible Markup Language, has often been described as a customizable version of HTML. Although this depiction is accurate to a degree, it doesn't really go far enough to distance it from HTML and characterize the language's strengths. To me, XML is pure structure. Each XML tag is only present to contribute to the structure of a document. Better still, the very name of each XML tag describes the content it contains, furthering the structural integrity of the document.

XML files begin with a statement that declares the XML version used. By default, Dreamweaver MX creates XML version 1.0 documents that specify the encoding:

```
<?xml version="1.0" encoding="iso-8859-1"?>
```

Internally, XML syntax is similar to HTML with a few key differences:

- Empty XML elements or tags include a closing slash, like this:

```
<bookImage src="jloweryImage.jpg" width="150" height="150" />
```

- The values of attributes must be quoted.

- Standalone attributes are not permitted. That is, checked as an attribute is not permitted, but checked="true" is.

- To avoid processing tags within text data, XML uses the CDATA element. CDATA stands for *character data*, and it is designated by surrounding the text with <![CDATA[and]]>. Here's an example:

```
<![CDATA[To designate a table of contents item, enclose the entry
with a <toc>...</toc> tag pair.]]>
```

Structurally, XML documents tend to be made up of multiple sets of tags following the same format. For example, if I were to describe a series of books I've read, the basic form might look like this:

```xml
<?xml version="1.0" encoding="iso-8859-1"?>
<books>
  <book>
    <bookTitle name="">
    <authorName name="">
    <bookDescription>
      <![CDATA[]]>
    </bookDescription>
  <book>
</books>
```

With a number of entries completed, the XML file would look like this:

```xml
<?xml version="1.0" encoding="iso-8859-1"?>
<books>
  <book>
    <bookTitle name="Critical Space">
    <authorName name="Greg Rucka">
    <bookDescription>
      <![CDATA[Bodyguard Atticus Kodiak is hired by someone who
      attempted to once kill him.]]>
    </bookDescription>
  <book>
  <book>
    <bookTitle name="Blackwater Sound">
    <authorName name="James W. Hall">
    <bookDescription>
      <![CDATA[Thorn abandons his role as Florida fisherman to
      stop the injustice brought by the rich and powerful
      Brasswell family.]]>
    </bookDescription>
  <book>
```

First of three children

continues

```
<book>
  <bookTitle name="Pursuit">
  <authorName name="Thomas Perry">
  <bookDescription>
    <![CDATA[Who is the hunter and who is the hunted in
    this book of criminologist vs. serial killer?]]>
  </bookDescription>
  <book>
</books>
```

In this example, the overall structural element is the `<books>` tag, which has three nodes or *children* in the `<book>` tags. Within each `<book>` child, the same descriptive tags are used with varying values. We'll see this exact type of format when we examine XML documents that are exported from Dreamweaver.

Exporting Template Content to XML

Most of Dreamweaver's XML focus is dedicated to working with templates and template-derived documents. Dreamweaver regards the locked areas of a template as the presentation layer of a document and the content within the editable and repeating regions as well as some other template markup as the data. Dreamweaver can only pull XML data from an instance of a template and, similarly, import XML data into a template instance.

Exporting a Single Document

As noted earlier, Dreamweaver provides a direct menu command for extracting the XML content from templates: File, Export, Template Data as XML. When invoking this command—which becomes active only when the current document is template derived—the Export Template Data as XML dialog box is displayed (see Figure 4.1). For basic templates—ones that use only editable regions—Dreamweaver can format the XML output in one of two ways. The standard Dreamweaver XML approach lists every region as an `<item>` tag, identified separately by the `name` attribute. For example, if a template had three editable regions—such as `bookTitle`, `authorName`, and `bookDescription`—then selecting the Use Standard Dreamweaver XML Tags option would output the following:

NOTE: You might find it helpful to examine output from Dreamweaver's Export Template Data as XML command; you'll find examples in Listing 4-1 (standard items sample) and Listing 4-2 (editable regions sample) at the end of this section.

```
<item name="bookTitle"><![CDATA[Critical Space]]></item>
<item name="authorName"><![CDATA[Greg Rucka]]></item>
<item name="bookDescription">><![CDATA[Bodyguard Atticus Kodiak is
hired by someone who attempted to once kill him.]]></item>
```

In contrast, the Use Editable Region Names as XML Tags option formats
the data like this:

```
<bookTitle>![CDATA[Critical Space]]></bookTitle>
<authorName><![CDATA[Greg Rucka]]></authorName>
<bookDescription><![CDATA[Bodyguard Atticus Kodiak is hired by
someone who attempted to once kill him.]]></bookDescription>
```

*Note
constant
use of
CDATA*

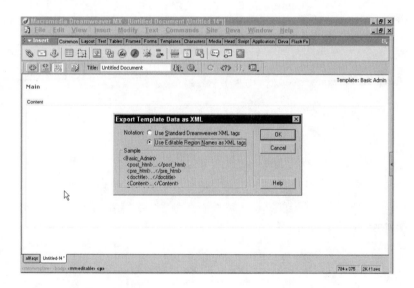

4.1

The Export Template Data
as XML dialog box offers
two export styles—as long
as the only template
markup tags in the
document are editable
regions.

There are other differences as well. For instance, the syntax for the master
template under the standard Dreamweaver XML tags is this:

```
<templateItems template="/Templates/BasicBookList.dwt"
codeOutsideHTMLIsLocked="false">
...
</templateItems>
```

as opposed to this:

```
<BasicBookList template="/Templates/BasicBookList.dwt"
codeOutsideHTMLIsLocked="false">
...
</BasicBookList>
```

NOTE: Don't get the idea that template data can only be exported from static pages. Dynamic pages, which often include code outside of the <html> tag pair, can also be exported. Dreamweaver uses a special syntax for code that appears before the opening <html> tag:
`<item name="(code before HTML tag)">`
or
`<pre_html>`
Similar tags are used for code that appears after the closing </html> tag.

As noted, complex template documents—those that have repeating regions or template parameters as well as editable regions—can only be output in the standard Dreamweaver format. Several additional tags are used to note the enhanced template markup. A template parameter—the only evidence of a conditional region—looks like this:

```
<parameter name="dbOnSale" type="boolean"
passthrough="false"><![CDATA[true]]></parameter>
```

A repeating region is coded this way:

```
<repeat name="RepeatRegion1">
  <repeatEntry>
    <item name="BookTitle"><![CDATA[Critical Space]]></item>
    <item name="AuthorName"><![CDATA[Greg Rucka]]></item>
    <item name="MainCharacter"><![CDATA[Atticus Kodiak]]></item>
  </repeatEntry>
  <repeatEntry>
    <item name="BookTitle"><![CDATA[Blackwater Sound]]></item>
    <item name="AuthorName"><![CDATA[James W. Hall]]></item>
    <item name="MainCharacter"><![CDATA[Thorn]]></item>
  </repeatEntry>
</repeat>
```

NOTE: If your template region names include special characters—including spaces or underscores—then Dreamweaver only lets you export using the standard Dreamweaver method.

That's it. The following listings show the completed code.

Listing 4-1   **Standard Items Sample** (04_standarditems.xml)

```xml
<?xml version="1.0"?>
<templateItems template="/Templates/Basic Admin.dwt"
codeOutsideHTMLIsLocked="false">
    <item name="(code after HTML tag)"><![CDATA[
]]></item>
    <item name="(code before HTML
tag)"><![CDATA[<%@LANGUAGE="VBSCRIPT"%>
]]></item>
    <item name="doctitle"><![CDATA[
<title>Untitled Document</title>
]]></item>
    <item name="Content"><![CDATA[
<p>The content goes here.</p>
<p> </p>
]]></item>
</templateItems>
```

Listing 4-2   **Editable Regions Sample** (04_editableregions.xml)

```xml
<?xml version="1.0"?>
<Basic_Admin template="/Templates/Basic Admin.dwt"
codeOutsideHTMLIsLocked="false">
    <post_html><![CDATA[]]></post_html>
    <pre_html><![CDATA[<%@LANGUAGE="VBSCRIPT"%>
</pre_html>
    <doctitle><![CDATA[
<title>Untitled Document</title>
]]></doctitle>
    <Content><![CDATA[
<p>The content goes here.</p>
<p> </p>
]]></Content>
</Basic_Admin>
```

Exporting an Entire Site

Undoubtedly, the Export, Template Data as XML command is quite useful at extracting the content from a templated page; unfortunately, it's also somewhat tedious. If you are responsible for exporting the content from an entire site, you have quite a repetitive task ahead of you when you're using just this feature. Luckily, Dreamweaver includes an equally powerful command for extracting all the data from all the template-derived pages in a site.

Although the command for exporting a single page is front and center, you really have to dig to find the equivalent site-wide command. In fact, you have to perform an entirely different—somewhat antithetical—operation to get the XML output. Dreamweaver MX includes the ability to export a site, completely stripping out all the template markup from template-derived documents. When you choose Modify, Templates, Export Without Markup, the dialog box shown in Figure 4.2 is displayed.

4.2

To extract all the data as XML from a site, you first must choose Templates > Export Without Markup.

NOTE: To avoid having to ask for individual names for each file exported, Dreamweaver automatically appends the .xml extension to whatever the original filename is— including the extension. For example, marchbooklist.htm becomes marchbooklist.htm.xml.

To enable the XML operation, make sure that the Keep Template Data Files option is selected. This is the signal to Dreamweaver to make two copies of template-derived documents: one without template markup and another in XML data format. Dreamweaver stores both files in the same folder. If you've previously exported the site and want to update the data files, select Extract Only Changed Files.

Exporting Selected Files in a Site

So far, we've seen how Dreamweaver can export XML data from a single page or from an entire site. However, what if you need something in between? What if you need to export the five files you're working on or only a couple of folders of files? What if you don't want to make a template-less copy of the site to get the exported files?

Although Dreamweaver makes exporting template data as XML programmatically appear straightforward, there's an aptly named function, dw.exportTemplateDataAsXML(). It's not as easy as it seems. Every time the exportTemplateDataAsXML() function is called, the Export Template Data as XML dialog box opens, disrupting the automatic nature of the operation. Luckily, Dreamweaver makes it fairly easy to get an array of all the editable regions in a document with another API function, dom.getEditableRegionList(). That function serves as the basis for the Export XML extension.

The Export XML extension (see Figure 4.3) allows the user to select the scope of the operation (Current Document, All Open Documents, Selected Files in Site Panel or Entire Site), which template to declare in the XML file, and where to store the files.

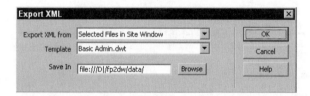

4.3

Export XML uses Massimo Foti's site-wide library to work with a wide range of file selections.

Another real challenge is developing a system to supply the file URLs as needed, whether it's just from the current document, from the selected files, or from the entire site. Although Macromedia hasn't seen fit to provide this functionality, a robust solution has emerged from Dreamweaver's premier third-party developer, Massimo Foti. Fairly early on in the development of his extensions, Massimo came across this very problem: How do you process a single command across a site?

Over the years, Massimo has refined his library numerous times, and it is quite full featured and extremely useful. Although the code is too lengthy to reproduce and analyze in this chapter, I have included it as Bonus Listing 4-A (Massimo Foti's Site-Wide Library [04_siteutils.js]) on the book's web site, with Massimo's permission, as well as a small extension to demonstrate its use, shown here in listing 4-3.

TIP: To see the full range of Massimo Foti's work, visit www.massimocorner.com.

Listing 4-3   **Export XML** (04_exportxml.mxp)

```
<html>
<head>
<title>Export XML</title>
```

continues

```javascript
<script language="javascript"
src="../Shared/Beyond/Scripts/Beyond_Site.js"></script>
<script language="JavaScript" src="../Shared/MM/Scripts/CMN/UI.js"
type="text/JavaScript"></script>
<script language='javascript'>

//init globals ****************************************************
var theSelect = findObject('fileList');
var theWildText = findObject('wildText');
var theTemplateList = findObject("template_list");
var theXML = "";


//******************* Primary Functions **************************

function commandButtons(){
    return new Array( 'OK', 'doCommand()', 'Cancel',
    'window.close()', 'Help', 'getHelp(theHelpFile)')
}
function exportXML(theURL) {
    var theDOM = dw.getDocumentDOM();
    if(theDOM.documentElement.innerHTML.indexOf("InstanceBegin
    template=") != -1) {
        var theERs = theDOM.getEditableRegionList();
        var theName, theData
        theXML = "";
        for (i = 0; i < theERs.length; ++i) {
            theName = theERs[i].getAttribute("name");
            theData = theERs[i].innerHTML;
            theXML += '<item name="' + theName + '"><![CDATA[' +
            theData + ']]></item>' + '\n';
        }
        var theXMLHeader = "";
        theTemplate = theTemplateList.options
        [theTemplateList.selectedIndex].text;
        var theTemplateFile = dw.getSiteRoot() + "Templates/" +
        theTemplate;
```

```
        theXMLHeader += '<?xml version="1.0"?>' + '\n';
        theXMLHeader += '<templateItems template="/Templates/' +
        theTemplate + '" codeOutsideHTMLIsLocked="false">' + '\n';
        theXML = theXMLHeader + theXML + '\n' + '</templateItems>'
        + '\n';
        var fileURL = findObject("folder_text").value +
        theURL.substr(theURL.lastIndexOf("/") + 1) + ".xml";
        r = DWfile.write(fileURL, theXML);
    }
    dw.releaseDocument(theDOM);
}


function doCommand() {
    var selectArray = new Array("currentDoc","openedDocs",
    "siteSelected","wholeSite");
    var theRes = 1
    var theWildCards = ".htm;.html;.shtm;.shtml;.asp;.cfm;.cfml;
    .php;.php3"

    for (var i=0; i<theSelect.options.length; i++){
        if (theSelect.options[i].selected){
            whichFiles = selectArray[i];
        }
    }
    switch (whichFiles){

        case "currentDoc":
            urlArray = getCurrentDoc();
            if(urlArray){
                exportXML(urlArray);
            }
            break;

        case "openedDocs":
            agree = confirm("This command cannot be undone.
            Proceed?");
```

continues

```
                    //If it's ok, go
                    if (agree){
                        openFilesArray = new Array();
                        //Get the currently opened files
                        openFilesArray = getOpenedDocs();
                        //Filter them to get just the ones matching extensions
                        urlArray = filterFiles(theWildCards,openFilesArray);
                        for (var i=0; i<openFilesArray.length; i++){
                            exportXML(urlArray[i]);
                        }
                    } else {
                        return;
                    }
                    break;

                case "siteSelected":
                 var siteFocus,agree;
                 siteSelectedArray = new Array();
                 writeSiteSelectedArray = new Array();
                 siteFocus = site.getFocus();
                 if(siteFocus == "local" || "site map"){
                     //Ask the user
                     agree = confirm("This command cannot be undone.
                     Proceed?");
                     //If it's ok, go
                     if (agree){
                         //Get the urls of the files selected inside
                         //the site window
                          siteSelectedArray = site.getSelection();
                         if (siteSelectedArray.length == 0 ||
                         siteSelectedArray[0].indexOf(".") == -1) {
                             alert("No files in Site window selected.
                             \nChoose another Generate From option.")
                             return;
                         }
                         //Filter them to get just the matching extensions
```

```
            urlArray = filterFiles(theWildCards,
            siteSelectedArray);
            for (var i=0; i<urlArray.length; i++){
                exportXML(urlArray[i]);
            }
        } else {
            return;
        }
    }
    else{
        alert("This command can affect only local files");
    }
    break;


case "wholeSite":
    var agree;
    wholeSiteArray = new Array();
    writeFilesArray = new Array();
    //Ask the user
    agree = confirm("This command cannot be undone.
    Proceed?");
    //If it's ok, go
    if (agree){
        //Get all the urls of files in the site with
        //matching extensions
        wholeSiteArray = getWholeSite();
        //Filter them to get just the matching extensions
        urlArray = filterFiles(theWildCards,wholeSiteArray);
        for (var i=0; i<urlArray.length; i++){
            exportXML(urlArray[i]);
        }
    } else {
        return;
    }
    break;
}
window.close();
```

continues

```
        return;
    }

    function findFolder() {
        findObject("folder_text").value = dw.browseForFolderURL();
    }

    function getTemplateList() {
        //returns a list of templates in site
        var theTemplateDir = dw.getSiteRoot() + "Templates/";
        var theTemplates = new Array();
        theTemplates = DWfile.listFolder(theTemplateDir + "*.dwt",
        "files");
        if (theTemplates){
            loadSelectList(theTemplateList,theTemplates);
        }
    }

    function initUI() {
        getTemplateList();
    }

    </script>
    </head>

    <body onLoad="initUI()">
    <form name="theForm">
      <table border="0">
        <tr>
          <td nowrap> <div align="right">Export XML from</div></td>
          <td nowrap> <select name="fileList" style="width:220px">
             <option selected>Current Document</option>
             <option>All Open Documents</option>
             <option>Selected Files in Site Window </option>
             <option>Entire Site</option>
            </select> </td>
```

```
    </tr>
    <tr>
      <td nowrap><div align="right">Template</div></td>
      <td nowrap><select name="template_list" id="template_list"
      style="width:220">
          <option selected>Loading templates.............</option>
        </select></td>
    </tr>
    <tr>
      <td><div align="right">Save In</div></td>
      <td><input name="folder_text" type="text" id="folder_text"
      style="width:155">
        <input type="button" name="Button" value="Browse"
        onClick="findFolder()"></td>
    </tr>
  </table>
</form></body>
</html>
```

After Massimo's function does the heavy lifting of finding all the required
file URLs, that information is passed to the exportXML() function in the
extension. As is often the case, the Document Object Model (DOM) for the
document is first appropriated and put into a variable. Then the function
tests to make sure that the document is derived from a template and that it's
possible to export XML from it. Again, there is a Macromedia API function
intended for this purpose—and again, we can't use it because it requires the
document to be open before it will work. Because I don't want to open and
close every document, I found another way to determine whether the file is
template derived:

```
if(theDOM.documentElement.innerHTML.indexOf("InstanceBegin
template=") != -1)
```

This code walks down the DOM a bit and looks for the key words that
indicate the document is a template instance. If so, we're ready for the
process to begin by getting all the editable regions in the file:

```
var theERs = theDOM.getEditableRegionList();
```

The next significant action takes place in a loop where the editable region name and innerHTML are extracted and inserted into an XML format:

```
for (i = 0; i < theERs.length; ++i) {
    theName = theERs[i].getAttribute("name");
    theData = theERs[i].innerHTML;
    theXML += '<item name="' + theName + '"><![CDATA[' + theData +
']]></item>' + '\n';
}
```

Added to format output

Next, we're ready to set up the template name variable, which we'll soon insert into the XML file:

```
theTemplate = theTemplateList.options[theTemplateList.
selectedIndex].text;
```

The header for the XML file is constructed next, integrating the template name:

```
theXMLHeader += '<?xml version="1.0"?>' + '\n';
theXMLHeader += '<templateItems template="/Templates/' +
theTemplate + '" codeOutsideHTMLIsLocked="false">' + '\n';
```

Now the entire XML file is concatenated into one string:

```
theXML = theXMLHeader + theXML + '\n' + '</templateItems>' + '\n';
```

Closing XML tag

After building the file URL to store the XML file, the DWfile API is used to write it out:

```
var fileURL = findObject("folder_text").value +
theURL.substr(theURL.lastIndexOf("/") + 1) + ".xml";
r = DWfile.write(fileURL, theXML);
```

The final instruction in the code is used to release the memory used to work with the DOM—a necessary step when possibly processing an entire site:

```
dw.releaseDocument(theDOM);
```

Manually Importing from XML

On the flip side of exporting XML data from templates, Dreamweaver has the capability to import XML data into a template to create a new template-derived document. For the import operation to work as intended, the XML must be in a specific format. Each XML tag corresponds to a template region or markup. Both XML syntax used during export—the standard Dreamweaver <item> syntax and the editable region names as XML tags—are supported for import, with the same restrictions. For complex templates, including any template markup other than just editable regions, the standard Dreamweaver syntax must be used.

Perhaps the best way to understand the format required for import is to examine an exported XML file. Here's a simple example:

```
<?xml version="1.0"?>
<templateItems template="/Templates/planet.dwt"
codeOutsideHTMLIsLocked="false">
    <item name="diameter"><![CDATA[
        <P> 7926 miles
        ]]></item>
    <item name="moons"><![CDATA[
        <P> 1
        ]]></item>
    <item name="planetImage"><![CDATA[<IMG
SRC="assets/Images/earth.gif" ALIGN="TOP" WIDTH="72" HEIGHT="72"
VSPACE="0" HSPACE="0" ALT="Earth Photo" BORDER="0">]]></item>
    <item name="doctitle"><![CDATA[
<TITLE>Earth</TITLE>
]]></item>
    <item name="orbital_period"><![CDATA[
        <P> 365 days, 6 hours, 9 minutes, 13 seconds
        ]]></item>
</templateItems>
```

Link to Template

Note placement in file

The first thing to notice is the tag identifying the template from which the document was derived. Another important aspect is the order—or rather the lack of order—of the item entries. In the original file, the editable regions appeared in this sequence: `doctitle`, `planetImage`, `diameter`, `orbital_period`, and `moons`. In the exported data file, they are written in this order: `diameter`, `moons`, `planetImage`, `doctitle`, and `orbital_period`. This is one of the major advantages of an XML file over a less structured layout of information—the order the data is written is irrelevant to the order of its final presentation.

Dreamweaver imports XML files written in both standard and editable region-based syntax. Either of the following two formats is supported:

```
<templateItems template="/Templates/planet.dwt"
codeOutsideHTMLIsLocked="false">...</templateItems>

<planet template="/Templates/planet.dwt">...</planet>
```

When the File, Import, XML into Template command is given and a properly formatted XML file is selected, the data and the template instance are merged and a new document is created immediately.

Automated Import to Template

Again, we're faced with a powerful command that does exactly what we want—except that it does it with only one document at a time. What's clearly needed here is a parallel to the Export XML extension—one that permits the same choices in scope (current document, open documents, selected files in site panel, or entire site) and stores all the HTML documents generated from importing XML files in a single folder. Constructing this extension takes even less time because much of the work (looping through the selected files, for example) has already been done once before. A key point to take away from this section—aside from how to build the function—is how you can leverage work in one extension to make another.

Let's start by defining how we expect the new extension, Import XML, to work:

1. From the Extension dialog box, the user selects which XML files should be included in the operation.

2. The user also selects a folder to store the generated pages.

3. When the command executes, the program gathers the URL of each XML file.

NOTE: The approach described in this section is not the only way to combine data and templates to create new pages. To see how you can generate HTML pages directly from a data source, look at Chapter 5, "Automating Static Page Production from a Data Source."

NOTE: To View the completed code, see Listing 4-4 at the end of this section.

4. The URL is passed to a function that first creates a blank document to hold the template instance and then imports the XML data.

5. The new file is saved and closed—and the next XML file, if any, is processed.

The process and the Import XML extension are pretty straightforward. Best of all, we have a starting point to jump off from: the Export XML extension. In a situation like this where so much is duplicated from one extension to the next, I typically open the original extension and do a File, Save As to create a new extension. I save the new file in the appropriate Configuration folder; in this case, that would be Commands.

Next, I change the title of the extension. The title is displayed in the title bar of the Extension dialog box. Changing the title is a small thing, but I often forget to do it if I don't do it right away. Now we can begin to seriously modify the base extension, starting with the user interface. In this case, we'll take away an element found in Export XML that is not needed in Import XML: the Template drop-down list. For this version of Import XML, it is assumed that all the XML files declared their associated template. Why? The primary reason is that the key API function we will be using, dw.importXMLIntoTemplate(), requires it. It also greatly simplifies our coding.

With the Template drop-down list and its label deleted, the Import XML extension (see Figure 4.4) is ready for user input.

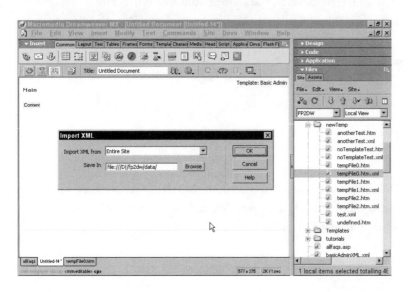

TIP: Remember that Dreamweaver MX now supports multiuser configurations. If you are working with a multiuser-compatible OS (such as Windows 2000 or Mac OS X), the custom extensions need to be saved in the appropriate user/Macromedia/ Dreamweaver MX/ Configuration folder. Extensions for single-user systems are stored in the Programs/Macromedia/ Dreamweaver MX/ Configuration folder (Windows) or in the Applications:Macromedia: Dreamweaver MX: Configuration folder (Macintosh).

4.4

Why rebuild when you can duplicate? The Import XML extension is a duplicate of Export XML with one user interface element removed.

I need to make only one small change to code within the `doCommand()` function of Import XML. In the Export XML extension, the `Wildcards` variable was set to allow almost every type of Web document extension: .htm, .html, .shtm, .shtml, .asp, .cfm, .cfml, .php, and .php3. For the Import XML extension, the selection needs to be limited to just one file type: .xml.

As before, the main function is separated from the code that takes the user's selection of which files to be processed. Here, that function is named `importXML()`, whereas in the original extension, it was named `exportXML()`. Because the user selection code calls the function for each choice of scope potentially made, the easiest way to modify the code is to do a find and replace.

The first line in the `importXML()` function serves to create a new, blank document:

```
var theTempDOM = dw.createDocument();
```

If this is not done, the template instance is loaded onto the current document.

The next bit of code represents one of the real pitfalls of extension programming: incorrect documentation. According to the *Extending Dreamweaver* manual, the `importXMLIntoTemplate()` function takes a file URL as its only argument. Unfortunately, that's wrong. Although it does take a URL pointing to an XML file, the string should be formatted as a file path, like this:

```
D:\fp2dw\newTemp\anotherTest.xml
```

instead of a file URL, like this:

```
file:///D|/fp2dw/newTemp/anotherTest.xml
```

Dreamweaver provides a function in the MMNotes API collection that converts a file URL to a file path. We can use that without including any other JavaScript file:

```
var theNewURL = MMNotes.localURLToFilePath(theURL);
```

With our new URL created, we're ready to perform the key operation of importing the XML into a template:

```
dw.importXMLIntoTemplate(theNewURL);
```

Now we create a new document name based on the XML filename and save the file. The new name substitutes an .htm extension for the file's original.xml one and incorporates the user-selected path to a folder:

```
docName = findObject("folder_text").value +
theURL.substring(theURL.lastIndexOf("/") + 1, theURL.length - 4) +
".htm";
res = dw.saveDocument(theTempDOM, docName);
```

Finally, if the save operation was successful, the document is closed and control passes back to the doCommand() function to get another URL for processing, if necessary.

```
if (res) {
    dw.closeDocument(theTempDOM);
}
return;
```

The most common error to watch for when using an extension like this is malformed XML. If you encounter problems, check the XML file by choosing Validate Current Document as XML from the Validation panel.

Listing 4-4   Import XML (04_importXML.mxp)

```
<html>
<head>
<title>Import XML</title>

<script language="javascript"
src="../Shared/Beyond/Scripts/Beyond_Site.js"></script>
<script language="JavaScript" src="../Shared/MM/Scripts/CMN/UI.js"
type="text/JavaScript"></script>
<script language='javascript'>
```

continues

```javascript
//init globals ****************************************************
var theSelect = findObject('fileList');
var theWildText = findObject('wildText');
var theXML = "";



//******************** Primary Functions ************************

function commandButtons(){
    return new Array( 'OK', 'doCommand()', 'Cancel',
    'window.close()', 'Help', 'getHelp(theHelpFile)')
}


function importXML(theURL) {
   var theTempDOM = dw.createDocument();
   var theNewURL = MMNotes.localURLToFilePath(theURL);
   dw.importXMLIntoTemplate(theNewURL);
   docName = findObject("folder_text").value +
   theURL.substring(theURL.lastIndexOf("/") + 1, theURL.length -
   4) + ".htm";
   res = dw.saveDocument(theTempDOM, docName);
   if (res) {
      dw.closeDocument(theTempDOM);
   }
   return;
}



function doCommand() {
   var selectArray = new Array("currentDoc","openedDocs",
   "siteSelected","wholeSite");
   var theRes = 1
   var theWildCards = ".xml"

   for (var i=0; i<theSelect.options.length; i++){
      if (theSelect.options[i].selected){
         whichFiles = selectArray[i];
```

```
    }
}
switch (whichFiles){

    case "currentDoc":
        urlArray = getCurrentDoc();
        if(urlArray){
            importXML(urlArray);
        }
        break;


    case "openedDocs":
        agree = confirm("This command cannot be undone.
        Proceed?");
        //If it's ok, go
        if (agree){
            openFilesArray = new Array();
            //Get the currently opened files
            openFilesArray = getOpenedDocs();
            //Filter them to get just the ones matching extensions
            urlArray = filterFiles(theWildCards,openFilesArray);
            for (var i=0; i<openFilesArray.length; i++){
                importXML(urlArray[i]);
            }
        } else {
            return;
        }
        break;

      case "siteSelected":
       var siteFocus,agree;
       siteSelectedArray = new Array();
       writeSiteSelectedArray = new Array();
       siteFocus = site.getFocus();
       if(siteFocus == "local" || "site map"){
           //Ask the user
```

continues

```
            agree = confirm("This command cannot be undone.
        Proceed?");
        //If it's ok, go
        if (agree){
            //Get the urls of the files selected inside the
            //site window
             siteSelectedArray = site.getSelection();
            if (siteSelectedArray.length == 0 ||
            siteSelectedArray[0].indexOf(".") == -1) {
                alert("No files in Site window selected.\nChoose
                another Generate From option.")
                return;
            }
            //Filter them to get just the matching extensions
            urlArray = filterFiles(theWildCards,
            siteSelectedArray);
            for (var i=0; i<urlArray.length; i++){
                importXML(urlArray[i]);
            }
        } else {
            return;
        }
    }
    else{
        alert("This command can affect only local files");
    }
    break;

case "wholeSite":
    var agree;
    wholeSiteArray = new Array();
    writeFilesArray = new Array();
    //Ask the user
    agree = confirm("This command cannot be undone.
    Proceed?");
    //If it's ok, go
    if (agree){
```

```
                //Get all the urls of files in the site with matching
                //extensions
                wholeSiteArray = getWholeSite();
                //Filter them to get just the matching extensions
                urlArray = filterFiles(theWildCards,wholeSiteArray);
                for (var i=0; i<urlArray.length; i++){
                    importXML(urlArray[i]);
                }
            } else {
                return;
            }
            break;
    }
    window.close();
    return;
}


function findFolder() {
    findObject("folder_text").value = dw.browseForFolderURL();
}


function findFile() {
    findObject("file_text").value = dw.browseForFileURL("select");
}


function getTemplateList() {
    //returns a list of templates in site
    var theTemplateDir = dw.getSiteRoot() + "Templates/";
    var theTemplates = new Array();
    theTemplates = DWfile.listFolder(theTemplateDir + "*.dwt",
    "files");
    if (theTemplates){
        loadSelectList(theTemplateList,theTemplates);
    }
}
```

continues

```
function initUI() {
}

</script>
</head>

<body onLoad="initUI()">
<form name="theForm">
  <table border="0">
    <tr>
      <td nowrap> <div align="right">Import XML from</div></td>
      <td nowrap> <select name="fileList" style="width:220px">
          <option selected>Current Document</option>
          <option>All Open Documents</option>
          <option>Selected Files in Site Window </option>
          <option>Entire Site</option>
        </select> </td>
    </tr>
    <tr>
      <td><div align="right">Save In</div></td>
      <td><input name="folder_text" type="text" id="folder_text"
      style="width:155">
        <input type="button" name="Button" value="Browse"
        onClick="findFolder()"></td>
    </tr>
  </table>
</form></body>
</html>
```

Chapter 5

Automating Static Page Production from a Data Source

On first blush, creating static Web pages dynamically appears to be an oxymoron, if not just a bad idea. Data-driven or dynamic pages are often highly touted as the next evolutionary step for static HTML, so why would anyone ever want to go back? Home pages are often static, although increasingly, they are beginning to include some form of dynamic content. Static pages are often created within a dynamic site to provide a context for search engines to engage. Moreover, some clients just have not made the leap to dynamic site.

Whatever the reason, if your production environment would benefit from dynamically generated static pages, Dreamweaver is up to the task. Besides Dreamweaver, the techniques described in this chapter require some type of application server or *middleware*, such as ASP, ColdFusion, or PHP server. Although this chapter's examples all use a local development server, remote application servers can also be used.

The enhanced template power found in Dreamweaver MX opens up the possibilities for static page generation. In this chapter, we'll first look at the general technique for extracting data from a data source and then how to integrate that data with Dreamweaver's editable regions. Later in this chapter, you'll see how to show or hide template-embedded content, depending on data-derived values. We'll also examine how to programmatically increase the number of entries in a Dreamweaver template repeating region. Finally, we'll discuss a method for replacing third-party tags with external content in case your shop does not use Dreamweaver templates.

Overview of the Technique

Before diving into details, let's get a bird's-eye view of what's involved:

TIP: Here's one thought to keep in mind as you are involved with the data side of the process: The data that is inserted into the page goes in as HTML. Many fields contain straight text that, when replaced in the template, take on the formatting of the surrounding area; you can, however, add your own tags—either HTML or CSS styling. If you are inserting multiple paragraphs, be sure to enclose each with the <p> tags so that they will render properly.

- One or more templates with editable regions are constructed and stored in a Dreamweaver site.

- The data that is intended to replace the content in the editable regions is stored in a data source, such as an Access or SQL Server database.

- A Web application page that extracts the data from the data source and restyles it in a text format is created.

- A request is sent from a Dreamweaver extension to an application server (either local or remote) for the Web application page.

- Dreamweaver parses the data and inserts it into the proper places in an instance of a template.

- The new document—derived from a template and complete with the integrated data—is stored as a standard HTML page.

To help you understand the concept more completely, this workflow is diagrammed in Figure 5.1.

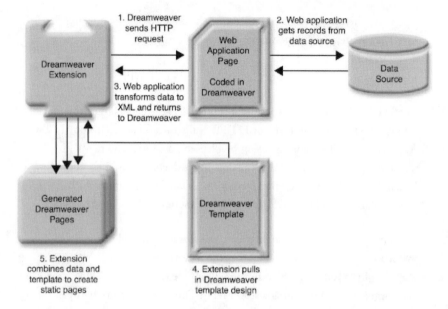

5.1

With the aid of a custom extension, Dreamweaver can combine external data and Dreamweaver templates to generate static pages.

This chapter assumes you know how to create templates in Dreamweaver and have data available in a data source. Before we discuss the development of the Web application page, you need to understand how Dreamweaver makes the connection and what format specifications are involved.

Connecting with the HTTP API

Dreamweaver MX enables the user to easily create Web applications that connect to data sources and populate pages with all manner of data. These Web applications must be processed by a specified application server, whether the application is ASP, ColdFusion, or something else, before the data can be displayed. Even Live Data view, which shows the actual data in the page, is constructed by sending a copy of the page being designed to the application server and then extracting and integrating the data. Rather than taking the Live Data route, which involves a great deal of extremely complex translation, Dreamweaver provides another apparatus for processing a Web application page and extracting the results: the HTTP API.

The HTTP API works, as you might suspect, by sending and receiving data via hypertext transfer protocol, or HTTP. Numerous functions in the HTTP API—seven in all—allow extension builders to post form data to a Web server and get responses; all the functionality is documented in Extending Dreamweaver (Help, Extending Dreamweaver) under the Utility APIs section. All of the HTTP API functions are methods of the `MMHttp` object.

To connect to a Web application server and extract data, only two related `MMHttp` functions are required: `MMHttp.getFile()` and `MMHttp.getFileCallback()`. Both methods are similar, each taking a URL as an argument and returning a server reply. The only difference between the two methods is that `getFileCallback()` calls a specified function after the data object has been received; the function you use depends on how your extension is constructed.

The `getFile()` function requires only one argument: the URL of the page to be processed:

```
var theFile = MMHttp.getFile("http://localhost/beyond/ch05_ex.asp");
```

Other optional arguments allow the returned file object to be saved under user control. However, in an automated production extension, where many pages are being generated, it's more expedient to save the files programmatically. Therefore, the optional arguments are not explored here.

If you are using the `getFileCallback()` function, the syntax includes the name of the function to be called:

```
var theFile = MMHttp.getFileCallback("convertFile()",
"http://localhost/beyond/ch05_ex.asp");
```

Let's look next at the application page.

Writing the Data Source Page

Exactly how the application page is coded varies greatly according to the
server model, the language, and the results desired. The overall structure of
the page translates well from one application to the next. You can even use
Dreamweaver to handle much of the foundation coding for you.

Basically, the application page needs to do four things:

- Connect to a data source.

- Extract a recordset.

- Convert the data to an XML-based file.

- Return the file to Dreamweaver.

The first two tasks are typical for application development, with or without
Dreamweaver. If you're using Dreamweaver, simply create the recordset
desired on an otherwise blank, dynamic page. Then, because the page should
execute but never display, delete all the standard HTML code, including the
<!DOCTYPE> declaration. At this point, if you are working in ASP/VBScript,
the page will look like this one:

```
<%@LANGUAGE="VBSCRIPT"%>
<!--#include file="../Connections/Extension.asp" -->
<%
Dim rsEx
Dim rsEx_numRows

Set rsEx = Server.CreateObject("ADODB.Recordset")
rsEx.ActiveConnection = MM_Extension_STRING
rsEx.Source = "SELECT * FROM extensions"
rsEx.CursorType = 0
rsEx.CursorLocation = 2
rsEx.LockType = 1
rsEx.Open()

rsEx_numRows = 0
%>
```

> **NOTE:** To view the completed code, see Listing 5-1 at the end of this section.

```
<%
rsEx.Close()
Set rsEx = Nothing
%>
```

Because Dreamweaver maintains a powerful Document Object Model (DOM) extensibility feature set, it's easy to extract data from a page if the page is structured as or like XML. Dreamweaver doesn't require a page to be in XML-compliant format to work this way. All that's necessary is a structured document with a clear separation of parameters and their content. Here's a simple example:

```
<main>
   <item name="dbName">Joseph Lowery</item>
   <item name="dbEmail">jlowery@idest.com</item>
</main>
```

After a recordset has been established, you can replace the static values (Joseph Lowery and `jlowery@idest.com`) with dynamic values, like these in ASP:

```
<main>
   <item name="dbName">(rsEx.Fields.Item("dbName").Value)</item>
   <item name="dbEmail">(rsEx.Fields.Item("dbEmail").Value)</item>
</main>
```

The `MMHttp.getFile()` function retrieves a text-based file, so the static and dynamic values must be concatenated into one long string and returned like this:

```
<%
Dim theString
theString = "<main>" & _
   "   <item name='dbName'>" & (rsEx.Fields.Item("dbName").Value) &
"</item>" &
   "   <item name='dbEmail'>" & (rsEx.Fields.Item("dbEmail").Value) &
"</item>" &
```

Concatenates next line

```
"</main>"
Response.Write(theString)
%>
```
Output string for return

Although each application page that is designed to generate data for static pages is different, one trait is virtually certain to be shared: Each page needs to be able to easily move through the recordset, returning one record after another on demand. This is a fairly common task for an experienced Web application developer. Dreamweaver can insert the necessary code for you, although this time with a bit of "sleight of hand." Here's how it's done:

1. Before the standard HTML code has been removed, drag a field or two from the Bindings panel onto the page.

   This field is really only inserted to indicate the change from one record to the next.

2. Press Enter (Return) and add a text phrase such as Next Record to the page.

   This is a dummy phrase that will be deleted later.

3. Select the text phrase and enter a hash mark in the Link field of the Property inspector to create a null link.

4. With the newly applied link selected, from the Server Behavior panel, add a Move to Next Record server behavior.

   Dreamweaver adds all the necessary code to handle recordset paging.

5. Select the entire text phrase, including the <a> tag surrounding it, and delete it.

   Dreamweaver alerts you that not all of the server behavior has been removed. In fact, only the smallest portion of the behavior, the event call, has been removed. All of the recordset paging code is still intact and ready for use.

NOTE: The process is slightly different for ColdFusion because you need to add a Move to Next Page server behavior and restrict the number of entries on a page to one.

You can test the effectiveness of Dreamweaver's paging server-side code fairly easily. While in Design view, enter into Live Data View mode to see the results returned for the first record. In the Live Data toolbar field, enter the following:

```
offset=1
```

After you press Enter or click back into Design view, the Live Data View updates to display the second record. An extension can use this added facility to page through the recordset for each new generated page.

Reading the Results

As noted earlier, the `getFile()` and `getFileCallback()` functions return a reply from the server. The reply is either an error code—designating everything from an unknown file error to a disk full error—or a file URL to the retrieved file. Although these functions can be used to retrieve standard HTML files from the Web, they are much more beneficial for our purposes when they retrieve pages processed by an application server. After processing, they are, like all files viewed in the browser, essentially text files. Unlike a technology such as Flash Remoting, Dreamweaver cannot process data objects such as recordsets directly. However, Dreamweaver is quite capable of handling XML and XML-styled documents.

TIP: You'll find a complete listing of status codes and their meaning in the Extending Dreamweaver document, available under the Help menu.

After you have retrieved the results by using the `MMHttp.getFile()` function, you need to perform some error checking. Status codes are returned with the function to indicate a successful operation—where the status code is 200—or a problem—which returns any other number. Code like the following reports a general error if one is encountered, but otherwise allows the operation to proceed:

```
var theResult = MMHttp.getFile(theURL);
    if (theResult.statusCode != 200) {
        return alert('HTTP Error: ' + theResult.statusCode + ' at '
        + theURL);
    }
```

Remember that besides the status code, the `getFile()` function returns the file URL of where the retrieved file is stored. Next, the file URL is extracted from the result using the `.data` property:

```
var theFile = theResult.data;
```

Unless specified, this file is stored in the Dreamweaver MX/Configuration/
Temp folder as a TMP file; such files are automatically deleted when
Dreamweaver is shut down. With the file URL known, check first to make
sure that the file is valid:

```
if ( (theFile == null) || (theFile == '') ){
    return alert('HTTP Error: Unknown File Error');
}
```

Now, we're ready to begin the process of reading the file. First, we'll get the
DOM and check to make sure it is readable:

```
var theDOM = dreamweaver.getDocumentDOM(theFile);
if (theDOM == null) {
    return alert('HTTP Error: File Not Properly Formed');
}
```

If the application file output data in the `<item>` tag syntax (described in the
previous section), then you can use the DOM function
`getElementsByTagName()`:

```
var theItems = theDOM.getElementsByTagName('item');
if ( (theItems == null) || (theItems.length == 0) ){
    return alert('HTTP Error: No Items In File');
}
```

This puts all of the `<item>` tags and their contents into an array where they
can be easily compared to a template's editable regions, as described in the
next section.

Listing 5-1   **Sample Application Page.asp** (05_sampleapp.asp)

```asp
<%@LANGUAGE="VBSCRIPT"%>
<!--#include file="../Connections/Extension.asp" -->
<%
Dim rsEx
```

continues

```
Dim rsEx_numRows

Set rsEx = Server.CreateObject("ADODB.Recordset")
rsEx.ActiveConnection = MM_Extension_STRING
rsEx.Source = "SELECT * FROM extensions"
rsEx.CursorType = 0
rsEx.CursorLocation = 2
rsEx.LockType = 1
rsEx.Open()

rsEx_numRows = 0
%>


<%
rsEx.Close()
Set rsEx = Nothing
%>
```

Replacing Editable Regions with Data

Editable regions are the most basic building block of Dreamweaver
templates. Although it's possible to generate static pages dynamically without
using templates (as described in the final section of this chapter), doing so
foregoes numerous advantages. First, templates are visual. With placeholder
graphics and text, it is easy to achieve and maintain an overall look and feel.
Second, if all the generated pages share common elements such as logos or
navigation, these elements can be incorporated into a template without difficulty. Third, and perhaps most importantly, is the ability to update all the
template-derived pages into a single operation.

The simplest approach to combining data with editable regions requires a
minor bit of planning and coordination. When inserting an editable region
into a template, give the region the same name as the field that is supplying
the data. With matching names, you can compare an array of data fields to
each of the editable regions. If you find a match, you can replace the contents
of the editable region with that of the data field.

Two basic comparison techniques are available—one quite a bit more flexible than the other. For situations in which the scope of the project is somewhat limited—either in the number of fields and editable regions or in the number of different application pages and template combinations—editable region names are compared to elements of the data array. Dreamweaver provides an API function to gather a list of all the editable regions in a template:

```
var theERs = theDOM.getEditableRegionList();
```

If you know the order in which the editable regions appear in the array (it parallels their position in the code), you can address the desired region. This technique employs a series of if-else if statements, as follows:

```
var theERs = theDOM.getEditableRegionList();
for (var j=0; j<theItems.length; j++) {
    var theItem = theItems[j];
    var theItemName = theItem.getAttribute('name');
    if (theItemName.toLowerCase() == 'dbName')
    {
        theERs[2].innerHTML = theItem.innerHTML;
    }
    else if (theItemName.toLowerCase() == 'dbDescription')
    {
        theERs[3].innerHTML = theItem.innerHTML;
    }
    else if (theItemName.toLowerCase() == 'dbInfo')
    {
        theERs[4].innerHTML = theItem.innerHTML;
    }
    else if (theItemName.toLowerCase() == 'dbPrice')
    {
        theERs[5].innerHTML = theItem.innerHTML;
    }
}
```

When a particular data field is found, the content—the innerHTML property—is replaced with the innerHTML of the corresponding editable region.

The second method is a bit more complex from a code perspective, but it's also far more flexible. In this technique, the two arrays (the data field items and the editable regions) are compared to one another:

```
var theERs = theDOM.getEditableRegionList();
for (i = 0; i < theItems.length; ++i) {
    for (k = 0; k < theERs.length; ++k) {
        if(theItems[i].getAttribute("name") ==
        theERs[k].getAttribute("name")) {
            theERs[k].innerHTML = theItems[i].innerHTML;
            break;
        }
    }
}
```

The Static from Dynamic Extension

NOTE: To view the completed code, see Listing 5-2 at the end of this section.

I've intentionally tried to keep the concepts separate from an actual implementation knowing full well that each extension requires a high degree of customization. However, before proceeding into more advanced template topics such as optional regions and template parameters, I thought a look at an extension example that pulls it all together would be beneficial.

The Static from Dynamic extension, shown in Figure 5.2, parameterizes a number of the values necessary for the command:

- A drop-down list of available templates for the current site.

- A text field for entering the application page's URL. I pre-filled the box with what I thought was the most common prefix.

- An option to process all records found or to enter a number.

- A text field for the path to store the generated pages—complete with a Browse button so that you can easily select the folder.

- Another drop-down list showing all the fields found in the application page. After a field is selected, the data in that field provides the base name for the generated files. This list populates after a proper address is entered into the URL field.

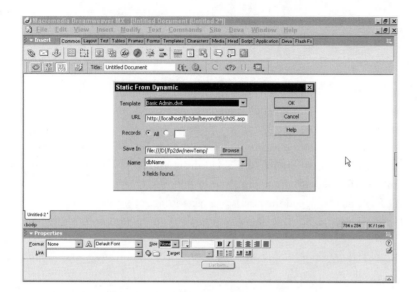

5.2

The Static from Dynamic extension works on a per-site basis and automatically lists all the templates available within the current site.

One additional element completes the interface. Underneath the Name list is a bit of text that initially reads as follows: `Enter URL to Load Fields for Name`. After you have entered the URL, the text shows the number of fields found. When the command is generating the static pages, the text area acts as a progress indicator and states, for example, `Processing 3 of 25`.

Let's look at the primary function of the Static From Dynamic command, `runCommand()`, which is called when the user selects OK. Several variables are declared at the outset by using the `findObject()` function to simplify the coding:

```
var theBaseURL = findObject("url_text").value;
var theRB = findObject("records_rb");
var theLimit;
flag = "last"
```

I also set a variable, `flag`, that another function, `checkFile()`, uses to determine how to proceed. Next, I set `theLimit` variable, which determines how many records to process. If the first option button, All, is selected, then all of the records are available. Otherwise, the upper limit is determined by whatever number is entered into the number text field.

TIP: If you're looking for a similar way to generate Web graphics dynamically, check out my Data-Driven Graphics Wizard available in Fireworks MX, which combines an XML data file with variables embedded into a Fireworks template.

```
if (theRB[0].checked == true) { //all
    theLimit = theItems.length;
} else {
    theLimit = parseInt(findObject("number_text").value);
}
```

Now we're ready for the main loop. After we have entered the looping condition, we construct the `theURL` variable, which is required for the `MMHttp` function. The variable is composed of the base URL, which is pulled from the URL text field, and the offset argument string. The offset string (`?offset=3`), you'll recall, is used to page through the recordset.

```
for (z=0; z < theLimit; ++z) {
    theURL = theBaseURL + "?offset=" + z;
```

Next, we execute the application file and check the results. Why am I using `getFileCallback()` rather than just `getFile()`? The `getFile()` function is fine for processing one file at a time as we did in the earlier examples, but when we're executing one file after another, it is necessary to make sure the results from one file are received and verified before proceeding to the next. The callback function (`checkFile()`) not only makes sure that the results received are as expected, but it also slows down the processing sufficiently to avoid data overwriting:

```
theResult = MMHttp.getFileCallback("checkFile",theURL);
```

With data in hand—or rather, in `theResult`—we're ready to create a new document based on the template chosen from the pull-down menu. Note that although a `dw.newFromTemplate()` command is available, it actually applies the template to the current document. Rather than making the user close all of his open files, I create a new, blank document before I call `newFromTemplate()`:

```
var theList = findObject("template_list");
var theTemplate = dw.getSiteRoot() + "Templates/" +
theList.options[theList.selectedIndex].text;

var theTempDOM = dw.createDocument();
dw.newFromTemplate(theTemplate);
```

Makes blank page

Applies template

The next function is an implementation of the technique for replacing
content inside of editable regions with the data, described earlier in this
chapter:

```
var theERs = theTempDOM.getEditableRegionList();
for (i = 0; i < theItems.length; ++i) {
    for (k = 0; k < theERs.length; ++k) {
        if(theItems[i].getAttribute("name") ==
        theERs[k].getAttribute("name")) {
            theERs[k].innerHTML = theItems[i].innerHTML;
            break;
        }
    }
}
```

All the content has been inserted, and now it's time to save the document.
User-defined values for both the filename and the path to the folder are
employed:

```
docName = findObject("folder_text").value +
theNameList.options[theList.selectedIndex].text + ".htm";
```

User-selected folder

Data field for name

```
res = dw.saveDocument(theTempDOM, docName);
```

Listing 5-2 **StaticfromDynamic.htm** (05_staticdynamic.mxp)

```
<!DOCTYPE HTML PUBLIC "-//W3C//DTD HTML 4.01 Transitional//EN">
<html>
<head>
<title>Static From Dynamic</title>
```

continues

```
<meta http-equiv="Content-Type" content="text/html;
charset=iso-8859-1">
<script language="JavaScript"
src="../Shared/Common/Scripts/dwscripts.js"
type="text/JavaScript"></script>
<script language="JavaScript" src="../Shared/MM/Scripts/CMN/UI.js"
type="text/JavaScript"></script>
<script language="JavaScript">
<!--
//*************** Global Variables
var theResult, theFile, theItems, theHelpText, z;
var theNameList = findObject("name_list");
var flag = "first";

function commandButtons(){
    return new Array( 'OK', 'runCommand()', 'Cancel',
    'window.close()', 'Help', 'getHelp(theHelpFile)');
}


function checkFile() {
   var theBaseURL = findObject("url_text").value;
   if (flag == "first") {
      theResult = MMHttp.getFile(theBaseURL);
   }
   if (theResult.statusCode != 200) {
      return alert('HTTP Error: ' + theResult.statusCode + ' at '
      + theURL);
   }

   theFile = theResult.data;
   if ( (theFile == null) || (theFile == '') ){
      return alert('HTTP Error: Unknown File Error');
   }

   var theDataDOM = dreamweaver.getDocumentDOM(theFile);
   if (theDataDOM == null) {
```

```
        return alert('HTTP Error: File Not Properly Formed');
    }


    theItems = theDataDOM.getElementsByTagName('item');
    if ( (theItems == null) || (theItems.length == 0) ){
        return alert('HTTP Error: No Items In File');
    }


    var theFields = new Array();
    for (i=0; i < theItems.length; ++i) {
        theFields[i] = theItems[i].getAttribute("name");
    }
    if (flag == "first") {
        theHelpText = document.getElementsByTagName("helptext");
        loadSelectList(theNameList,theFields);
        theHelpText[0].innerHTML = theItems.length + " fields
        found.";
    } else {
        var theMsg = "Processing " + z + " of " + theItems.length;
        theHelpText[0].innerHTML = theMsg;
    }
    return;
}


function runCommand(){
    //set URL
    var theBaseURL = findObject("url_text").value;
    flag = "last"
    //get data
    var theLimit;
    var theRB = findObject("records_rb");
    if (theRB[0].checked == true)    { //all
        theLimit = theItems.length;
    } else {
        theLimit = parseInt(findObject("number_text").value);
    }
```

continues

```
for (z=0; z < theLimit; ++z) {
    theURL = theBaseURL + "?offset=" + z;
    theResult = MMHttp.getFileCallback("checkFile",theURL);
    //create document from template
    var theList = findObject("template_list");
    var theTemplate = dw.getSiteRoot() + "Templates/" +
    theList.options[theList.selectedIndex].text;
    var theTempDOM = dw.createDocument();
    dw.newFromTemplate(theTemplate);
    var theERs = theTempDOM.getEditableRegionList();
    //replace editable regions with data
    for (i = 0; i < theItems.length; ++i) {
        for (k = 0; k < theERs.length; ++k) {
            if(theItems[i].getAttribute("name") ==
            theERs[k].getAttribute("name")) {
                theERs[k].innerHTML = theItems[i].innerHTML;
                alert("here");
                break;
            }
        }
    }
    //store document
    docName = findObject("folder_text").value +
    theNameList.options[theList.selectedIndex].text + ".htm";
    res = dw.saveDocument(theTempDOM, docName);
}
window.close()
}


function findFolder() {
    findObject("folder_text").value = dw.browseForFolderURL();
}


function getTemplateList() {
    //returns a list of templates in site
    var theTemplateDir = dw.getSiteRoot() + "Templates/";
```

```
      var theTemplates = new Array();
      theTemplates = DWfile.listFolder(theTemplateDir + "*.dwt",
      "files");
      if (theTemplates){
          var theList = findObject("template_list");
          loadSelectList(theList,theTemplates);
      }
}


function initUI() {
    getTemplateList();
}


//-->
</script>
</head>

<body onLoad="initUI()">
<form name="form1" method="post" action="">
  <table border="0">
    <tr>
      <td><div align="right">Template</div></td>
      <td><select name="template_list" id="template_list"
      style="width:220">
          <option selected>Loading templates.............</option>
        </select></td>
    </tr>
    <tr>
      <td><div align="right">URL</div></td>
      <td><input name="url_text" type="text" id="url_text"
      style="width:220" value="http://localhost/fp2dw/beyond05/
      ch05.asp" onBlur="checkFile()"></td>
    </tr>
    <tr>
      <td><div align="right">Records</div></td>
```

continues

```
            <td><input name="records_rb" type="radio" value="all"
              checked>
            All
            <input name="records_rb" type="radio" value="some">
            <input name="number_text" type="text" id="number_text"
            size="5"></td>
        </tr>
        <tr>
          <td><div align="right">Save In</div></td>
          <td><input name="folder_text" type="text" id="folder_text"
          style="width:150">
            <input type="button" name="Button" value="Browse"
            onClick="findFolder()"></td>
        </tr>
        <tr>
          <td><div align="right">Name</div></td>
          <td><select name="name_list" id="name_list"
          style="width:220">
              <option selected>Choose Base Name</option>
            </select></td>
        </tr>
        <tr>
          <td> </td>
          <td><helptext>Enter URL to Load Fields for
          Name</helptext></td>
        </tr>
      </table>
    </form>
  </body>
</html>
```

Optional Regions and Template Parameters

Dreamweaver MX introduced several powerful template features to complement the standard editable regions. Optional regions permit a designated
area of a template-derived document to either be shown or hidden at design
time. A catalog page might, for example, include an embedded "now on sale"
banner in an optional region allowing the graphic to be displayed only for
appropriate products. In this section, we look at ways of driving optional
regions dynamically; it is assumed that you're familiar with inserting them in
the standard fashion.

Optional regions use two different sets of tags for both the template and the
template-derived document. Within the template, one set of tags surrounds
the content in the `<body>`:

```
<!-- TemplateBeginIf cond="dbOnSale" -->
<img src="../images/onsale.gif" width="152" height="71">
<!-- TemplateEndIf -->
```

Another related tag is inserted into the template's `<head>` area:

```
<!-- TemplateParam name="dbOnSale" type="boolean" value="true" -->
```

If the `value` attribute of the `TemplateParam` tag is set to `true`, the optional
region is displayed; if it is `false`, all content within the region is hidden.

When an instance of the template is created, the syntax of the tags changes
significantly. The tags that mark the optional regions are not visible in the
code, regardless of whether the region is designated to be shown. However,
the counterpart to the `TemplateParam` tag is still present in the `<head>`,
although now it is has become an `InstanceParam` tag, like this:

```
<!-- InstanceParam name="dbOnSale" type="boolean" value="true" -->
```

The `InstanceParam` tag is our target for dynamically driving the optional
region. Building on the procedure outlined in the previous sections, you
would require four elements:

- A boolean (true/false) field in the data source with the same name as the optional region

- An application page that extracts the boolean field and outputs it into XML-like syntax

- A template that includes an optional region

- A routine in a Dreamweaver extension to write the boolean value supplied by the data into the InstanceParam tag

The fourth point represents the only difficult task—and it's only difficult because it can be a little problematic locating InstanceParam tags to replace them. Because Dreamweaver template tags are HTML-comment based instead of Dreamweaver-specific tags—<! InstanceParam... --> as opposed to <MM:InstanceParam...>—they cannot be as easy isolated as a standard tag. Typically, when looking for a specific tag, the getElementsByTagName() function is used to retrieve an array of all of one type of tag on the same page. Any further search for a particular tag is then handled by looping through the array, looking for a specific attribute or value. That method won't work with comment-based tags.

To find a particular InstanceParam tag, we rely on two bits of information. First, all InstanceParam tags are placed in the <head> area, which limits our search quite explicitly. Second, InstanceParam tags are never placed within another tag; they are *first children* of the <head> tag. Armed with that little bit of knowledge, we're ready to begin the hunt for the elusive InstanceParam.

First, we employ the getElementsByTagName() function to get the contents of the <head> tag:

```
var theDOM = dw.getDocumentDOM().getElementsByTagName("head")
```

Next, we gather all of the first children of the <head> tag object into an array:

```
var theNodes = theDOM[0].childNodes;
```

Now we're ready to loop through the array, looking for a particular name associated with the optional region and the `InstanceParam` tag. In this example, we're looking for `dbOnSale`. When we find it, we want to change the attribute from `true` to `false`:

```
for (i=0; i < theNodes.length; ++i) {
  if(theNodes[i].getAttribute("name")) {
    if ( theNodes[i].getAttribute("name") == "dbOnSale") {
      theNodes[i].setAttribute("value","false");
      break;
    }
  }
}
```

One final step is necessary to update an instance of a template. Again, an API call is ready to lend a hand:

```
dw.getDocumentDOM().dom.updateCurrentPage() ;
```

The `updateCurrentPage()` function is the same one called when we select Modify, Template, Update Page.

Programmatically Adding Repeating Regions

Repeating regions are another Dreamweaver MX template innovation. Typically, a repeating region surrounds a table row containing one or more editable regions. After creating an instance of the template, the designer can manipulate the number of rows—adding or removing them as needed and even changing their order. To add a row in a repeating region, you need to make sure the View > Visual Aids > Invisible Elements option is turned on. Then select the Add (+) button above the repeating region. This system works well for individual pages, but it might be a roadblock in a production situation. In this section, I'll show you how to programmatically add any number of additional rows—or whatever the repeating region encloses.

The structure of a repeating region is similar to other template region types, but it is different enough to require alternative handling. Here is a sample repeating region with three editable regions, one in each table cell, as inserted into a template:

```
<!-- TemplateBeginRepeat name="RepeatRegion1" -->
  <tr>
    <td><!-- TemplateBeginEditable name="EditRegion6" --> 
    <!-- TemplateEndEditable --></td>
    <td><!-- TemplateBeginEditable name="EditRegion7" --> 
    <!-- TemplateEndEditable --></td>
    <td><!-- TemplateBeginEditable name="EditRegion8" --> 
    <!-- TemplateEndEditable --></td>
  </tr>
<!-- TemplateEndRepeat -->
```

The template syntax seems straightforward enough, but look what happens when a document is created from the template:

```
<!-- InstanceBeginRepeat name="RepeatRegion1" -->
  <!-- InstanceBeginRepeatEntry -->
  <tr>
    <td><!-- InstanceBeginEditable name="EditRegion6" --> 
    <!-- InstanceEndEditable --></td>
    <td><!-- InstanceBeginEditable name="EditRegion7" --> 
    <!-- InstanceEndEditable --></td>
    <td><!-- InstanceBeginEditable name="EditRegion8" --> 
    <!-- InstanceEndEditable --></td>
  </tr>
  <!-- InstanceEndRepeatEntry -->
<!-- InstanceEndRepeat -->
```

Added in Instance — points to `<!-- InstanceBeginRepeatEntry -->`

Added in Instance — points to `<!-- InstanceEndRepeatEntry -->`

Notice the additional repeat entry identifying tags. From a DOM point of view, these nodes within the outer repeating region node make it a bit more difficult to select an inner editable region programmatically. Luckily, the Dreamweaver engineers have provided a significant aid for situations like these. Within the Shared folder, you'll find a collection of functions used by Macromedia commands to perform their magic; for Dreamweaver MX templates, the assisting file is called TemplateUtils.js. Found in the Shared/MM/Scripts/CMN folder, the TemplateUtils.js file has more than 90 template-related functions. Although it is beyond the scope of this book to discuss all of those functions, we will cover several that are used for our purpose. If you are working in-depth with templates, be sure to examine TemplateUtils.js closely.

To demonstrate the techniques in this section, I've created a sample extension, Add to Repeating Region, . This extension (see figure 5.3), given the name of a repeating region and a number, adds the specified number of rows to the region.

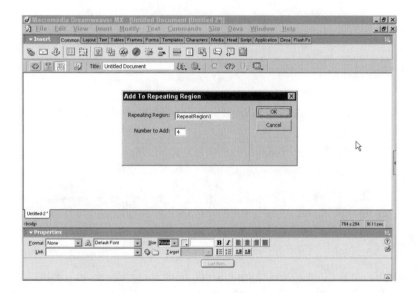

One of the first lines of code in the example extension includes the TemplateUtils.js file:

```
<script language="JavaScript" src="../Shared/MM/Scripts/CMN/
TemplateUtils.js" type="text/JavaScript"></script>
```

Unfortunately, despite the range of the functions available in TemplateUtils.js, not one exactly fits the first goal: to find a repeating region by name on a template-derived document. However, we're not completely out of luck. One function, findNamedRepeatRegion(), is close:

```
function findNamedRepeatingRegion(regionName, targetDom)
  {
  var curDOM = (targetDom == null) ? dw.getDocumentDOM
  ('document') : targetDom;
```

NOTE: To view the completed code, see Listing 5-3 at the end of this section.

5.3

This custom extension adds repeating rows to the end of the region, although you can easily add them to the top, if desired.

NOTE: This represents a little behind-the-scenes magic managed by the Dreamweaver engineers. This code works in all installations of Dreamweaver—including multiuser configurations. In multiuser configurations, custom extensions like this one are installed in the user Dreamweaver folder, not the system folder, where the Shared scripts are stored. In effect, Dreamweaver understands what you are trying to accomplish, and rather than literally trying to locate the specified file one level up in the nonexistent user Shared folder, Dreamweaver knows to look in the system Shared folder.

```
            var scopeNode = findTemplateScopeNode(curDOM);


        if (scopeNode == null)
            return null;


        //For some reason, this seems to be case sensitive when
        //looking for XML style tags.
        var params = scopeNode.getElementsByTagName
        ("MMTemplate:Repeat");
```

Works with templates only ⎯⎯⎯

```
            for (i=0;i<params.length;i++)
            {
            if (dwscripts.minEntityNameDecode(params.item(i).name) ==
            regionName)
                return params.item(i);
            }


        return null;
        } //findNamedRepeatingRegion
```

As pointed out in the callout, this function finds repeating regions within templates. There is a different syntax for repeating regions within instances of templates. To get the functionality needed for our extension, follow these steps:

1. From the TemplateUtils.js folder, copy the findNamedRepeatRegion() function.

2. Locate the line of code that reads as follows:

```
var params = scopeNode.getElementsByTagName("MMTemplate:Repeat");
```

3. Change "MMTemplate:Repeat" to "MMTInstance:RepeatEntry".

4. Rename the function to findNamedRepeatingRegionInstance().

   What you choose to name the function is really optional; it's only important that you do rename any modified functions to avoid conflicts.

Even though we have included a modified version of a TemplateUtils.js function, it is still necessary to include the entire file. Even the modified function uses other support functions, such as `findTemplateScopeNode()`.

The next modification necessary for this function comes down to style. Rather than including yet another, rather lengthy file, I'd prefer to use some built-in functionality. The original function called out an external script and function to check for a matching name:

```
if (dwscripts.minEntityNameDecode(params.item(i).name) ==
regionName)
```

However, I found that I could get the same results with a DOM function:

```
if (params[i].parentNode.getAttribute("name") == regionName)
```

The `parentNode` property is needed to take the additional InstanceRepeatEntry nodes into account. The point here is that after you have begun to customize a function, you can code it in your own style.

If we find a matching region, we can then look for an editable region within the repeating region. To add a new row using this technique, we need to have a portion within the repeating region selected. Because the one commonality that repeating regions used in this way share is an editable region, that's what we look for:

```
var theER = findChildEditableRegion(params[i])
```

The `findChildEditableRegion()` function is another useful tool from the TemplateUtil.js file. After we identify the editable region, we select it:

```
var theOffs = curDOM.nodeToOffsets(theER);
curDOM.setSelection(theOffs[0], theOffs[1]);
```

Now we're ready to perform the actual operation of the extension. After getting the user-supplied value, we'll take advantage of another bit of built-in Macromedia functionality to add the rows:

```
var theNum = parseInt(findObject("number_text").value);
for (x = 0; x < theNum; ++x) {
  dw.runCommand("InsertRepeatEntry.htm",null,null,"listEnd");
}
```

TIP: The final argument, listEnd, determines where the row is added in the repeating region. Other valid values for this argument are listBegin, beforeEntry, and afterEntry. The latter two values refer to the current cursor position within the region.

As you can see, the custom extension executes a standard Dreamweaver command: InsertRepeatEntry.htm. This command is used whenever Modify > Templates > Repeating Entry > New Entry at End is selected, or whenever the cursor is in the last row of a repeating region and the Add (+) button is selected.

Listing 5-3   **Add to Repeating Region.htm** (05_addrepeating.mxp)

```
<!DOCTYPE HTML PUBLIC "-//W3C//DTD HTML 4.01 Transitional//EN">
<html>
<head>
<title>Add To Repeating Region</title>
<meta http-equiv="Content-Type" content="text/html; charset=iso-
8859-1">
<script language="JavaScript" src="../Shared/MM/Scripts/CMN/UI.js"
type="text/JavaScript"></script>
<script language="JavaScript"
src="../Shared/MM/Scripts/CMN/TemplateUtils.js"
type="text/JavaScript"></script>
<script language="JavaScript">
<!--
//*************** Global Variables

function commandButtons(){
    return new Array( 'OK', 'runCommand()', 'Cancel',
    'window.close()');
}

function findNamedRepeatingRegionInstance(regionName, targetDom)
    {
    var curDOM = (targetDom == null) ? dw.getDocumentDOM
    ('document') : targetDom;
```

```
    var scopeNode = findTemplateScopeNode(curDOM);
    if (scopeNode == null)
        return null;


    //For some reason, this seems to be case sensitive when
    //looking for XML style tags.
    var params = scopeNode.getElementsByTagName
    ("MMTInstance:RepeatEntry");
    for (i=0;i<params.length;i++)
        {
        if (params[i].parentNode.getAttribute("name") ==
        regionName)
            var theER = findChildEditableRegion(params[i])
            var theOffs = curDOM.nodeToOffsets(theER);
            curDOM.setSelection(theOffs[0], theOffs[1]);
            var theNum = parseInt(findObject("number_text").value);
            for (x = 0; x < theNum; ++x) {
                dw.runCommand("InsertRepeatEntry.htm",null,null,
                "listEnd");
            }
        }
    return null;
    }


function runCommand() {
    var theDOM = dw.getDocumentDOM();
    var theRR = findObject("name_text").value;
    var theData = findNamedRepeatingRegionInstance(theRR, theDOM);
    window.close();
}

//-->
</script>
</head>
```

continues

```
<body>
<form name="form1" method="post" action="">
  <table border="0">
    <tr>
      <td nowrap>
<div align="right">Repeating Region:</div></td>
      <td><input name="name_text" type="text"
      value="RepeatRegion1"></td>
    </tr>
    <tr>
      <td><div align="right">Number to Add: </div></td>
      <td><input name="number_text" type="text" id="number_text2"
      value="2" size="5"></td>
    </tr>
  </table>
</form>
<p> </p></body>
</html>
```

Working without Templates

Although I'm pretty biased in favor of templates, I've seen circumstances where they just don't fit in the production workflow. Some companies have legacy systems in place that depend on their own custom tag(s). Dreamweaver has little problem accepting and working with third-party tags. It even has the ability to display custom icons in the Design view to represent a custom tag. Thanks to the power of the DOM in Dreamweaver extensibility, you can also incorporate third-party tags to generate static pages in much the same way demonstrated earlier in this chapter.

Let's assume, for example, that you're building a web catalog for several car models. The page layout is the same for each page, but the model name, image, description, and price are different. These different variables could easily be represented by custom tags (in bold), like this:

```
<p class="modelHead"><varModel></p>
<p class="modelBody"><varDesc></p>
<p class="modelPrice">Only $<varPrice>!</p>
```

Dreamweaver's DOM is robust enough to recognize third-party tags such as these. To reference a specific tag, use the `getElementsByTagName()` function:

```
var theDOM = dw.getDocumentDOM();
var theModel = theDOM.getElementsByTagName("varModel");
```

The `getElementsByTagName()` function returns an array of all specified tags on a page. To reference the first—and, in cases such as this example, the only—tag, use the syntax `theModel[0]`.

Remember the two techniques used for replacing editable regions with data (discussed in the "Replacing Editable Regions with Data" section)? You can use the same basic techniques without templates with minor modification. Perhaps the easiest way to accomplish this is to create an array of the third-party tags used, like this:

```
var theTags = new Array("varModel","varDesc","varPrice");
```

Then the first method would look like this:

```
var theTags = new Array("varModel","varDesc","varPrice");
for (var j=0; j<theItems.length; j++) {
   var theItem = theItems[j];
   var theItemName = theItem.getAttribute('name');
   if (theItemName == 'varModel')
   {
      theTags[0].outerHTML = theItem.innerHTML;
   }
   else if (theItemName == 'varDesc')
   {
      theTags[1].outerHTML = theItem.innerHTML;
   }
```

```
    else if (theItemName == 'varPrice')
    {
        theTags[2].outerHTML = theItem.innerHTML;
    }
}
```

Note that instead of replacing the innerHTML of an editable region, we're replacing the outerHTML of a non-empty tag—in essence replacing the entire tag. The second method of looking for a match between data and third-party tags would look like this:

```
var theTags = new Array("varModel","varDesc","varPrice");
for (i = 0; i < theItems.length; ++i) {
   for (k = 0; k < theTags.length; ++k) {
      if(theItems[i].getAttribute("name") == theTags[k]) {
          theTags[k].outerHTML = theItems[i].innerHTML;
          break;
      }
   }
}
```

If you'd prefer to leave the third-party tags in the final output, use a tag pair, such as <varmodel></varmodel>, and replace the innerHTML of the tag.

✳ _____

Chapter 6

Templating Navigation Systems

Much of the power of the web derives from its ability to link from anywhere to anywhere. Sometimes, however, a linear or sequential navigation is key. Tutorials, help systems, and even static catalog pages often employ navigational elements to move progressively from one page to the next. Many designers also include a Previous or Back link to step through the sequential pages in reverse.

Although the initial coding—typically done manually—of sequential navigation systems is at best tedious, maintaining such sets of pages can be a nightmare. Let's say you have a five-page tutorial on training a puppy:

- getting_started.htm

- soft_biting.htm

- housebreaking.htm

- socializing.htm

- further_training.htm

Even if you use a template for basic layout, you'll need to link one page to the other, in both directions. If you add a new page, such as placing teaching_tricks.htm after socializing.htm, you'll have to change two links—one on socializing.htm and one on further_training.htm—in addition to adding the links for the new page. Changing the sequence—moving housebreaking.htm before soft_biting.htm, for example—is even more involved and requires six different modifications.

You can see how even on a small scale, managing sequential links is maintenance intensive. On larger sites, with multiple sequences spread over thousands of pages, manual updates and modifications are highly inefficient and impractical.

Several strategies have emerged for constructing and maintaining sequential pages. In this chapter, we'll look at three approaches:

- **Template expressions**—With a bit of planning and careful coding, Dreamweaver MX's template expressions feature offers a static page alternative to data-driven flexibility. This is recommended for smaller sites.

- **JavaScript based**—If you're working with a medium-to-large static page site, a sequential navigation method that uses JavaScript arrays might work best for you.

- **Dynamic**—For large sites, data-driven navigation is probably the best answer. Centralizing the linking elements in a data source makes them highly maintainable.

You'll find code and examples for all three methods posted on the Beyond Dreamweaver web site.

Using Template Expressions

Dreamweaver MX introduced several extremely powerful template features, including optional regions, repeating regions, and nested templates. Although more obscure than these high-profile options, the new template expressions feature offers a great deal of flexibility and power. You can even use template expressions as the base for a linear navigation system, as you'll see in this section.

In essence, a template expression is a variable or *parameter* established in the template that can be set independently in each template-derived document or *instance*. There are several types of template parameters: boolean (true/false), text, number, color, or URL. When entered into the template, the TemplateParam tag is used:

```
<!-- TemplateParam name="saleURL" type="URL"
value="../sale/special.htm" -->
<!-- TemplateParam name="onsale" type="boolean" value="true" -->
```

If entered by hand, `TemplateParam` code should be placed in the `<head>` section. The user interface for creating template parameters is somewhat hidden. This type of code is also generated whenever an editable attribute is created. You'll see how to create an editable attribute in the next section.

After the template parameter is set up, we can place references to the parameter—known as *template expressions*—anywhere in the page. Template expressions are written in two ways:

- As a comment:

```
<!-- TemplateExpr: expr = "onsale"-->
```

- As a parenthetical:

```
@@(onsale)@@
```

The two formats are interchangeable; I typically use the parenthetical format for two reasons. First, it's shorter and quicker to write. Second, it has the advantage of displaying in the Design view with its own symbol, as seen in Figure 6.1. This symbol can be seen only when Invisible Elements is turned on.

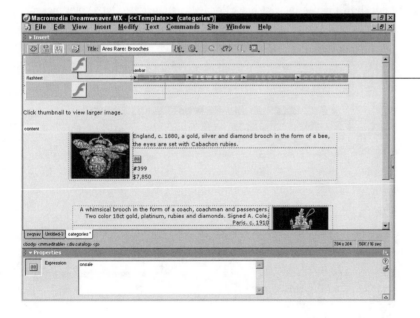

Template expression symbol

6.1

Template expressions should be hand-coded or entered through the Property inspector; use the parenthetical syntax to display a special template expressions symbol.

When Dreamweaver makes an instance of a template that contains a template expression, the code syntax changes. The `TemplateParam` tag becomes an `InstanceParam` tag:

```
<!-- InstanceParam name="saleURL" type="URL"
value="sale/special.htm" -->
<!-- InstanceParam name="onsale" type="boolean" value="true" -->
```

Any template expressions that are embedded in the template are displayed with their current values in the code. For example, a link using the `saleURL` parameter would look like this:

```
<a href="sale/special.htm">On Sale Now!</a>
```

To change the parameter's value, choose Modify, Template Properties. The Template Properties dialog box (see Figure 6.2) contains a list of all the template parameters in the current page. Select any entry and alter the fields that follow as needed. Most of the template parameter types (text, number, and URL) use text fields; boolean type parameters use a check box to show or not show the parameter while color type parameters offer a color picker.

6.2

We must make all modifications to template parameters through the Template Properties dialog box. Changes we make by hand are not recognized until the Template Properties dialog box is opened.

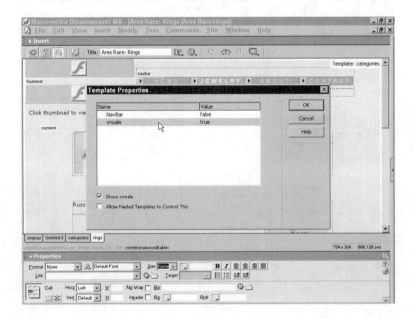

Preparing the Template

The strategy described in this section for creating navigation links using template parameters and expressions relies on files with sequentially numbered names, such as tutorial1.htm, tutorial2.htm, and so on. After the basic naming scheme has been established, the template is ready to be prepared. Here's how the process works:

1. A template parameter is inserted into the template `<head>` section either by hand or by creating an editable attribute. This parameter holds the number in the filename sequence of the current page.

2. Evaluated template expressions, based on the template parameter, are entered as `href` values in the Previous and Next links.

3. In the template-derived document, the template parameter is updated to reflect the instance's filename number. For example, the parameter for tutorial5.htm would be 5.

Although steps 1 and 2 only need to be performed one per template, step 3 is performed for each instance of the template that is created. However, because each instance needs custom attention anyway to add individual content, changing the template parameter value is not really an onerous burden.

The following procedure assumes that you are familiar with templates in general and have, for the sake of discussion, created a template with both Previous and Next links (either text or graphics). Best practice dictates that the navigation links in this technique would be placed in a locked, non-editable region. That's because you want to keep the navigation constant after all, although it's possible to insert them into an editable region.

Entering the Template Parameter

As mentioned earlier, template parameters are either entered by hand or by using Dreamweaver's editable attribute user interface. If the template parameter is entered manually, place this code in the `<head>` section:

```
<!-- TemplateParam name="currentFile" type="number" value="1" -->
```

This code creates a template parameter named `baseLink` with a default value of 1. To create the same code via Dreamweaver's point-and-click interface, follow these steps:

1. From the Tag Selector, choose the `<a>` tag surrounding the Previous text or button.

2. Select Modify, Templates, Make Attribute Editable.

3. In the Editable Tag Attributes dialog box (see Figure 6.3), select Add (+) and then enter an attribute name, such as `thefilenum`.

   The attribute name is used for setup purposes. Naturally, you want to select an attribute name that browsers will ignore rather than a real attribute.

6.3

All modifications to template parameters must be made through the Template Properties dialog box. Changes made by hand are not recognized until the Template Properties dialog box opens.

4. Make sure that Make Attribute Editable is selected.

5. In the Label field, enter the name that you want the template parameter being established to have.

   In this example, I'm using `currentFile` as the template parameter name.

6. From the drop-down list, choose Number as the attribute type.

7. In the Default field, enter a number. This number should be an integer for easy calculation; in this example, I entered the number 1.

After you click OK, Dreamweaver writes the template parameter code seen previously:

```
<!-- TemplateParam name="currentFile" type="number" value="1" -->
```

Dreamweaver also includes the dummy attribute created in the <a> tag:

```
thefilenum="@@(currentFile)@@"
```

You're free at this point to delete the false attribute and its value; the important code—the template parameter—remains in the document regardless of whether the attribute is removed.

Automating the Link Creation

In this next step, the previously established template parameter is added to each of the navigation links in slightly different formulas. One of the most powerful aspects of template expressions is that they are evaluated at design time. Numerous types of operations—including mathematical, string, and binary—are available for use. This example combines both math and string concatenation to create links to both the previous and next pages in the sequence.

Here are the steps necessary for inserting a template expression as a navigation link:

1. On the template page, select the Next button or text link.

2. In the Property inspector, enter code similar to the following in the Link field:

```
@@('template' + (currentFile + 1) + '.htm')@@
```

In this example, the sequential files are all within the same folder and named template1.htm, template2.htm, and so on. My template parameter, defined in the previous section, is called currentFile. Note that single rather than double quotes are used; this is done because the entire template expression is enclosed in quotes in the <a> tag:

TIP: Want to make your navigation really slick? Use Dreamweaver MX's optional region feature to hide the Previous link if the template parameter was set to 1; in that circumstance, there is no previous page. Likewise, if you know the number of the final page in the series, wrap an optional region around the Next link to hide it when the template parameter is equal to the last value.

```
<a href="@@('template' + (currentFile + 1) + '.htm')@@">NEXT</a>
```

3. Select the Previous button to perform a similar operation.

4. In the Link field, enter code like this:

```
@@('template' + (currentFile - 1) + '.htm')@@
```

For the Previous link, instead of adding a number to the base value, as was done for the Next link, one is subtracted.

Setting the Instance Parameter

NOTE: Be sure to save your template before proceeding to the next series of steps. If you have already created one or more instances, update the files as requested by Dreamweaver after the save.

Now that the template work is done, all that is left is to set the parameter for each instance. Although it might sound burdensome, it's a fairly straightforward operation that you can accomplish right after the file is created from the template.

1. Select Modify > Template Properties.

2. In the Template Properties dialog box, choose the parameter set up in the template.

   In our example, the parameter would be currentFile.

3. In the text field, insert the number that matches the value in the filename of the current page.

   For example, if the file is template23.htm, enter 23.

After you close the Template Properties dialog box, check the code. Where the template expressions were inserted in the Next and Previous links, the fully resolved filenames appear. With a value of 23 for the parameter, the code will be similar to this:

```
<a href="template22.htm">Next</a> - <a href="template24.htm">
Previous</a>
```

If the links are not being formed correctly, check to make sure that you defined the template parameter as a number.

Taking a JavaScript Approach

The template expression technique described in the previous section works well for sequentially numbered files. Life isn't always that tidy, however. Frequently, a sequence is composed of a series of static files with disparate names, such as beads.htm, necklaces.htm, earrings.htm, and so on. In situations such as these, JavaScript provides the needed functionality and flexibility.

The technique described in this section relies on three core JavaScript abilities: arrays, string manipulation, and browser control. Here's how it works:

- An array is created that contains the filenames in the series in the desired order.

- JavaScript functions are added to the Previous and Next links that trigger the process.

- A JavaScript function retrieves the path to the current file and extracts the filename.

- The filename is compared to elements of the array and, when a match is found, its location in the array—and thus, the sequence—is recorded.

- The browser loads a new file which, depending on the link selected, is either the next or the previous filename in the sequence.

To keep it easy to update, two basic files are needed: a JavaScript include and a Dreamweaver template for basic page presentation and to call the JavaScript (see Bonus Listing 6-A, shown on the book's web site).

NOTE: To view the completed code, see Listing 6-1 at the end of this section.

Creating the Array

Much of the flexibility of this technique comes from the array element. Because the array—and all of the other JavaScript code—is maintained in an external JavaScript file, modifications have to be made in only one file to alter the entire sequence. New files are easily added into the array and just as easily removed or rearranged.

There's only one small condition for coding this segment of the technique: The array should be entered in the root of the JavaScript file so that it is available globally. A typical array might look like this:

```
var fileNameArr = new
Array("beads.htm","necklaces.htm","earrings.htm","brooches.htm");
```

TIP: With larger sites or
multiple sequential navigation series, you'll probably
want to find some way to
automate the creation of
the array to avoid both
typographical errors and
extreme tedium. I've
created such a tool for use
with Deva Tools: the
JavaScript Navigation Array
Builder. This tool is available both on the book's
web site and at
www.devahelp.com.

One more global variable is needed to hold the pathname; in this example code, that variable is named `thePath`.

Adding Function Calls

Next we add a function call to both the Previous and Next links contained in the template file. In this example, the function is named `goPage()`, and it takes a single argument: `direction`. For Next links, the `direction` value is `forward`; for Previous links, the `direction` value is `back`. Here is some sample code for a pair of text links:

```
<a href="javascript:;" onClick="goPage('back');">Previous</a>
<a href="javascript:;" onClick="goPage('forward');">Next</a>
```

TIP: Alternatively, we could
write this code without the
`onClick` event, like this:

```
<a href="javascript:
goPage('back');"
>Previous</a>
```

I prefer to use the
`onClick` event for clarity
and in case I want to use
additional events, such
as `onMouseOver` or
`onMouseOut`.

Naturally, you can enter this code by hand through Code view. For brief edits like this, I am quite fond of using the Quick Tag Editor. Here's how you would enter the same code in the Design view:

1. Select the text or image serving as your Next link.

2. In the Property inspector, enter `javascript:;` in the Link field to create a link.

3. Choose the `<a>` tag from the Tag Selector.

4. Select the Quick Tag Editor button from the Property inspector or use the keyboard shortcut Ctrl+T (Command-T).

   The Quick Tag Editor displays the code snippet for the `<a>` tag in Edit Tag mode, as shown in Figure 6.4.

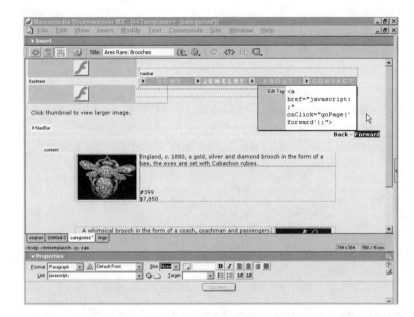

6.4

The Quick Tag Editor
toggles through three
modes: Edit Tag, Insert
HTML, and Wrap Tag.

5. Tab to the end of the tag and enter the following code:

```
onClick="goPage('forward');"
```

6. Press Enter (Return) to close the Quick Tag Editor.

7. Repeat these steps for the Previous link.

As in the template expressions method, it's best to place your links in a
locked region of the template. With these types of automatic links, the
navigation code probably won't need to be edited.

Getting the Filename

Getting the filename in a JavaScript function is really a two-part process.
First, the document.URL property is used to get the full path to the current
file, like this:

```
var theFile = document.URL
```

The variable, `theFile`, would contain something like this:

```
http://www.aresrare.com/specialorder/beads.htm
```

Only the filename is needed. The second part of the process is to extract the filename from the path. To accomplish this, you use the standard `substring()` function in conjunction with the `lastIndexOf()` property:

```
theFile = theFile.substring(theFile.lastIndexOf('/')+1);
```

These two code lines are the first entries in the function used ultimately to find a match between the filename and an item in the array. In the example code, the function is called `findIndex()`.

Comparing the Filename to the Array

With the filename identified, a matching entry in the array is ready to be found. After it's discovered, the entry's location in the array is returned to the calling function—where it will be used to calculate the next or previous item in the array.

Here is the filename-array matching code, in bold, placed in the context of the containing function:

```
function findIndex() {
    var theFile = document.URL
    theFile = theFile.substring(theFile.lastIndexOf('/')+1);
    for (i=0; i < fileNameArr.length; ++i) {
        if (fileNameArr[i] == theFile) {
            return i;
        }
    }
    return "noMatch";
}
```

This function is set up to return the matching array item index number (the variable i) if a match is found. If not, noMatch is returned instead to allow for error checking in the calling function. This is covered next in the final step.

Opening the Requested Page

Remember the goPage() function called from the Next and Previous links? It's time to bring in that function and finish off this technique. When goPage() is initially called, it calls the findIndex() function which, as noted in the previous step, compares the current filename to the array items and returns its location in the array. The location is stored in a variable called theIndex:

```
var theIndex = findIndex();
```

If no match is found, theIndex variable contains noMatch; an error message is displayed:

```
alert("No matching item in array. Check filename.");
```

Obviously, this is the bare minimum of what could or should be done if an error is encountered. Another tactic would be to redirect the user to another page on the site with more information and a request to email the webmaster concerning the problem. Here's one way to send a user to another page:

```
window.location = "/help/nomatch.htm";
```

If no error is encountered, the argument passed by the links when calling goPage() is inspected. If the argument, theDirection, is equal to "forward", then theIndex variable is incremented; otherwise, theDirection is implicitly "back" and theIndex is decremented.

```
if (theDirection == "forward") {
   theIndex = parseInt(theIndex) + 1
} else {    //go backwards
   theIndex = parseInt(theIndex) - 1
}
```

After the desired index is established, the filename corresponding to that index is extracted and set to another variable, `thePath`:

```
thePath = fileNameArr[theIndex];
```

The final step—of the `goPage()` function as well as of the entire process—is to load the new file into the browser. This transition is handled with the `window.location` object, like this:

```
window.location = thePath;
```

In this routine, the `window.location` transition is enclosed by a `setTimeout()` function. The `setTimeout()` function delays execution of the enclosed argument by a specified number of milliseconds; a value of 1,000 equals 1 second. The `setTimeout()` function is a necessary wrapper for `window.location` to function properly—even if the delay is only 1/10th of one second.

Here's the entire `goPage()` function so that you can see how it all fits together:

```
function goPage(theDirection) {
    if (theIndex == "noMatch") {
        alert("No matching item in array. Check filename.");
    } else {
        if (theDirection == "forward") {
            theIndex = parseInt(theIndex) + 1;
        } else {      //go backwards
            theIndex = parseInt(theIndex) - 1;
        }
    }
    thePath = fileNameArr[theIndex];
    setTimeout("window.location = thePath;",100);
}
```

Listing 6-1   **JavaScript Navigation Functions** (06_jvsnav.js)

```javascript
// JavaScript Document
var fileNameArr = new
Array("beads.htm","bracelets.htm","various.htm","brooches.htm",
"earrings.htm");
var thePath, thePathForward, thePathBack;

function findIndex() {
    var theFile = document.URL
    thePath = theFile.substring(0,theFile.lastIndexOf('/')+1);
    theFile = theFile.substring(theFile.lastIndexOf('/')+1);
    for (i=0; i < fileNameArr.length; ++i) {
        if (fileNameArr[i] == theFile) {
            return i;
        }
    }
    return "noMatch";
}

function goPage(theDirection) {
    var theIndex = findIndex();
    if (theIndex == "noMatch") {
        alert("No matching item in array. Check filename.");
    } else {
        if (theDirection == "forward") {
            theIndex = parseInt(theIndex) + 1
        } else {//go backwards
            theIndex = parseInt(theIndex) - 1
        }
    }
    thePath = fileNameArr[theIndex];
    setTimeout("window.location = thePath;", 100);
}
```

Going Dynamic

The final sequential navigation technique is intended for data-driven or dynamic sites. The technique is similar to the JavaScript method in that arrays are used in both, but the dynamic method completely separates the navigation sequence from the page. As with many data-driven sites, the separation between front end and back end is a major boost to scalability and productiveness.

TIP: The technique described in this section is intended for sites where the pages differ so much in design that replacing content on the page dynamically is not practical. If the page is highly structured, use Dreamweaver's built-in recordset navigation server behaviors (Move to Next Record, Move to Previous Record) to fill each page with dynamic content.

Here's how the dynamic sequential navigation technique works:

1. The data source is constructed in such a way that each record contains a filename and a sequencing value.

2. In Dreamweaver, the connection and recordset are established.

3. The recordset is passed into an array.

4. The filename is dynamically retrieved by a server-side script.

5. The array is searched to locate an entry matching the filename.

6. The links are built according to the position of the filename in the array.

NOTE: To view the completed code, see Listing 6-2 at the end of this section.

The following technique, created by Dan Short (www.web-shorts.com), uses the ASP server model and is written in VBScript. Similar capabilities are available with the other server models. The script is highly portable.

Building the Data Source Schema

When designing the data source schema for this technique, three fields, at a minimum, are required:

- **ID**—A key or autonumber field, which provides each record with a unique ID

- **Filename**—A text field to contain the filename of each file in the series

- **Sequence**—A number field to hold the sequencing order

Here's an example data source table:

ID	Sequence	Filename
1	10	beads.asp
2	20	bracelets.asp
3	30	brooches.asp
4	40	earrings.asp

For maximum flexibility, enter only the name of the file into the Filename field; the path to the file should not be included. When it comes time to bind the image filename to the src attribute, any necessary path can be included, like this:

```
/images/<%=(rsFiles.Fields.Item("images").Value)%>
```
Added path

Although the Sequence field values are up to the developer, I recommend using a series of numbers with a fair degree of separation. In other words, it's better to use 10, 20, 30 as opposed to 1, 2, 3. Why? Having a little "air" between the values makes it much simpler to insert one or more pages in the middle of the sequence. If, for example, I wanted to move earrings.asp between bracelets.asp and brooches.asp, I just need to change the sequence value from 40 to 25, like this table.

ID	Sequence	Filename
1	10	beads.asp
2	20	bracelets.asp
3	30	brooches.asp
4	25	earrings.asp

TIP: One of the key advantages in a data-driven site is that the data can be added or modified at any point. In the early stage of developing this application, it is only important that a small amount of data, suitable for testing, is entered into the data source.

When the data source is sorted into the recordset, the series will be in the desired order—without having to renumber additional records.

Setting Up Connection and Recordset

After the data source is designed and initially populated, two more pieces of the foundation must be laid: the data source connection and the recordset. Both of these tasks are accomplished easily in Dreamweaver.

The most direct route to establish a data source connection in Dreamweaver MX is through the Databases panel. Click Add (+) to choose either the Custom Connection String or Data Source Name (DSN) option, which is available for the ASP server model. Your server model might have a different option. For this example, I set up a DSN named aresfiles pointing to an Access database of the same name. These are the steps I took to accomplish this:

1. From the Databases panel, select Add (+) and choose Data Source Name (DSN).

2. In the Data Source Name (DSN) dialog box, select the DSN from the drop-down list. If you need to create a DSN, choose Define.

   DSN creation is handled through the ODBC Data Source Administrator on Windows 2000 systems; your system might have a slightly different name.

3. Enter any username and password information, if necessary.

4. Make sure the data source connection is working properly by selecting Test.

After you have defined the data source connection, it is displayed in the Databases panel. Although it is possible to drag the connection from the Databases panel onto a page in Code view, I typically let Dreamweaver handle it—which it does automatically when a recordset is defined.

The recordset for this technique is straightforward. Because the application is working with all the data, the SQL statement is basic and Dreamweaver's point-and-click user interface for creating simple recordsets is all that is required.

1. From the Bindings panel, choose Add (+) and select Recordset (Query).

   The Recordset dialog box opens; the interface that is displayed depends on which of the two interfaces (Simple or Advanced) was previously used. To follow along with this example, make sure the Simple interface (see Figure 6.5) is shown.

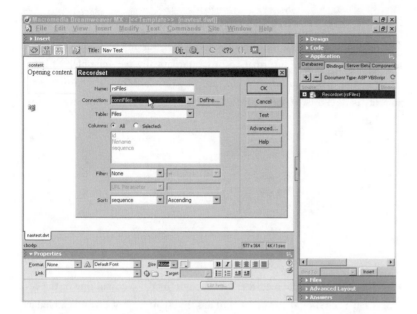

6.5

Choosing a connection in
the Recordset dialog
automatically inserts the
proper data source connection code.

2. Give the recordset a name. Traditionally, I use a name with an rs
    prefix, such as rsFiles.

3. Choose a connection from the drop-down list. If you neglected to
    create one previously, you can do so now by choosing Define.

    In this example, the connection is called connFiles.

4. Select the table that contains the filename and sequence fields.

    Make sure those fields are included by either choosing All or
    Selected. Then highlight the necessary fields.

5. Unless the table contains multiple groups of files for sequencing, leave
    Filter set to None.

6. In the Sort area, set the field containing the sequencing values to
    Ascending.

7. Make sure the results are as expected by selecting Test.

After closing the dialog box, you'll find the new recordset available from the
Bindings panel; if you switch to Code view, you'll see that the code for the
connection has been automatically added right before the recordset code.

Putting the Recordset into an Array

The next step requires a bit of hand-coding. For our application to access the sequence and filename information programmatically, we must place it into an array. The VBScript function for inserting the data from a recordset into an array is `GetRows`. If the recordset is called `rsFiles`, the code would look like this:

```
<%
Dim MyArray, i
MyArray = rsFiles.GetRows
rsFiles.MoveFirst()
%>
```

TIP: If you plan to use this technique often, you might want to download the custom RS into the Array server behavior available from the Beyond Dreamweaver web site.

Place the code after the recordset has been defined. The final line of the code block, `rsFiles.MoveFirst()`, is not absolutely necessary, but it is added as a good programming practice. After the `GetRows` function is complete, the recordset pointer is at the end of the recordset; `MoveFirst()` resets the pointer to the beginning in case there is further recordset interaction.

Getting the Filename

As with the JavaScript technique, a primary step in the dynamic navigation technique is to get the filename. All server models have a method for getting the name of the current file. In ASP VBScript, that method is to use the `Request` object in combination with the `ServerVariables("SCRIPT_NAME")` property, like this:

```
PageName = Request.ServerVariables("SCRIPT_NAME")
```

After you have retrieved the full pathname, you must extract the filename. One way to do this in VBScript is to split the string into elements on an array; the `Split()` function uses the forward slash of the URL as the delimiter. This makes the last element of the array the filename:

```
PageArray = Split(PageName, "/")
PageName = PageArray(Ubound(PageArray))
FullPageName = UCase(PageName)
```

Filename uppercased for easy comparison

Matching the Filename to the Array

With the array populated and the filename safely stored, the next step is to
match one to the other. After a match has been found, the filename's location
in the array is set to a variable—in this example, pos—for use in the final
building of the links.

```
Dim pos
For i = 0 to UBound(MyArray,2)
    If UCase(MyArray(1,i)) = FullPageName Then
        pos = i
        Exit For
    End If
Next
```

Examines filename field

Building the Links

To create the Previous and Next links, you directly enter the reference to the
array into the code for the tag:

```
Response.Write "<a href=""" & MyArray(1,pos-1) & """>Previous</a>
 - <a href=""" & MyArray(1,pos+1) & """>Next</a>"
```

As in the JavaScript technique, the Previous link is set to the filename before
the current file in the array, whereas the Next link uses the filename that is
after the current file.

In the template expression technique, I pointed out that you could use
Dreamweaver template optional regions to hide the Previous and Next link
when appropriate. With the power of server-side scripting, this functionality
is easily included in our basic technique. However, rather than hide the entire
link, we just remove the <a> tag, leaving just the Previous or Next text. Here
are the three routines necessary to cover all circumstances:

```
If pos = 0 Then
    Response.Write "Previous | - <a href=""" & MyArray(1,pos+1) & """>
    Next</a>"
```

First in array

```
                    ElseIf pos = UBound(MyArray,2) Then
Last in array ────────┘   Response.Write "<a href=""" & MyArray(1,pos-1) & """>
                          Previous</a> - Next"


Middle of array ──────  Else
                          Response.Write "<a href=""" & MyArray(1,pos-1) & """>
                          Previous</a> - <a href=""" & MyArray(1,pos+1) & """>Next</a>"
                    End If
```

You could, of course, add numerous enhancements to this technique. For example, you could add code to jump to the next major topic when the end of a sequence is reached.

Listing 6-2 Dynamic Navigation Functions (06_dynnav.dwt.asp)

```asp
<%@LANGUAGE="VBSCRIPT" CODEPAGE="1252"%>
<% Option Explicit %>
<!--#include file="../Connections/connFiles.asp" -->
<%
Dim rsFiles
Dim rsFiles_numRows

Set rsFiles = Server.CreateObject("ADODB.Recordset")
rsFiles.ActiveConnection = MM_connFiles_STRING
rsFiles.Source = "SELECT * FROM Files ORDER BY sequence ASC"
rsFiles.CursorType = 0
rsFiles.CursorLocation = 2
rsFiles.LockType = 1
rsFiles.Open()

rsFiles_numRows = 0
%>
<%
'Put our pages in an array.
Dim MyArray, i
MyArray = rsFiles.GetRows
```

```
'MyArray(0,0) = ID
'MyArray(1,0) = Page Name
'MyArray(2,0) = Sequence
rsFiles.MoveFirst()
%>
<html>
<head>
<!-- TemplateInfo codeOutsideHTMLIsLocked="true" -->
<!-- TemplateBeginEditable name="doctitle" -->
<title>Nav Test</title>
<!-- TemplateEndEditable -->
<meta http-equiv="Content-Type" content="text/html;
charset=iso-8859-1">
<!-- TemplateBeginEditable name="head" -->
<!-- TemplateEndEditable -->
</head>

<body>
<!-- TemplateBeginEditable name="content" -->
<p>Opening content.</p>
<p> </p>
<!-- TemplateEndEditable -->
<%
'Get Page Name
Dim PageName, PageArray, FullPageName
'Get Page Name
'Get the URL
PageName = Request.ServerVariables("SCRIPT_NAME")
'Split it into pieces based on the /
PageArray = Split(PageName, "/")
'Make the page name (while we'll use for linking) the last item
in the array
PageName = PageArray(Ubound(PageArray))
'Make an all uppercase version for testing for matching documents
FullPageName = UCase(PageArray(Ubound(PageArray)))
```

continues

```
'Find our page in the Recordset Array
Dim pos 'Use to store page position
For i = 0 to UBound(MyArray,2)
    If UCase(MyArray(1,i)) = FullPageName Then
        pos = i
        Exit For
    End If
Next


'Build the links
'Is this the first page in the list?
If pos = 0 Then
    Response.Write "Previous | - <a href=""" & MyArray(1,pos+1) & """>
    Next</a>"


'Is this the last page in the list?
ElseIf pos = UBound(MyArray,2) Then
    Response.Write "<a href=""" & MyArray(1,pos-1) & """>
    Previous</a> - Next"


'Must be a middle page
Else
    Response.Write "<a href=""" & MyArray(1,pos-1) & """>
    Previous</a> - <a href=""" & MyArray(1,pos+1) & """>Next</a>"
End If
%>
</body>
</html>
<%
rsFiles.Close()
Set rsFiles = Nothing
%>
```

Part III

Extensions

Chapter 7

Communicating with Fireworks

Any way you look at it, Dreamweaver is a big application. Yet, even the
biggest web-authoring tool has its limitations—and rightfully so. You
wouldn't expect your coding environment to also create your graphics or rich
media; dedicated applications such as Fireworks or Flash are far better suited
for such specialized tasks. However, Dreamweaver's architecture extends the
boundary of the program's functionality to embrace the power of other
software within the Macromedia product line.

In this chapter, we'll look at techniques I used to build cross-application
extensions with Dreamweaver, Fireworks, and Flash. The Dreamweaver-
Fireworks connection is a little older and more developed than the one
between Dreamweaver and Flash; numerous extensions that utilize the
Fireworks graphics engine from within Dreamweaver are widely available.
We'll examine how that communication is handled and demonstrate with
a sample application I built—Thumbnail Builder.

The boundary between Dreamweaver and Flash is somewhat in flux, but
enough stability exists to permit specialized extensions. Dreamweaver 4 introduced the Flash Objects architecture, along with its first manifestations—
Flash Buttons and Flash Text. Flash Objects rely on Generator templates for
their basic functionality. Currently, Generator templates must be authored in
Flash 5 because Generator is no longer available in Flash MX. Macromedia
has hinted at the development of a technology aimed to replace Generator,

but nothing has been officially announced as of this writing. Luckily, the underlying power of Flash Objects is quite extensive and worthy of the in-depth exploration you'll find later in this chapter.

Controlling Fireworks from Dreamweaver

Dreamweaver and Fireworks enjoy a robust integration. In the standard shipping configuration, it's easy to go back and forth between the two products. To bring in graphics created in Fireworks, you can export to Dreamweaver in a variety of flavors:

- Images only

- Sliced or hotspot images and the corresponding HTML/XHTML code

- Sliced or hotspot images with Dreamweaver-style behaviors, modifiable within Dreamweaver

- Images and code formatted as Dreamweaver Library items

After the code is exported, you can also make modifications on the Fireworks side and update the HTML; those HTML changes are automatically incorporated into Dreamweaver. Moreover, you can export the code to a file and use Dreamweaver's dedicated Insert Fireworks object, or you can copy it directly to the Clipboard in Fireworks for a straightforward paste operation in Dreamweaver.

Controlling Fireworks from within Dreamweaver provides just as many options. Dreamweaver recognizes Fireworks-generated code and designates it with its own Property inspector. Such recognition is important because with it, Dreamweaver has the option to edit the web-optimized graphic inserted into its document *or* modify the Fireworks source PNG format file. In addition, Dreamweaver and Fireworks maintain the capability to edit the table structure for sliced images; this means you can make modifications on the Dreamweaver side—such as converting an image slice to a HTML slice—and the change will be respected when edited in Fireworks.

Finally, Dreamweaver also includes an Optimize in Fireworks command for resizing, rescaling, cropping, or otherwise optimizing an embedded graphic. This command, however, does not use the full Fireworks program; instead, only Fireworks' Export Preview dialog box is launched, as shown in Figure 7.1. This functionality is contained within a DLL found within Dreamweaver's JSExtension folder called FWLaunch.dll. This same DLL also holds the key to controlling Fireworks from within Dreamweaver.

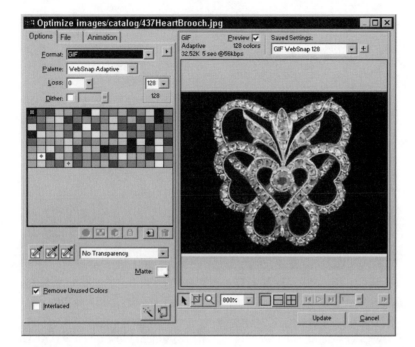

7.1

Dreamweaver's Optimize in Fireworks command opens a subset of the Fireworks engine in Dreamweaver.

Existing Extensions

Several notable extensions take advantage of the power contained within FWLaunch.dll. One standard command, Create Web Photo Album, uses Fireworks to batch process a series of images into thumbnails; a more enhanced version of this command (Web Photo Album 2.0) is available on the Dreamweaver Exchange under the Productivity category. Also on the Exchange is a suite of three cross-application extensions known collectively as the InstaGraphics Extensions:

- **Convert Text to Graphics**—Takes selected text or text within specific tags (h1–h6 or any custom tag) and renders it in the font, font size, and Fireworks style of your choosing. After the graphic is completed, both the exported GIF and source PNG files are stored.

NOTE: In the interest of full disclosure, it should be noted that I authored two Dreamweaver-to-Fireworks commands that evolved into Convert Text to Graphics and Convert Bullets to Graphics. Macromedia took over and enhanced my initial commands, named StyleBuilder and BulletBuilder respectively, to be incorporated into the InstaGraphics extension.

- **Convert Bullets to Graphics**—Changes HTML unordered list items to standard text and replaces the bullets with one of 10 different graphics shapes (star, diamond, triangle, and so on) in any Fireworks style in a user-selected size. The command can be applied to a single list, as shown in Figure 7.2, or in all the lists on the page.

- **Fireworks Button Object**—Makes graphics buttons with user-defined text according to predesigned or custom templates. All buttons generated have simple, two-state rollover behaviors automatically attached; again, both the exported file and the source file are saved for easy editing.

7.2

Both the Convert Text to Graphics and the Convert Bullets to Graphics commands (shown here) have the ability to incorporate custom Fireworks styles via the Update Styles button.

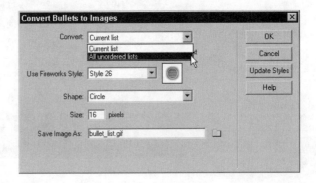

All of these Dreamweaver extensions use the same basic technique for cross-application communication with Fireworks—and they all take advantage of Fireworks capabilities exposed through its Document Object Model (DOM) and API. As you'll see in the following section, these extensions all use a single function call contained within the FWLaunch DLL—FWexec()—to control Fireworks.

Constructing Fireworks Commands

To better understand all that is involved in the programming of cross-application extensions, you need to have a firm grasp of the user experience. When you understand the end result, the reasoning behind the coding process becomes much clearer.

NOTE: Cross-application extensions are found listed under the Commands menu; however, the Extension Manager can install them wherever the author deems appropriate. You can access the Fireworks Button object, for example, through Media—it's own category—in the Insert panel.

Running the Command: The User Experience

Let's step through a sample command. Although the following example uses screen shots from the Convert Text to Image command, the basic procedure is the same for any such extension:

1. The user invokes the command in Dreamweaver.

2. The command's dialog box, like the one for Convert Text to Image in Figure 7.3, appears.

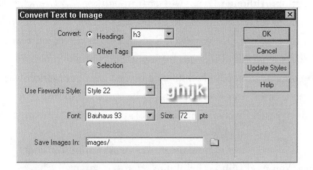

7.3

As with other Dreamweaver extensions, the dialog box is the primary user interface for specifying parameters. The key difference with a cross-application extension like Convert Text to Graphics is that these parameters are eventually passed to Fireworks for processing.

3. The user clicks OK to run the command after all the parameters are selected.

4. A small message box appears that says `Waiting for Fireworks`.

   As you'll see in the next section, this message box is actually a separate command launched from the Convert Text to Image command.

5. Fireworks opens or, if it is already open, it is brought to the front.

6. The Fireworks-related commands are executed and a small dialog box appears indicating that a script is being processed.

   When you're finished in Fireworks, Dreamweaver comes back to the front and the small message box and dialog box close. Any changes to image or text are then incorporated into the Dreamweaver document.

TIP: One of the cool features of the Convert Text to Image command is the swatch that shows an example of the selected Fireworks style. These swatches are actually created programmatically from within the extension by pressing the Update Styles button.

TIP: You can customize the processing message by changing the `App.batchStatusString` property when you execute the Fireworks command. To see this effect in action, select Update Styles from either the Convert Text to Image or Convert Bullets to Image commands.

Depending on the complexity of the command and the speed of the system involved, the whole procedure might happen so fast that the user is not aware of all of these steps. All that the end user really has to do is click the OK button. The programmer's task, as you'll see, is a tad more complex. Now, let's pop that hood and see what's really going on.

Behind the Scenes: The Developer's Experience

The biggest problem in creating cross-application extensions is one-way communication. Although Dreamweaver (through the FWLaunch DLL) is clearly able to send a command to Fireworks for execution, Fireworks cannot, in turn, talk to Dreamweaver. Rather, Dreamweaver must wait for a response to its request to Fireworks before it can continue processing. This restricted communication is the rationale behind the code workflow found in cross-application extensions. You might be surprised to find that such an application typically involves a minimum of five different JavaScript files.

Let's look at an overview of how the process works, from the coding perspective. You might find it helpful to refer to diagram 7.4.

7.4

The cross-application extension workflow from a code point-of-view.

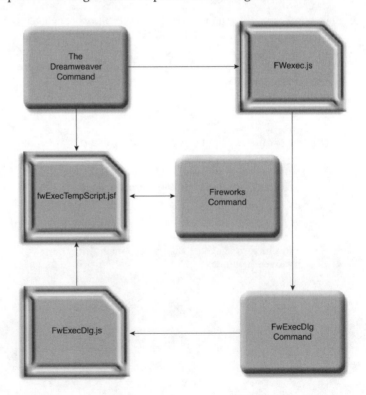

1. The user executes the Dreamweaver command, stored in the Commands folder.

2. The user presses the OK button, and then several key events take place:

   - All of the user-selected parameters are entered into their appropriate variables.

   - These variables are passed to Fireworks via the `execFunctionInFireworks()` function, stored in Shared/Fireworks/FwExec.js.

   - The actual commands to be processed within Fireworks are written to a temporary file, fwExecTempScript.jsf, which is stored in the Shared/MM/Scripts/ folder. The .jsf extension designates a Fireworks JavaScript file.

3. The `execFunctionInFireworks` runs a separate command, `FwExecDlg`, to pop up the `Waiting for Fireworks` notice.

   The `FwExecDlg` command is a "hidden" command found in the file, FwExecDlg.htm. The HTML comment, `<!-- MENU-LOCATION=NONE -->`, before the opening `<html>` tag prevents the extension from appearing in the Commands folder.

4. When the `FwExecDlg` command loads, it calls one function: `fwexec_execJsInFireworksAndWaitForResponse()`. This function is founded in the external JavaScript file, FwExecDlg.js.

   The key function call contained within `fwexec_execJsInFireworksAndWaitForResponse()` is `FWLaunch.execJsInFireworks()`, which executes a temporary JavaScript file created on-the-fly and stored in Shared/MM/Scripts/fwExecTempScript.jsf.

Although this whole procedure might appear quite convoluted, it's actually fairly straightforward to implement. With the standard Macromedia files (FwExec.js, FwExecDlg.htm, and FwExecDlg.js) in place, all the back-end interprocess communication is handled for you. As a programmer, you can concentrate on coding the commands to execute in Fireworks and Dreamweaver—and you'll find an example of how it's done in the next section.

NOTE: Dreamweaver commands may be split into two or more files within the Commands folder, an HTML file and a JavaScript file. The HTML page holds the form and form elements that make up the dialog box as well as `<script>` tag linking to the JavaScript file. The JavaScript file contains most, if not all, of the JavaScript functions necessary. This file often also defines text strings in a series of global variables to make localization easier. All of Macromedia's commands use the two-file design.

Example: Cross-Application Extension: Thumbnail Builder

As noted earlier, Dreamweaver comes with Create Web Photo Album, which is a tool for creating thumbnails. However, this command is intended for batch-processing a series of images. What if you want to create thumbnails one at a time? I wrote the Thumbnail Builder extension to fill just that need (see Listing 7-1).

Listing 7-1 **Thumbnail Builder.htm** (07_ThumbnailBuilder.mxp)

```html
<!-- MENU-LOCATION=NONE -->
<html>
<head>
<title>Thumbnail Builder</title>
<!-- By Joseph Lowery,
    Author of the Dreamweaver Bible series,
    the Fireworks Bible series and Beyond Dreamweaver
    jlowery@idest.com
-->
<script src="../Shared/Fireworks/FwExec.js"></script>
<script language="javascript"
src="../Shared/MM/Scripts/CMN/UI.js"></script>
<script language="javascript"
src="../Shared/MM/Scripts/CMN/FILE.js"></script>
<script language="javascript"
src="../Shared/MM/Scripts/CMN/enableControl.js"></script>
<script language="javascript"
src="../Shared/MM/Scripts/CMN/enableControl.js"></script>
<script language="javascript"
src="../Shared/MM/Scripts/CMN/docInfo.js"></script>
<script src="ThumbnailBuilder.js"></script>
<link rel="stylesheet" href="mmres://user_interface_dialog.css">
<style type="text/css">
<!--
.textbox {  width: 30px; height: 15px}
-->
</style>
```

```
</head>
<body onLoad="initUI()">
<form name="theForm">
  <table border="0">
    <tr>
      <td colspan="4" nowrap><currentsize>Current Image: W: xx
        H:
        xx</currentsize></td>
    </tr>
    <tr>
      <td colspan="4"><newsize>Thumbnail: W:
          H:</newsize></td>
    </tr>
    <tr>
      <td colspan="4">
        <hr>
      </td>
    </tr>
    <tr>
      <td>Size:</td>
      <td>
        <div align="right">
          <input name="sizeRB" type="radio"
          onClick="javascript:document.theForm.widthText.focus()"
          value="width" checked>
        </div>
      </td>
      <td>Width</td>
      <td nowrap>
        <input type="text" name="widthText" class="textbox"
        onBlur="checkField(this.name)">
        pixels </td>
    </tr>
    <tr>
      <td> </td>
      <td>
```

continues

```
                    <div align="right">
                      <input type="radio" name="sizeRB" value="height"
                      onClick="javascript:document.theForm.
                      heightText.focus()">
                    </div>
                  </td>
                  <td>Height</td>
                  <td nowrap>
                    <input type="text" name="heightText" class="textbox"
                    onBlur="checkField(this.name)">
                    pixels </td>
              </tr>
              <tr>
                  <td> </td>
                  <td>
                    <div align="right">
                      <input type="radio" name="sizeRB" value="percentage"
                      onClick="javascript:document.theForm.
                      percentageText.focus()">
                    </div>
                  </td>
                  <td>Percentage</td>
                  <td nowrap>
                    <input type="text" name="percentageText" class="textbox"
                    onBlur="checkField(this.name)">
                    % </td>
              </tr>
              <tr>
                  <td colspan="4">
                    <hr>
                  </td>
              </tr>
              <tr>
                  <td>Border:</td>
                  <td>
                    <div align="right">
                      <input type="checkbox" name="htmlCB" value="html">
```

```
      </div>
    </td>
    <td>HTML</td>
    <td>  </td>
</tr>
<tr>
    <td> </td>
    <td>
      <div align="right">
        <input type="checkbox" name="bevelCB" value="checkbox">
      </div>
    </td>
    <td>Bevel</td>
    <td>  </td>
</tr>
<tr>
    <td> </td>
    <td>
      <div align="right">
        <input type="checkbox" name="dropshadowCB"
        value="checkbox">
      </div>
    </td>
    <td nowrap>Drop Shadow</td>
    <td> </td>
</tr>
<tr>
    <td colspan="4">
      <hr>
    </td>
</tr>
<tr>
    <td nowrap>Target:</td>
    <td>
      <div align="right">
        <input type="radio" name="targetRB" value="jspw">
      </div>
```

continues

```
        </td>
        <td colspan="2">Just So Picture Window</td>
      </tr>
      <tr>
        <td> </td>
        <td>
          <div align="right">
            <input type="radio" name="targetRB" value="radiobutton">
          </div>
        </td>
        <td colspan="2">_blank page</td>
      </tr>
    </table>
</form></body>
</html>
```

Here's how the command is used:

1. The user selects an image to convert to a thumbnail and run the command.

   The user must select an image for the command to become active in the menu.

2. In the Thumbnail Builder dialog box, the user must enter the size of the thumbnail first. An image can be sized in one of three ways:

   • Width—The entered value sets the width of the thumbnail in pixels; the height is proportionately calculated.

   • Height—The user sets the thumbnail's height in pixels; again, the other dimension—in this case width—is automatically calculated according to the width to height ratio of the original image.

   • Percentage—The width and height are calculated according to the entered percentage value.

   After the user selects the method and enters the value, the new dimensions are presented just below the original dimensions, as shown in Figure 7.5.

Thumbnail Builder ☒

Current Image: W: 239 H: 214
Thumbnail: **W: 119   H: 107**

OK

Help

Cancel

Size: ○ Width   [   ] pixels

        ○ Height   [   ] pixels

        ◉ Percentage [50] %

Border: ☐ HTML

         ☑ Bevel

         ☐ Drop Shadow

Target: ◉ Just So Picture Window

         ○ _self page

7.5

The Thumbnail Builder interface displays the settings from the previous session to enhance user productivity.

3. Next, the user selects the type of effects to be applied to the thumbnail. Again, the user has three choices: HTML, which places a standard 1-pixel wide border around the image, indicating it is a link; Bevel, which applies Fireworks' built-in Bevel effect to the thumbnail; and Drop Shadow, which, as expected, adds a Fireworks drop shadow to the thumbnail.

   The effects can be used in combination with each other, although combining HTML with the Drop Shadow option might not create the desired look because the HTML border wraps around the entire image, including the shadow.

4. The final choice determines how the original image is displayed after the thumbnail is clicked. If the user has the Just So Picture Window extension by E. Michael Brandt installed, that option becomes available; if selected, the original image opens in a separate window, sized to fit the graphic. Otherwise, the image is targeted to open in the same browser window as the current document.

5. After the user selects the options and clicks OK, the thumbnail is built in Fireworks and stored in the same folder as the original image; the same original filename plus a suffix of _small is used.

6. In Dreamweaver, the original image is replaced with the new thumbnail, complete with a link to the larger image. In the code, this line:

NOTE: Only one extension (a command) is calling another (a behavior) here, but arguments are being passed to the second extension from the first. You'll see how it's done later in the section "Executing the Thumbnail Builder Command."

```
<img src="images/tiger.jpg" width="407" height="256">
```

is replaced with this line:

```
<a href="images/tiger.jpg"><img src="images/tiger_small.jpg"
width="407" height="256"></a>
```

If the Just So Picture Window option is selected, an `onClick` function call is added to the `<a>` tag in addition to the necessary behavior function being written to the `<head>` section.

Next, we'll deconstruct the primary code from the Thumbnail Builder extension. Not only will you find a carefully drawn roadmap to create your own cross-application extensions in the following sections, but I've also included numerous tips and techniques for successfully building extensions of any type.

Controlling Menu Access

In versions prior to Dreamweaver MX, any command placed in the Configuration/Commands folder was automatically placed in the Commands menu—unless a special snippet of code was placed at the top of the file. To avoid having your command placed at the bottom of the Commands menu, you need to include the first line you see here from the start of my command file, 07_ThumbnailBuilder.mxp:

```
<!-- MENU-LOCATION=NONE -->
<html>
<head>
<title>Thumbnail Builder</title>
```

With `<!-- MENU-LOCATION=NONE -->` in place, you're free to specify where and how you would like the command to be accessed. When the Extension Manager packages the command for installation, menu placement is noted in the .mxi file under the `<configuration-changes>` section (see Listing 7-2).

Listing 7-2   **ThumbnailBuilder.mxp** (07_ThumbnailBuilder.mxp)

```
<macromedia-extension
    name="Thumbnail Builder"
    version="1.0.0"
    type="Command">

    <!-- List the required/compatible products -->

    <products>
        <product name="Dreamweaver" version="6" primary="true" />
        <product name="Fireworks" version="3" primary="false" />
    </products>

    <!-- Describe the author -->

    <author name="Joseph Lowery" />

    <!-- Describe the extension -->

    <description>
<![CDATA[
Thumbnail Builder creates a thumbnail from a selected image,
replaces the original image with the thumbnail and then creates a
link to the larger image. Thumbnail size may be specified by the
width, height or percentage. A variety of border attributes (HTML,
bevel and drop shadow) are available).

The original image can appear in the current browser window or, if
you have E. Michael Brandt's Just So Picture Window installed, in
its own window.
]]>
    </description>

    <!-- Describe where the extension shows in the UI of the product -->

    <ui-access>
<![CDATA[
```

continues

```
                You'll find this command in the Commands menu and in the image
                context menu.
                ]]>
                </ui-access>


                <!-- Describe the files that comprise the extension -->


                <files>
                    <file name="Commands/ThumbnailBuilder.htm"
            destination="$dreamweaver/configuration/commands" shared="true"/>
                    <file name="Commands/ThumbnailBuilder.js"
            destination="$dreamweaver/configuration/commands" />
                    <file name="Commands/FwExecDlg.htm"
            destination="$dreamweaver/configuration/commands" shared="true" />
                    <file name="Commands/FwExecDlg.js"
            destination="$dreamweaver/configuration/commands" shared="true" />
                    <file name="Shared/Fireworks/FwExec.js"
            destination="$dreamweaver/configuration/Shared/Fireworks"
            shared="true" />
                </files>


                <!-- Describe the changes to the configuration -->


            <configuration-changes>
            <menu-insert insertAfter="DWMenu_Commands_OptimizeInFW">
              <menuitem name="Thumbnail Builder..."
            file="Commands/ThumbnailBuilder.htm" id="DWMenu_ThumbnailBuilder" />
            </menu-insert>
            <menu-insert insertAfter="DWContext_Image_OptimizeInFW">
              <menuitem name="Thumbnail Builder..."
            file="Commands/ThumbnailBuilder.htm"
            id="DWContext_Image_ThumbnailBuilder" />
            </menu-insert>


            </configuration-changes>
            </macromedia-extension>
```

For the Thumbnail Builder command, I wanted to offer two options for access. The first option is under the Commands menu, after another cross-application extension, the Optimize in Fireworks entry. Wherever possible, I like to group related commands. The second option is in the context or pop-up menu for images, again after the Optimize in Fireworks command. After looking up the ID labels for the two Optimize in Fireworks entries in the Configuration/Menus/menus.xml file, I insert the following code at the end of my .mxi file:

```
<configuration-changes>

    <menu-insert insertAfter = "DWMenu_Commands_OptimizeInFW">

        <menuitem name = "Thumbnail Builder..." file =
        "Commands/ThumbnailBuilder.htm" id="DWMenu_ThumbnailBuilder" />

    </menu-insert>

    <menu-insert insertAfter = "DWContext_Image_OptimizeInFW">

        <menuitem name = "Thumbnail Builder..." file =
        "Commands/ThumbnailBuilder.htm" id =
        "DWContext_Image_ThumbnailBuilder" />

    </menu-insert>

</configuration-changes>
```

Regular menu entry

Context menu entry

The two `<menu-insert>` entries do the same job and are identical except for the `id` property value, which must be unique.

Including the Proper Files

The next segment of code in the ThumbnailBuilder.htm file is made up of a series of includes. Aside from all the power offered by its DOM and JavaScript API, Dreamweaver includes a wealth of programming routines that are available for private use. Most of these files are located in the Configuration/Shared/MM folder and can be referenced with a `<script scr="fileName"></script>` code.

In ThumbnailBuilder.htm, five such files are included from Macromedia's script cache and one from one mine:

TIP: If you're not familiar with the .mxi format or the process of packaging extensions, you can find all the necessary documentation from within the Extension Manager. Choose Help, Creating and Submitting Extensions for an overview of the procedure. Within the section on packaging an extension, you'll find a link to a document detailing the Macromedia Exchange Installation (MXI) file format.

Installed with extension ———

```
<script src="../Shared/Fireworks/FwExec.js"></script>
<script language="javascript"
src="../Shared/MM/Scripts/CMN/UI.js"></script>
<script language="javascript"
src="../Shared/MM/Scripts/CMN/FILE.js"></script>
<script language="javascript"
src="../Shared/MM/Scripts/CMN/enableControl.js"></script>
<script language="javascript"
src="../Shared/MM/Scripts/CMN/docInfo.js"></script>
<script src="ThumbnailBuilder.js"></script>
```

Standard ———

The first included file, FwExec.js, is necessary for smooth communication with Fireworks, as described earlier in this chapter. The next four files contain specific functions that are called within my command. The UI.js file, for example, is included in almost every extension I write because it contains the extraordinarily useful function, `findObject()`, which allows form elements to be properly located regardless of their location in the file. Some JavaScript files contain more specialized functions that are useful only in certain circumstances, such as the `SetEnabled()` function found in the enableControl.js file; this function is used to enable or disable form elements programmatically.

Styling the Dialog Box

Unknown to many extension developers, Dreamweaver uses its own built-in CSS style sheets to achieve a consistent look and feel throughout its many user interfaces. One such style sheet, `user_interface_dialog.css`, controls the appearance of all text and form input fields. To access this style sheet, link to it in this manner:

```
<link rel="stylesheet" href="mmres://user_interface_dialog.css">
```

The `mmres://` protocol designates a particular namespace recognized within Dreamweaver.

I also employ another style sheet declaration; rather than a link to an external file, this is an internal declaration for the custom class `.textbox`. I apply this CSS class to the various text fields for a consistent width that I control.

```
<style type="text/css">
<!--
.textbox {  width: 30px; height: 15px}
-->
</style>
```

Not only do these style sheet declarations ensure the appearance of the dialog box at runtime, but they also help during design time.

Adding Text Dynamically

In Thumbnail Builder, I need to show both the size of the original image and the dimensions of the new thumbnail. The original image dimensions depend on the selected image; therefore, they might vary one use to another. The thumbnail dimensions, on the other hand, are user determined and could change repeatedly while the user tries out different values.

To show both of these varyingly dynamic bits of information, two custom tags are used: `<currentsize>` and `<newsize>`. The two tags are embedded in the body text of the form as shown in the following code:

```
<td colspan="4" nowrap><currentsize>Current Image: W: xx          Placeholder text
  H: xx</currentsize></td>

...

<td colspan="4" nowrap><newsize>Thumbnail: W:               Placeholder text
    H:</newsize></td>
```

The `<currentsize>` text is calculated when the extension first loads. You'll find this code in the `initUI()` function:

```
theCurrentSize =
dw.getNaturalSize(getFullPath(theSelObj.getAttribute("src")));

var theHeading = document.getElementsByTagName('currentsize');     Refers to dialog box

theHeading[0].innerHTML = "Current Image: W: " + theCurrentSize[0]
+ "   H: " + theCurrentSize[1]
```

The `getNaturalSize()` function returns a two-element array representing the width and height respectively. The `document.getElementsByTagName` `('currentsize')` function call is used to display the dimensions in the dialog box. Note that the document DOM is addressed for the `getElementsByTagName()` function rather than the more commonly seen `dw.getDocumentDOM()`. Here, "document" refers to the extension interface, the dialog box, rather than the current Dreamweaver document. The `getElementsByTagName()` function also returns an array—stored in my variable, `theHeading`—but because only one `<currentsize>` tag is available, I can replace the `innerHTML` of the first element with my new text, as shown in the third line of the preceding code snippet.

A similar strategy is used to display the dimensions of the thumbnail in the function `updateSize()`. This function is called upon initialization and whenever a new value is entered in one of the three size text fields. The `updateSize()` function first retrieves the selected image dimension to be used to calculate the new thumbnail size:

```
dw.getNaturalSize(getFullPath(theSelObj.getAttribute("src")));
```

Next, we set up to replace the `<newsize>` text in the dialog box, as we did with the original size text:

```
var theNewSizeText = document.getElementsByTagName('newsize');
```

Now we're ready to see which option is checked and react accordingly. In each case, one dimension is gathered from the user input and the second dimension is calculated. The calculations vary according to the option chosen, but notice that in each circumstance, the `parseInt()` function is used to convert the text of the submitted value into a number:

```
if (theSizeChoice[0].checked) {    //width
    theNewWidth = parseInt(findObject("widthText").value);
    theNewHeight = parseInt((theNewWidth / parseInt(theOldSize[0]))
* parseInt(theOldSize[1]));
}
```

```
if (theSizeChoice[1].checked) {    //height
   theNewHeight = parseInt(findObject("heightText").value);
   theNewWidth = parseInt((theNewHeight / parseInt(theOldSize[1]))
* parseInt(theOldSize[0]));
}
if (theSizeChoice[2].checked) {    //percentage
   var thePercent = parseInt(findObject("percentageText").value);
   theNewWidth = parseInt((thePercent / 100) * theOldSize[0]);
   theNewHeight = parseInt((thePercent / 100) * theOldSize[1]);
}
```

After the calculations are all done, the inner HTML of the `<newsize>` tag is
replaced with the desired text string:

```
theNewSizeText[0].innerHTML = "Thumbnail: <b>W: " + theNewWidth +
"   H: " + theNewHeight + "</b>";
}
```

The bold and non-breaking space tags are added to give the dimensions a bit
of emphasis and structure.

Crafting the Input Fields

One of my goals in structuring an interface is to make the user experience as
intuitive as possible. The next bit of code illustrates one method of achieving
that goal. Thumbnail Builder has a series of radio buttons, each with an
associated text field, as shown in Figure 7.6. I know that when users select a
particular radio button—Width, for example—they intend to enter a value in
the associated text field. The following bit of code uses inline JavaScript to
set the focus to the proper text field after a radio button is selected.

7.6

The Size section depends on a couple of custom JavaScript functions to make it intuitive for users to change selections.

Size option radio buttons

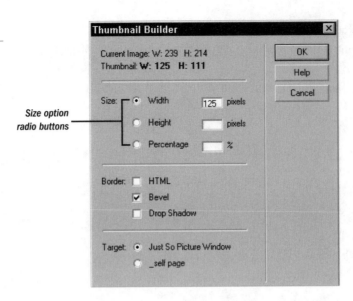

```
<input type="radio" name="sizeRB" value="width"
onClick="javascript:document.theForm.widthText.focus()">
```

This code eliminates the need for a second click and makes it easy for the user to quickly enter his value. The reverse assumption also holds true: If I, as a user, enter a value in the Width text field, it can be assumed that I want to choose the Width option. Although simple in concept, these automatic selections requires a bit more coding, so here I'll call a custom function after the value has been entered and the field has been exited:

```
<input type="text" name="widthText" class="textbox"
onBlur="checkField(this.name)">
```

The checkField() function checks to see which text field is being used and then performs two operations. First, it clears the other two text fields. If I had an old value in Percentage, and I entered a new value in Width, I wouldn't want the old value anymore, would I? Second, checkField() sets the appropriate radio button. Moreover, when those operations are completed, the updateSize() function (discussed in the previous section) is called so that my new thumbnail dimensions are displayed:

```
function checkField(theFieldName) {
    var theField = findObject(theFieldName);
    if (theField.value != "") {
        if (theFieldName == "widthText") {
            findObject("heightText").value = "";
            findObject("percentageText").value = "";
            findObject("sizeRB")[0].checked = true
        }
        if (theFieldName == "heightText") {
            findObject("widthText").value = "";
            findObject("percentageText").value = "";
            findObject("sizeRB")[1].checked = true
        }
        if (theFieldName == "percentageText") {
            findObject("heightText").value = "";
            findObject("widthText").value = "";
            findObject("sizeRB")[2].checked = true
        }
    }
    updateSize();
}
```

Clears text field

Selects radio button

There is, as usual, a number of ways this function could have been written;
you could, for example, structure it using a series of **case** statements rather
than the **if** clauses as I did here.

Limiting the Command's Use

That completes our tour of the Thumbnailbuilder.htm file, which creates the
user interface and includes the necessary files. Now let's look at the compan-
ion file, 07_ThumbnailBuilder.mxp (see Listing 7-3).

Listing 7-3   **ThumbnailBuilder.mxp** (07_ThumbnailBuilder.mxp)

```
/******************** GLOBAL VARS ************************/
var theSizeChoice = findObject("sizeRB");
var theCurrentSize;
```

continues

```
var picWinHeight, picWinWidth, picWinAlt, picWinColor,
picWinHugger, picWinHugMargin;
/******************** GLOBAL CONSTANTS ********************/


/******************************************************/

function canAcceptCommand() {
   var theDom = dw.getDocumentDOM();
   var selection = dreamweaver.getSelection();
   var theSel = dreamweaver.offsetsToNode( selection[0],
   selection[1] );

   return(theSel != null && theSel.nodeType == Node.ELEMENT &&
   theSel.tagName == "IMG");
}

function commandButtons(){
    return new Array( 'OK', 'runCommand()', 'Help',
    'doHelp()','Cancel', 'window.close()');
}

function doHelp() {
dw.browseDocument('http://www.fp2dw.com/extensions/tbhelp.htm');

}

function fw_makeThumbnail(theFile,theSizeOption, theSizeValue,
theBevelOption, theShadowOption, theBG){
   var theMsg = "OK";
   theSizeValue = parseInt(theSizeValue);

   //lower the height/width value to accommodate for the shadow
   if (theShadowOption == "true" && theSizeOption != "scale") {
      theSizeValue = theSizeValue - 8;
   }
```

```
var theDoc = fw.openDocument(theFile,true);    //opens file as new
theDoc.setMatteColor(true, theBG);
var theWidth = theDoc.width;
var theHeight = theDoc.height;
if (theSizeOption == "width") {
    theSizeValue = theSizeValue / theWidth;
}
if (theSizeOption == "height") {
    theSizeValue = theSizeValue / theHeight;
}

if (theSizeOption == "scale") {
    theSizeValue = theSizeValue / 100;
}

theDoc.selectAll();
theDoc.scaleSelection(theSizeValue, theSizeValue,
"autoTrimImages transformAttributes");

if (theBevelOption == "true" && theShadowOption == "true")
{//do both
    fw.getDocumentDOM().applyEffects({ category:"Untitled",
    effects:[ { AngleSoftness:3, BevelContrast:75, BevelType:0,
    BevelWidth:10, ButtonState:0, DownBlendColor:"#0000003f",
    EdgeThreshold:0, EffectIsVisible:true,
    EffectMoaID:"{7fe61102-6ce2-11d1-8c76000502701850}",
    EmbossFaceColor:"#ffffff00", GlowStartDistance:0,
    GlowWidth:0, HiliteColor:"#ffffff",
    HitBlendColor:"#ffffff3f", LightAngle:135,
    LightDistance:100, MaskSoftness:0,
    OuterBevelColor:"#df0000", ShadowColor:"#000000",
    ShowObject:false, SlopeMultiplier:1, SlopeType:0,
    category:"Inner Bevel", name:"Inner Bevel" },
    { EffectIsVisible:true, EffectMoaID:"{a7944db8-6ce2-11d1-
    8c76000502701850}", ShadowAngle:315, ShadowBlur:4,
    ShadowColor:"#000000a5", ShadowDistance:7, ShadowType:0,
```

continues

```
            category:"Shadow and Glow", name:"Drop Shadow" } ],
            name:"Untitled" });
      } else if (theBevelOption == "true" && theShadowOption !=
      "true") {
            theDoc.applyEffects({ category:"Untitled", effects:[ {
            AngleSoftness:3, BevelContrast:75, BevelType:0,
            BevelWidth:10, ButtonState:0, DownBlendColor:"#0000003f",
            EdgeThreshold:0, EffectIsVisible:true,
            EffectMoaID:"{7fe61102-6ce2-11d1-8c76000502701850}",
            EmbossFaceColor:"#ffffff00", GlowStartDistance:0,
            GlowWidth:0, HiliteColor:"#ffffff",
            HitBlendColor:"#ffffff3f", LightAngle:135,
            LightDistance:100, MaskSoftness:0,
            OuterBevelColor:"#df0000", ShadowColor:"#000000",
            ShowObject:false, SlopeMultiplier:1, SlopeType:0,
            category:"Inner Bevel", name:"Inner Bevel" } ],
            name:"Untitled" });
      } else if (theShadowOption == "true" && theBevelOption !=
      "true") {
            theDoc.applyEffects({ category:"Untitled", effects:[ {
            EffectIsVisible:true, EffectMoaID:"{a7944db8-6ce2-11d1-
            8c76000502701850}", ShadowAngle:315, ShadowBlur:4,
            ShadowColor:"#000000a5", ShadowDistance:7, ShadowType:0,
            category:"Shadow and Glow", name:"Drop Shadow" } ],
            name:"Untitled" });
      }

      theDoc.setDocumentCanvasSizeToDocumentExtents(true); //allows
      the canvas to grow
      var theExt = theFile.substr(theFile.lastIndexOf('.'));
      theFile = theFile.substr(0,theFile.lastIndexOf('.')) +
      "_small";

      if (theExt.toLowerCase().indexOf('gif') != -1) {
            theDoc.setExportOptions({ exportFormat:"GIF",
            paletteTransparency:"index"});
      }
```

```
   if (theExt.toLowerCase().indexOf('jp') != -1) {
      theDoc.setExportOptions({ exportFormat:"JPEG"});
   }


   fw.saveDocument(theDoc,theFile + ".png");
   fw.exportDocumentAs(null, theFile, null);
   fw.closeDocument(theDoc,false);
   return theMsg;
}


function runCommand() {
   //Get the DOM of the user's document
   var theDom = dw.getDocumentDOM();
   var theBG = theDom.body.bgcolor?theDom.body.bgcolor:"#ffffff";
   var theSizeOption, theSizeValue;
   var theBevelOption = "false";
   var theShadowOption = "false";

   var offsets = theDom.getSelection();
   var theSelObj = dreamweaver.offsetsToNode(offsets[0],offsets[1]);
   var theFileBase = theSelObj.getAttribute("src");
   var jspwFileBase = theFileBase;
   var theFileURL = getFullPath(theFileBase);
   var thePath = "";
   if (theFileBase.lastIndexOf("/") != -1) {
      thePath =theFileBase.substr(0,theFileBase.lastIndexOf("/"));
      theFileBase = theFileBase.substr(theFileBase.lastIndexOf("/"));
   }


   if (theSizeChoice[0].checked) {
      theSizeOption = "width";
      theSizeValue = findObject("widthText").value;
      findObject("heightText").value = "";
      findObject("percentageText").value = "";
      if (theSizeValue == "" || isNaN(theSizeValue)) {
         alert("Please enter a numeric value in the Width field.");
```

continues

```
                    findObject("widthText").focus();
                    return;
                }
            }
            if (theSizeChoice[1].checked) {
                theSizeOption = "height";
                theSizeValue = findObject("heightText").value;
                findObject("widthText").value = "";
                findObject("percentageText").value = "";
                if (theSizeValue == "" || isNaN(theSizeValue)) {
                    alert("Please enter a numeric value in the Height
                    field.");
                    findObject("heightText").focus();
                    return;
                }
            }
            if (theSizeChoice[2].checked) {
                theSizeOption = "scale";
                theSizeValue = findObject("percentageText").value;
                findObject("widthText").value = "";
                findObject("heightText").value = "";
                if (theSizeValue == "" || isNaN(theSizeValue)) {
                    alert("Please enter a numeric value in the Scale
                    field.");
                    findObject("scaleText").focus();
                    return;
                }
            }

            if (findObject("bevelCB").checked) {
                theBevelOption = "true";
            }

            if (findObject("dropshadowCB").checked) {
                theShadowOption = "true";
            }
```

```
var thePicWin = 1;
getNotesPicWindow();
if (findObject('targetRB')[0].checked) {
   var jspwStr="JustSoPicWindow(" + jspwFileBase + "," +
   picWinWidth + "," + picWinHeight + "," + picWinAlt + "," +
   picWinColor + "," + picWinHugger + "," + picWinHugMargin + ")";
   if (thePicWin) thePicWin =
   dw.popupAction("JustSoPicWindow.htm",jspwStr);
   if (thePicWin == jspwStr) {// when the user Canceled jspw
      return;
   }
}


result = execFunctionInFireworks(fw_makeThumbnail, theFileURL,
theSizeOption, theSizeValue, theBevelOption, theShadowOption,
theBG);


// If execFunctionInFireworks returned NULL, everything went OK;
// time to insert the images
if (result == "OK"){
   var theExt = theFileBase.substr(theFileBase.lastIndexOf('.'));
   var theNewFile = theFileBase.substr
   (0,theFileBase.lastIndexOf('.')) + "_small";
   theNewFile = thePath + theNewFile + theExt;
   theNewFileURL = getFullPath(theNewFile);
   var theSizeArray = dw.getNaturalSize(theNewFileURL);
   var newID = makeUniqueName('IMG','tbb_')
   theSelObj.setAttribute("id",newID);
   theSelObj.setAttribute("src",theNewFile);
   theSelObj.setAttribute("width",theSizeArray[0]);
   theSelObj.setAttribute("height",theSizeArray[1]);
   var theBorder = "0";
   if (findObject('htmlCB').checked) {
      theBorder = "1";
      if (findObject('htmlText').value) {
         theBorder = findObject('htmlText').value;
```

continues

```
            }
        }
        theSelObj.setAttribute("border",theBorder);
        var theCode = theSelObj.innerHTML;
        if (findObject('targetRB')[0].checked) {//Just So Pic Win
            theSelObj.outerHTML = '<a href="javascript:;" onClick="'
            + thePicWin + ';return document.MM_returnValue' +
            '">' + theCode + '</a>';
        } else {
            theSelObj.outerHTML = '<a href="' + thePath +
            theFileBase + '">' + theCode + '</a>';
        }
    }

    saveRadioPreferences('sizeRB','targetRB');
    saveTextPreferences('widthText','heightText','percentageText',
    'htmlText','bevelText');
    saveBoxesPreferences('bevelCB','htmlCB','dropshadowCB');
    window.close();
    FWLaunch.bringDWToFront();
    return;
}

function saveTextPreferences(){//1.0
    if (typeof MMNotes == 'undefined') {return;} // Check for
    MMNotes extension.
    var theSettings,metaFile;
    theSettings = saveTextPreferences.arguments;
    metaFile = MMNotes.open(document.URL, true);
    if (metaFile) {
        for (var i=0; i<theSettings.length; i++){
            var settingName;
            //Assemble the name of the key inside the Design note
            settingName = "pref_"+theSettings[i];
            //Set the value of the key
            MMNotes.set(metaFile,settingName,findObject
            (theSettings[i]).value);
```

```
        }
        MMNotes.close(metaFile);
    }
}


//Get an array of text form elements and retrieve their setting
//Then, populate the elements with the relevant values
function getTextPreferences(){//1.0
    if (typeof MMNotes == 'undefined') {return;}
    // Check for MMNotes extension.
    var theSettings,metaFile;
    theSettings = getTextPreferences.arguments;
    metaFile = MMNotes.open(document.URL, true);
    if (metaFile) {
        for (var i=0; i<theSettings.length; i++){
            var settingName,settingValue;
            //Assemble the name of the key inside the Design note
            settingName = "pref_"+theSettings[i];
            //Get the value of the key
            settingValue = MMNotes.get(metaFile,settingName);
            //If we have a saved setting
            if(settingValue){
                //Set the status of the form element
                findObject(theSettings[i]).value = settingValue;
            }
        }
        MMNotes.close(metaFile);
    }
}


//Get an array of check boxes and save their setting
//Settings names are pref_nameOfFormElement
function saveBoxesPreferences(){//1.0
    if (typeof MMNotes == 'undefined') {return;} // Check for
    MMNotes extension.
    var theSettings,metaFile;
    theSettings = saveBoxesPreferences.arguments;
```

continues

```
        metaFile = MMNotes.open(document.URL, true);
        if (metaFile) {
            for (var i=0; i<theSettings.length; i++){
                var settingName;
                //Assemble the name of the key inside the Design note
                settingName = "pref_"+theSettings[i];
                //Set the value of the key

MMNotes.set(metaFile,settingName,findObject(theSettings[i]).checked);
            }
            MMNotes.close(metaFile);
        }
    }


//Get an array of checkboxes form elements and retrieve their
setting
//Then, change the status of the elements
function getBoxesPreferences(){//1.0
    if (typeof MMNotes == 'undefined') {return;} // Check for
    MMNotes extension.
    var theSettings,metaFile;
    theSettings = getBoxesPreferences.arguments;
    metaFile = MMNotes.open(document.URL, true);
    if (metaFile) {
        for (var i=0; i<theSettings.length; i++){
            var settingName,settingValue;
            //Assemble the name of the key inside the Design note
            settingName = "pref_"+theSettings[i];
            //Get the value of the key
            settingValue = MMNotes.get(metaFile,settingName);
            //If we have a saved setting
            if(settingValue){
                //Set the status of the form element
                findObject(theSettings[i]).checked = eval(settingValue);
            }
        }
```

```
            MMNotes.close(metaFile);
        }
    }



//Get an array of radio form elements and save their setting
//Settings names are pref_nameOfFormElement
function saveRadioPreferences(){//1.3
    if (typeof MMNotes == 'undefined') {return;} // Check for
    MMNotes extension.
    var theSettings,metaFile;
    theSettings = saveRadioPreferences.arguments;
    metaFile = MMNotes.open(document.URL, true);
    if (metaFile) {
        for (var i=0; i<theSettings.length; i++){
            var settingName;
            //Assemble the name of the key inside the Design note
            settingName = "pref_"+theSettings[i];
            //Find the selected element and set the value of the key
            for (var h=0; h<findObject(theSettings[i]).length; h++){
                if (findObject(theSettings[i])[h].checked){
                    MMNotes.set(metaFile,settingName,h);
                }
            }
        }
        MMNotes.close(metaFile);
    }
}


//Get an array of radio form elements and retrieve their setting
// change the status of the elements
function getRadioPreferences(){//1.3
    if (typeof MMNotes == 'undefined') {return;} // Check for
    MMNotes extension.
    var theSettings,metaFile;
    theSettings = getRadioPreferences.arguments;
```

continues

```
            metaFile = MMNotes.open(document.URL, true);
        if (metaFile) {
            for (var i=0; i<theSettings.length; i++){
                var settingName,settingValue;
                //Assemble the name of the key inside the Design note
                settingName = "pref_"+theSettings[i];
                //Get the value of the key
                settingValue = MMNotes.get(metaFile,settingName);
                //If we have a saved setting
                if(settingValue){
                    //Set the status of the form element
                    findObject(theSettings[i])[settingValue].checked =
                    true;
                }
            }
            MMNotes.close(metaFile);
        }
    }


    function checkField(theFieldName) {
    /*  activates onBlur
        checks to see if current text field is empty or with value
        if it's with a value, zeros out other text fields and
        sets the radio button
    */
        var theField = findObject(theFieldName);
        if (theField.value != "") {
            if (theFieldName == "widthText") {
                findObject("heightText").value = "";
                findObject("percentageText").value = "";
                findObject("sizeRB")[0].checked = true;
            }
            if (theFieldName == "heightText") {
                findObject("widthText").value = "";
                findObject("percentageText").value = "";
                findObject("sizeRB")[1].checked = true;
            }
```

```
        if (theFieldName == "percentageText") {
            findObject("heightText").value = "";
            findObject("widthText").value = "";
            findObject("sizeRB")[2].checked = true;
        }
    }
    updateSize();
}


function updateSize() {
    var theNewWidth, theNewHeight;
    var offsets = dw.getDocumentDOM().getSelection();
    var theSelObj = dreamweaver.offsetsToNode(offsets[0],offsets[1]);
    var theOldSize = dw.getNaturalSize(getFullPath
    (theSelObj.getAttribute("src")));
    var theNewSizeText = document.getElementsByTagName('newsize');

    if (theSizeChoice[0].checked) {//width
        theNewWidth = parseInt(findObject("widthText").value);
        theNewHeight = parseInt((theNewWidth / parseInt
        (theOldSize[0])) * parseInt(theOldSize[1]));
    }


    if (theSizeChoice[1].checked) {//height
        theNewHeight = parseInt(findObject("heightText").value);
        theNewWidth = parseInt((theNewHeight /
        parseInt(theOldSize[1])) * parseInt(theOldSize[0]));
    }
    if (theSizeChoice[2].checked) {//percentage
        var thePercent = parseInt(findObject("percentageText").value);
        theNewWidth = parseInt((thePercent / 100) * theOldSize[0]);
        theNewHeight = parseInt((thePercent / 100) * theOldSize[1]);
    }
    if (!(findObject("widthText").value == "" &&
findObject("heightText").value == "" &&
findObject("percentageText").value == "")) {//nothing to show first
time
```

continues

```
        theNewSizeText[0].innerHTML = "Thumbnail: <b>W: " +
        theNewWidth + "   H: " + theNewHeight + "</b>";
    }
}


function getNotesPicWindow(){
    if (parseInt(dw.appVersion) != 3){
        var handle=MMNotes.open(dw.getSiteRoot()+"vwd.mno",true) ;
        var PicWindowItems = MMNotes.get(handle,"picwindow");
        MMNotes.close(handle);
        PicWindowItems = PicWindowItems.split("_vwd_");
        if (PicWindowItems[0]) {
            picWinHugger = PicWindowItems[0] ;
            picWinHugMargin  = PicWindowItems[1] ;
            picWinAlt = PicWindowItems[2] ;
            picWinColor = PicWindowItems[3]   ;
        } else {
            picWinHugger =  "fullscreen";
            picWinHugMargin  = "0";
            picWinAlt = "* * Click screen to close * *";
            picWinColor = "#336699";
        }
        picWinWidth = theCurrentSize[0];
        picWinHeight = theCurrentSize[1];
    }
}



function initUI() {
    // Check for FW4; if not present, close the command dialog
    if (dw.getDocumentPath("document") == "" ) {
        alert("Please save document before using this command.")
        window.close();
    }
```

```
var theVersion = dw.appVersion.substr(0,4);
if (parseFloat(theVersion) < 6.00) {
    alert("You need Dreamweaver MX or higher for this
    command.");
    window.close;
}
if (!FWLaunch.validateFireworks(3.0)){
    alert("You need Fireworks 3 to run this command.");
    window.close();
} else {

    if (!DWfile.exists(dw.getConfigurationPath() +
    "/Behaviors/Actions/JustSoPicWindow.htm")) {
        SetEnabled(findObject("targetRB")[0],false);
        findObject("targetRB")[1].checked = true
    } else {
        SetEnabled(findObject("targetRB")[0],true);

    }

    var offsets = dw.getDocumentDOM().getSelection();
    var theSelObj = dreamweaver.offsetsToNode
    (offsets[0],offsets[1]);
    if (theSelObj.getAttribute("id")) {
        if (theSelObj.getAttribute("id").substr(0,4) == "tbb_") {
            alert("I like infinite regression as much as the next
            fellow, \nbut I'm afraid you can't make a thumbnail of
            a thumbnail.\n\nPlease choose a different image.")
            window.close();
        }
    }
    theCurrentSize = dw.getNaturalSize(getFullPath
    (theSelObj.getAttribute("src")));
    var theHeading = document.getElementsByTagName
    ('currentSize');
    theHeading[0].innerHTML = "Current Image: W: " +
    theCurrentSize[0] + "   H: " + theCurrentSize[1]
```

continues

```
        getRadioPreferences('sizeRB','targetRB');

getTextPreferences('widthText','heightText','percentageText','html
Text','bevelText');
        getBoxesPreferences('bevelCB','htmlCB','dropshadowCB');
        updateSize();
    }

}
```

First, we need to make sure that an image is actually selected. If the user does not have an image selected, we want the menu item for the command to appear inactive. To achieve this, we need only use one of the special Command API functions: canAcceptCommand(). The following code verifies first there is a selection, second, that the selected item is a tag of some kind (that is, not text or a comment) and, finally, that the selected item is an <img> tag.

```
function canAcceptCommand() {
    var theDom = dw.getDocumentDOM();
    var selection = dreamweaver.getSelection();
    var theSel = dreamweaver.offsetsToNode( selection[0],
    selection[1] );
    return(theSel != null && theSel.nodeType == Node.ELEMENT &&
    theSel.tagName == "IMG");
}
```

If canAcceptCommand() returns true, the menu item is available; if it returns false, the item is unselectable.

Setting Up the Buttons

Next, we need to set up the primary buttons to execute the command, cancel, or get help. Again, a special Command API function is employed: commandButtons(). The commandButtons() function uses a simple array of name-value pairs. Each pair consists of the buttons label and the function that is executed when that button is selected.

```
function commandButtons(){
    return new Array( 'OK', 'runCommand()', 'Help', 'doHelp()',
    'Cancel', 'window.close()');
}
```

The function is either a custom one, like those for OK and Help, or a built-in JavaScript function, like `window.close()` for Cancel.

For any extension other than those intended for my own use, I always try to provide some form of help. Not only is help the essence of user friendliness, but it also cuts down on the email queries I have to field. For simple extensions, my `doHelp()` function opens an alert with a brief explanation. For more complex explanations, I prefer to host a page on one of my web sites. The page can contain far more extensive help than an alert, and it is easily modified as required.

```
function doHelp() {
dw.browseDocument('http://www.fp2dw.com/extensions/tbhelp.htm');
}
```

The `browseDocument()` function opens the designated page in the user's primary browser.

Initializing the User Interface

So far in this analysis, I've mentioned a couple of functions that are called during initialization. Let's take a closer look at what else is going on in the `initUI()` function.

The first part of `initUI()` is devoted to error checking. First, we need to make sure the file is saved to avoid pathname hassles when storing the new thumbnail.

```
if (dw.getDocumentPath("document") == "" ) {
    alert("Please save document before using this command.")
    window.close();
}
```

Next, we need to verify that an appropriate version of Dreamweaver is running:

Change string to floating number

```
var theVersion = dw.appVersion.substr(0,4);
if (parseFloat(theVersion) < 4.01) {
    alert("You need Dreamweaver 4.01 or higher for this
    command.");
    window.close;
}
```

NOTE: The reason that Dreamweaver 4.01 or higher is specified rather than just version 4.0 is because 4.01, aside from fixing some bugs, included a function key to this extension, `dw.getNaturalSize()`, which is used to find the dimensions of the selected image.

Finally, we want to make sure that a capable version of Fireworks is in use. Fireworks 3 will do just fine:

```
if (!FWLaunch.validateFireworks(3.0)){
    alert("You need Fireworks 3 to run this command.");
    window.close();
```

The next bit of code checks to see whether the Just So Picture Window behavior is installed. If it is not, the appropriate radio button is disabled and the other choice is selected. If the behavior is found, the Just So Picture Window radio button is enabled.

Multiuser configuration automatically accounted for

```
if (!DWfile.exists(dw.getConfigurationPath() +
"/Behaviors/Actions/JustSoPicWindow.htm")) {
SetEnabled(findObject("targetRB")[0],false);
findObject("targetRB")[1].checked = true
    } else {
    SetEnabled(findObject("targetRB")[0],true);
}
```

During the beta test period, one of my testers decided to see what would happen if the extension was applied to an existing thumbnail. Let me just say it wasn't pretty, and it spawned the following bit of error-checking code. Here, I check to see whether the selected object has an `id` attribute that starts with `tbb_`, an identifier I place in all created thumbnails. If so, I respectfully request that the user make another choice and close the extension.

```
var offsets = dw.getDocumentDOM().getSelection();
var theSelObj = dreamweaver.offsetsToNode(offsets[0],offsets[1]);
if (theSelObj.getAttribute("id")) {
    if (theSelObj.getAttribute("id").substr(0,4) == "tbb_") {
        alert("I like infinite regression as much as the next fellow,
        \nbut I'm afraid you can't make a thumbnail of a
        thumbnail.\n\nPlease choose a different image.")
        window.close();
    }
}
```
Line feed character

The next section of `initUI()` displays the selected image's height and width
as discussed earlier. I included it here for the sake of completeness.

```
theCurrentSize = dw.getNaturalSize(getFullPath
(theSelObj.getAttribute("src")));


var theHeading = document.getElementsByTagName('currentSize');


theHeading[0].innerHTML = "Current Image: W: " + theCurrentSize[0]
+ "   H: " + theCurrentSize[1]
```

The next couple of code lines represent to me one of the hallmarks of a good
extension. In the interest of continued ease of use, most of my extensions
"remember" the settings from the previous session whenever possible. I've
found that most often, the user applies similar if not the same settings time
and again. To this end, I use a series of functions developed by Massimo Foti,
which get the previous choices (the "preferences") and store them in a Design
Note attached to the extension. Notice that I need only pass the names of the
elements to load their prior values.

```
getRadioPreferences('sizeRB','targetRB');
getTextPreferences('widthText','heightText','percentageText',
'htmlText','bevelText');
getBoxesPreferences('bevelCB','htmlCB','dropshadowCB');
```

When Thumbnail Builder is executed, a parallel set of functions stores the
user's current choices.

Writing the Fireworks Function

Now we come to the heart of the extension: the Fireworks function. This function is exactly as Fireworks; if you were to save this function as a separate .jsf file and supply the necessary arguments, Fireworks would execute it with no problem. This functionality is a major productivity boon. In essence, you can build and test the Fireworks function separately within Fireworks and, when it is completed, copy and paste it its entirety into your Dreamweaver extension.

Although you're under no obligation to do so, Fireworks functions in Dreamweaver traditionally start with `fw_`. My function, `fw_makeThumbnail()`, takes six arguments:

- `theFile`—The filename of the image that is selected in Dreamweaver, expressed as a file URL (that is, `file:///clients/bigco/images/newproduct.gif`)

- `theSizeOption`—The type of sizing that is chosen; can be width, height, or scale (percentage)

- `theSizeValue`—The value that is entered into the related text field

- `theBevelOption`—A boolean indicating whether Bevel was selected

- `theShadowOption`—A boolean indicating whether Drop Shadow was selected

- `theBG`—The background color of the Dreamweaver document that is necessary if the Drop Shadow option was chosen

The first line of code in the Fireworks function is extremely simple but vital:

```
var theMsg = "OK";
```

No matter what, `theMsg` is eventually returned to Dreamweaver and, if `theMsg` is `"OK"`, the Fireworks processing was successful. If the variable is set to something else, then something went wrong—either an error was encountered or the user cancelled the operation. Dreamweaver knows how to interpret the error codes and reacts appropriately. These provided error-handling routines are all in the FwExec.js and the FwExecDlg.htm files. Needless to say, these routines greatly simplify the programming life of the cross-application developer.

Although the next line might not make such an impact, it is key to writing Fireworks functions. With this code

```
theSizeValue = parseInt(theSizeValue);
```

the value passed in the argument theSizeValue is converted to a number. All values passed from Dreamweaver to Fireworks are received as strings. If the values are needed as numeric values, they must be converted to a number within the Fireworks function.

Next, we check to see whether the Drop Shadow option was selected and if either the Height or Width size methods were specified. If so, we reduce the dimensions slightly to compensate for the size of the drop shadow.

```
if (theShadowOption == "true" && theSizeOption != "scale") {
    theSizeValue = theSizeValue - 8;
}
```

Frankly, this routine is purely a judgment call. I figure that when someone says he wants the thumbnail to be 125 pixels, he wants the whole image to be 125 pixels, not 133 pixels including the drop shadow. As an extension developer, sometimes you're called on to make a best guess on the desired behavior.

We're ready now to open the selected image in Fireworks and start work. After we load the file, making sure it is not the original but a copy, we set the matte color and determine the dimensions:

```
var theDoc = fw.openDocument(theFile,true);
theDoc.setMatteColor(true, theBG);
var theWidth = theDoc.width;
var theHeight = theDoc.height;
```

Opens file as copy

Then we calculate theSizeValue variable according to the size option chosen. Note that theSizeValue is actually expressed as a percentage of the overall image. Fireworks requires percentages to properly scale an image.

```
if (theSizeOption == "width") {
    theSizeValue = theSizeValue / theWidth;
}
```

```
    if (theSizeOption == "height") {
        theSizeValue = theSizeValue / theHeight;
    }


    if (theSizeOption == "scale") {
        theSizeValue = theSizeValue / 100;
    }
```

Now, we're ready to resize the image to our desired dimensions. After first making sure that our image is selected, we apply the scaling function:

```
theDoc.selectAll();
theDoc.scaleSelection(theSizeValue, theSizeValue, "autoTrimImages
transformAttributes");
```

Why is theSizeValue repeated? In the scaleSelection() function, the first two arguments are the percentages of the desired width and height. Although you could scale these dimensions independently in Fireworks, we want to preserve the width to height ratio, so we use the same value.

The following code section makes up the bulk of the fw_makeThumbnail() function. In this series of if-then-else statements, the various effects are applied.

```
  if (theBevelOption == "true" && theShadowOption == "true") {
//do both
    fw.getDocumentDOM().applyEffects({ category:"Untitled",
    effects:[ { AngleSoftness:3, BevelContrast:75, BevelType:0,
    BevelWidth:10, ButtonState:0, DownBlendColor:"#0000003f",
    EdgeThreshold:0, EffectIsVisible:true, EffectMoaID:"{7fe61102-
    6ce2-11d1-8c76000502701850}", EmbossFaceColor:"#ffffff00",
    GlowStartDistance:0, GlowWidth:0, HiliteColor:"#ffffff",
    HitBlendColor:"#ffffff3f", LightAngle:135, LightDistance:100,
    MaskSoftness:0, OuterBevelColor:"#df0000",
    ShadowColor:"#000000", ShowObject:false, SlopeMultiplier:1,
    SlopeType:0, category:"Inner Bevel", name:"Inner Bevel" },
```

```
    { EffectIsVisible:true, EffectMoaID:"{a7944db8-6ce2-11d1-
    8c76000502701850}", ShadowAngle:315, ShadowBlur:4,
    ShadowColor:"#000000a5", ShadowDistance:7, ShadowType:0,
    category:"Shadow and Glow", name:"Drop Shadow" } ],
    name:"Untitled" });
} else if (theBevelOption == "true" && theShadowOption != "true") {
    theDoc.applyEffects({ category:"Untitled", effects:[ {
    AngleSoftness:3, BevelContrast:75, BevelType:0, BevelWidth:10,
    ButtonState:0, DownBlendColor:"#0000003f", EdgeThreshold:0,
    EffectIsVisible:true, EffectMoaID:"{7fe61102-6ce2-
    11d1-8c76000502701850}", EmbossFaceColor:"#ffffff00",
    GlowStartDistance:0, GlowWidth:0, HiliteColor:"#ffffff",
    HitBlendColor:"#ffffff3f", LightAngle:135, LightDistance:100,
    MaskSoftness:0, OuterBevelColor:"#df0000",
    ShadowColor:"#000000", ShowObject:false, SlopeMultiplier:1,
    SlopeType:0, category:"Inner Bevel", name:"Inner Bevel" } ],
    name:"Untitled" });
} else if (theShadowOption == "true" && theBevelOption != "true") {
    theDoc.applyEffects({ category:"Untitled", effects:[ {
    EffectIsVisible:true, EffectMoaID:"{a7944db8-6ce2-11d1-
    8c76000502701850}", ShadowAngle:315, ShadowBlur:4,
    ShadowColor:"#000000a5", ShadowDistance:7, ShadowType:0,
    category:"Shadow and Glow", name:"Drop Shadow" } ],
    name:"Untitled" });
}
```

Although these lines might seem overwhelming, they were among the easiest lines to code. Each `applyEffects()` function was copied from Fireworks' history panel and pasted directly into this function. To simplify matters, the default values were used; it is entirely possible, however, to substitute user-supplied values for attributes such as `ShadowColor` and `BevelWidth`.

Now that the graphic is rescaled and all the effects are applied, we fit the canvas to the image with the next function:

```
theDoc.setDocumentCanvasSizeToDocumentExtents(true);
```

After a few string manipulations to add a "_small" addendum to the filename

```
var theExt = theFile.substr(theFile.lastIndexOf('.'));
theFile = theFile.substr(0,theFile.lastIndexOf('.')) + "_small";
```

we're ready to set the export options. We use the extensions we retrieved to determine whether the file is GIF or JPEG format so that we can export the thumbnail in the same format.

```
if (theExt.toLowerCase().indexOf('gif') != -1) {
    theDoc.setExportOptions({ exportFormat:"GIF",
    paletteTransparency:"index"});
}
```

Could be 'jpeg' or 'jpg'

```
if (theExt.toLowerCase().indexOf('jp') != -1) {
    theDoc.setExportOptions({ exportFormat:"JPEG"});
}
```

The final four lines of the function are vital. After saving the image in the Fireworks native PNG format (so that modifications can be made easily), we export the image, close the file we created, and return our "OK" message:

```
fw.saveDocument(theDoc,theFile + ".png");
fw.exportDocumentAs(null, theFile, null);
fw.closeDocument(theDoc,false);
return theMsg;
```

Won't prompt to save with 'false' value

Executing the Thumbnail Builder Command

With all of our support function declared, we're ready to write the primary function that executes the Thumbnail Builder command. Because this function is fairly involved, let's take a moment to review its structure before we launch into the details:

In order of appearance, the primary code sections are as follows:

1. Define the local variables.

2. Get the image filename.

3. Set the argument variables according to user selections.

4. Execute the Fireworks function that is passing the argument variables.

5. Rewrite the HTML tag for the image if the Fireworks function processes without a problem.

6. Save the current user settings.

7. Finish up and close the dialog box.

As with many functions, the opening lines of the `runCommand()` function define needed local variables:

```
var theDom = dw.getDocumentDOM();
var theBG = theDom.body.bgcolor?theDom.body.bgcolor:"#ffffff";
var theSizeOption, theSizeValue;
var theBevelOption = "false";
var theShadowOption = "false";
```

Uses conditional operator

The second line of code merits a bit of explanation:

```
var theBG = theDom.body.bgcolor?theDom.body.bgcolor:"#ffffff";
```

In this line, I am declaring a variable to hold the background color of the current Dreamweaver document. If no background color is defined, in the body tag, I set the background to white (`#ffffff`).

The next section of code gets the file path of the selected image and then extracts just the filename. You might notice that I use the filename in two variables: `jspwFileBase` and `theFileBase`. The `jspwFileBase` variable is used to pass the full path of the image to the Just So Picture Window behavior while the Fireworks function uses the other variable.

```
var offsets = theDom.getSelection();
var theSelObj = dreamweaver.offsetsToNode(offsets[0],offsets[1]);
var theFileBase = theSelObj.getAttribute("src");
```

NOTE: You should realize that the background color is not properly picked up if it is set using a CSS style declaration, either internally or in an external style sheet. If the user selects the drop shadow option and has a CSS-type background color declared (other than white), the source PNG file will probably need to be modified to export the proper thumbnail.

```
var jspwFileBase = theFileBase;
var theFileURL = getFullPath(theFileBase);
var thePath = "";
if (theFileBase.lastIndexOf("/") != -1) {
    thePath = theFileBase.substr(0,theFileBase.lastIndexOf("/"));
    theFileBase = theFileBase.substr(theFileBase.lastIndexOf("/"));
}
```

The following three sections of code set the local variables to the various user-selected options. In the first section, the size option (width, height, and percentage) is examined. When the selected option is identified, the related value is inserted into theSizeValue variable and the other two values are set to empty strings. If the passed value is not a number, then the user is informed of the error and returned to correct the problem.

```
if (theSizeChoice[0].checked) {
    theSizeOption = "width";
    theSizeValue = findObject("widthText").value;
    findObject("heightText").value = "";
    findObject("percentageText").value = "";
    if (theSizeValue == "" || isNaN(theSizeValue)) {
        alert("Please enter a numeric value in the Width field.");
        findObject("widthText").focus();
        return;
    }
}
if (theSizeChoice[1].checked) {
    theSizeOption = "height";
    theSizeValue = findObject("heightText").value;
    findObject("widthText").value = "";
    findObject("percentageText").value = "";
    if (theSizeValue == "" || isNaN(theSizeValue)) {
        alert("Please enter a numeric value in the Height field.");
        findObject("heightText").focus();
        return;
    }
}
```

```
if (theSizeChoice[2].checked) {
    theSizeOption = "scale";
    theSizeValue = findObject("percentageText").value;
    findObject("widthText").value = "";
    findObject("heightText").value = "";
    if (theSizeValue == "" || isNaN(theSizeValue)) {
        alert("Please enter a numeric value in the Scale field.");
        findObject("scaleText").focus();
        return;
    }
}
```

The second set of user options looks to see what effects, if any, should be passed to Fireworks. The HTML option, if selected, is handled within Dreamweaver.

```
if (findObject("bevelCB").checked) {
    theBevelOption = "true";
}


if (findObject("dropshadowCB").checked) {
    theShadowOption = "true";
}
```

The following code block is a bit out of the norm—but all the more interesting for it. Here, after assembling the proper arguments, an entirely different extension—the Just So Picture Window behavior—is run via the popupAction() API call. Passing the string of arguments, jspwStr, is significant because it pre-fills the dialog box for the behavior as shown in Figure 7.7. This technique saves the user from having to select the image filename as well as enter other options. In most cases, the user only needs to verify the selections and click OK.

7.7

The popupAction API called is used to run a separate extension, automatically filling in the relevant user selections.

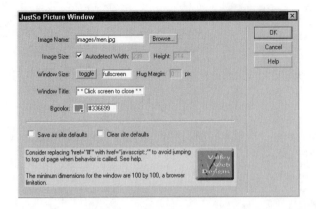

```
var thePicWin = 1;
getNotesPicWindow();
if (findObject('targetRB')[0].checked) {
    var jspwStr="JustSoPicWindow(" + jspwFileBase + "," +
    picWinWidth + "," + picWinHeight + "," + picWinAlt + "," +
    picWinColor + "," + picWinHugger + "," + picWinHugMargin +
    ")";
    if (thePicWin) thePicWin = dw.popupAction
    ("JustSoPicWindow.htm",jspwStr);
    if (thePicWin == jspwStr) {// when the user Canceled jspw
        return;
    }
}
```

Function and arguments

The next line of code puts the whole cross-application extension into action:

```
result = execFunctionInFireworks(fw_makeThumbnail, theFileURL,
theSizeOption, theSizeValue, theBevelOption, theShadowOption,
theBG);
```

You'll recall that the execFunctionInFireworks() call is stored in the included FwExec.js file. If the returned result is anything but "OK", the user is alerted to the specific error. If we're given the "OK", the next code block executes setting up the filename for the newly created thumbnail and gathering a few of its attributes (the dimensions and a unique ID).

```
// If execFunctionInFireworks returned NULL, everything went OK;
// time to insert the images
if (result == "OK"){
    var theExt = theFileBase.substr(theFileBase.lastIndexOf('.'));
    var theNewFile = theFileBase.substr(0,theFileBase.lastIndexOf
    ('.')) + "_small";
    theNewFile = thePath + theNewFile + theExt;
    theNewFileURL = getFullPath(theNewFile);
    var theSizeArray = dw.getNaturalSize(theNewFileURL);
    var newID = makeUniqueName('IMG','tbb_')
```
Gets size of actual image

All of the thumbnail attributes are set next: `id`, `src`, `width`, and `height`. If
the HTML border option is selected, a one-pixel border is added by default.
Should the user supply a different border width, that value is substituted.
The final line in this section prepares the new `<img>` tag for the thumbnail
to be written:

```
theSelObj.setAttribute("id",newID);
theSelObj.setAttribute("src",theNewFile);
theSelObj.setAttribute("width",theSizeArray[0]);
theSelObj.setAttribute("height",theSizeArray[1]);
var theBorder = "0";
if (findObject('htmlCB').checked) {
    theBorder = "1";
    if (findObject('htmlText').value) {
        theBorder = findObject('htmlText').value;
    }
}
theSelObj.setAttribute("border",theBorder);
var theCode = theSelObj.innerHTML;
```

In addition to the new `<img>` tag, a link to the original image is needed also
and is inserted into the following code:

```
                        if (findObject('targetRB')[0].checked) {    //Just So Pic Win
```

With Just So Picture
Window behavior

```
                            theSelObj.outerHTML = '<a href="javascript:;" onClick="' +
                            thePicWin + ';return document.MM_returnValue' + '">' +
                            theCode + '</a>';
                        } else {
```

Without the behavior

```
                            theSelObj.outerHTML = '<a href="' + thePath + theFileBase +
                            '">' + theCode + '</a>';
                        }
                    }
```

This link can take one of two forms. If the Just So Picture Window option is selected, the link looks something like this:

```
<a href="javascript:;"
onClick="JustSoPicWindow('images/SilverCoral.jpg','296','224','Clic
k to close','#EFEBEF','hug image','20');return
document.MM_returnValue"><img src="images/SilverCoral_small.jpg"
width="133" height="102"></a>
```

Otherwise, the link takes this form:

```
<a href="images/SilverCoral.jpg"><img src="images/
SilverCoral_small.jpg" width="133" height="102"></a>
```

We're almost done. The next section stores all the user's selections in the Design Note so that they are available the next time the command is run.

```
saveRadioPreferences('sizeRB','targetRB');
saveTextPreferences('widthText','heightText','percentageText','htm
lText','bevelText');
saveBoxesPreferences('bevelCB','htmlCB','dropshadowCB');
```

The final three lines are pure cleanup. The dialog box is closed, Dreamweaver is brought in front of Fireworks, and we end the function with a return.

```
window.close();
FWLaunch.bringDWToFront();
return;
```

A Key Fireworks Extension Development Technique

Without a doubt, the Fireworks extensibility model is quite robust. What's the best way to get a handle on it all—especially for someone coming from a Dreamweaver background? Short answer: the History panel. The History panel in Fireworks records actions taken to create Fireworks graphics. Like Dreamweaver's History panel, selected steps can be saved as a command to be executed at will. More importantly for our purposes, selected steps can also be copied to the Clipboard and then pasted into a text editor for examination and modification. I use this technique to create most of the core Fireworks routines for my extensions.

How do you apply this technique? As an example, let's say that as part of a new extension, you want to create a star-shaped graphic with a variable number of points. Here's how I would approach the problem:

1. Create a blank document to start with an uncluttered workspace.

2. Remove any existing History panel steps by choosing Clear History from the History panel options menu.

3. Select the Polygon tool from the Tools panel.

4. In the Property inspector, set the Shape to Star and the Sides to 5. (With a star shape as opposed to a polygon, the Sides option specifies the number of points.)

   You'll notice that no steps have yet to appear in the History panel. As in Dreamweaver, Fireworks does not record mouse movements or tool selections. Setting an object's properties also will not be recorded unless an object is selected. A key exception to the last statement is modifying the Fill color; this always generates a History panel step.

TIP: If you work with Fireworks extensions— either within Fireworks or combining both Dreamweaver and Fireworks—you'll need to use the Extending Fireworks manual. It's available in PDF format by choosing Help, Extending Fireworks. As of this writing, Macromedia is planning to have hard copy editions available at the online store.

5. Draw a star on the page.

   The History panel displays the step `Polygon tool`.

6. Choose the Polygon tool step in the History panel.

7. Copy the step either by choosing Copy Steps from the History panel options menu or by selecting the Copy Selected History Steps to the Clipboard button.

8. Open a text editor and paste in the contents of the Clipboard.

   The code posted will look like this:

   ```
   fw.getDocumentDOM().addNewStar(5, -1, true,
   {x:323, y:168}, {x:323, y:105});
   ```

   If you examine the `addNewStar()` function description in the Extending Fireworks documentation, you'll see that the first argument is the number of points.

9. To begin the process of parameterizing the points value, add a variable statement before the `addNewStar` function call, as in this example:

   ```
   var the Points = 8;
   ```

10. Now substitute the new variable for the points value, like this:

    ```
    fw.getDocumentDOM().addNewStar(thePoints, -1, true,
    {x:323, y:168}, {x:323, y:105});
    ```

    Substituted variable

11. To test your routine, save the text file with a .jsf extension. Then return to Fireworks to delete the existing star; Fireworks will insert the new star in the same location. It's better to see the changes this way.

12. Choose Commands, Run Script and locate the just saved .jsf file.

    Your new star with the desired number of points should appear.

To test a series of different values without modifying the .jsf file each time, set your variable to accept a prompt value, like this:

```
thePoints = prompt("Enter the number of points","");
```

This results in a prompt dialog—Fireworks' only native method of accepting user input outside of its new Flash user interface commands—as shown in Figure 7.8.

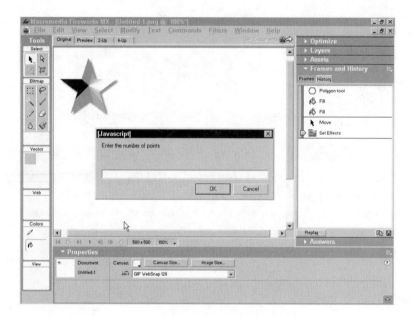

7.8

Prior to Fireworks MX, user interfaces for native Fireworks commands were limited to simple prompts like this one. In Fireworks MX, commands may employ a Flash user interface.

Any of the addNewStar() function's arguments can be set up for user interaction as seen in Figure 7.9.

7.9

Test your Fireworks functions interactively by setting a parameter equal to a `prompt()` function call. This page shows three stars created by using the command described in this section—with five, six, and seven points respectively—and the preparation for a fourth star with eight points. The gradient fill is picked up from a previous selection; however, the drop shadow effects were added later.

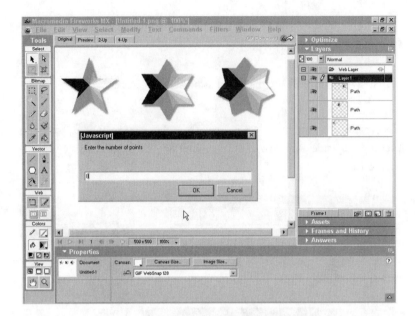

Not all arguments are as straightforward as our example, however. The star's position is given as the object's center point, rather than the top-left corner of the bounding rectangle shown in the Property inspector or the Info panel. Still, with a little effort, you can control virtually every aspect of Fireworks' drawing tools, which can add significantly to Dreamweaver's functionality.

Chapter 8

Making Flash Connections

Flash—by itself—is a remarkable web innovation. As a vector animation tool, it's second-to-none. And now, with Flash MX, the product is being positioned as a key element in developing rich Internet applications. However, as Macromedia is quick to acknowledge, HTML is far from dead. With their shared lineage and deep communication channels, Dreamweaver and Flash make a potent combination.

In this chapter, you'll see how to make the most of the various Dreamweaver-to-Flash-and-back communication possibilities. First, we'll look at the Flash Objects and describe a technique for creating custom navigation elements. Flash 5 is required to customize or extend Flash Objects.

Although Generator is no longer supported in Flash MX, a whole new avenue of Flash communication has opened up. In this chapter, you'll find three approaches: one that emulates Flash buttons on the client side; another that passes data—either static or dynamically generated—from a Dreamweaver coded page to a Flash movie; and a third that uses the new Flash Remoting feature, which allows Flash to send and receive more complex data structures.

Creating Custom Flash Buttons

With Flash Objects, introduced in Dreamweaver 4, Macromedia brought together two of its most powerful technologies. True to their underlying philosophy of extensibility, the Dreamweaver engineers provided an architecture for addressing Flash rather than just a feature. The implementation of Flash Objects included Flash Text and Flash Buttons; however, the architecture is capable of much more. One company, WebAssist (www.webassist.com), exploited this functionality to develop a commercial extension, Flash Charts, in several variations.

NOTE: Starting with Flash MX, Macromedia no longer includes support for Generator in Flash; however, you can still output Generator templates with Flash 5. Because Dreamweaver MX still includes Flash Objects, if you want to create custom Flash Buttons, you need to have Flash 5 available. The Generator Authoring Extensions for Flash 5 are available on the Macromedia site. As of this writing, you can find these extensions at www.macromedia.com/ software/generator/ download/extensions. html. There are a number of versions, corresponding to the different versions of Generator; make sure you download the proper version for your system.

All Flash Objects are based on Generator templates that are created in Flash 5. Dreamweaver uses the templates—recognizable by their .swt file extension—to create new Flash movies that use the .swf extension. The Generator templates have variables embedded in the Flash movies, such as {Button Font}. These variables are replaced by user-specified values when a Flash Object is inserted into Dreamweaver. Dreamweaver includes a fair number of Flash Buttons and Flash Text objects in the standard version of the program, and numerous other Flash Button collections are available on the Dreamweaver Exchange. Although these examples work fine, a custom-tailored solution is required occasionally, and clip-art—no matter how well executed—is not acceptable. Such custom Flash Objects—Flash Buttons and Flash Text—are created in Flash 5 with the aid of the Generator Authoring Extensions.

Although it's possible to make Flash Text templates, they are not used as frequently as Flash Buttons. The following procedure, which is specific to Flash Buttons, can easily be adapted to make a Flash Text template.

Preparing custom Flash Buttons is really a six-stage process, half of which takes place in Flash and half of which takes place in Dreamweaver:

1. Build a button in Flash 5.

2. Add one or more Generator objects to the button, specifying the necessary variables.

3. Save the button as a Generator template in the Dreamweaver user Configuration/Flash Objects/Flash Buttons folder.

4. In Dreamweaver, create a Flash Button based on the new template, specifying example text and commonly used fonts and font sizes.

5. Save the new Flash Button in the Dreamweaver user Configuration/Flash Objects/Flash Buttons Preview folder.

6. The next time you open the Flash Button dialog box, you'll find your custom button displayed with all the preset values.

The technique described in this section assumes that you are familiar with building buttons in Flash and inserting Flash Buttons in Dreamweaver. As with standard buttons built in Flash, your graphic should be converted to a button-type symbol, and it can use all four keyframes: Up, Over, Down, and Hit. After you've built the button, follow these steps to add the Generator functionality:

1. In Flash, choose Insert > New Symbol to hold the Generator object.

    Make sure your new symbol is set to Movie Clip; name the clip something like genText.

2. With the new symbol in Editing mode, choose Window > Generator Objects.

3. From the Generator Objects panel, drag the Insert Text object over the previously built button.

    Position the Insert Text object so that its center is over where you'd like your button text to appear.

4. When the Insert Text object is in place and selected, the Generator Insert Text panel displaying the appropriate properties appears, as shown in Figure 8.1.

NOTE: To add text variables in a Generator template, you need the Insert Text Generator object. The Insert Text object is a custom object created by Mike Chambers of Macromedia. It is currently available on the Flash Exchange at www.macromedia.com/exchange/flash.

8.1

Variables later used by
Dreamweaver are entered
into the Generator object
Properties panel; double-
click the Insert Text object
to reopen the panel.

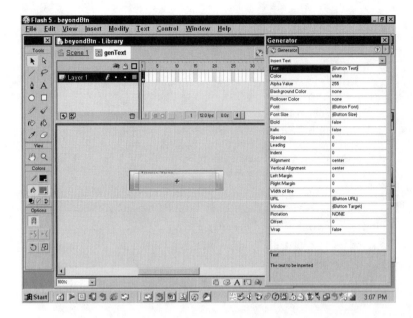

Within the panel, you need to set several parameters to placeholder
values so that the Insert Flash Button dialog box in Dreamweaver can
function properly. In each case, enter the value in the right column.

5. Enter the following values in the Generator Insert Text panel:

   • **Text**—Enter {Button Text}

   • **Font**—Enter {Button Font}

   • **Font Size**—Enter {Button Size}

   • **Alignment**—Enter either left, right, center, or justified.

   • **Vertical Alignment**—Enter either top, center, or bottom.

   Optionally, you can enter a text color in the Color field (as a recognized color name or hexadecimal value) and true or false in the Bold
   and/or Italic options.

6. Shrink the movie to the size of your button by dragging the button to
   the upper-left corner of the stage and choosing Modify > Movie. In
   the Modify Movie dialog box, change the dimensions to match those
   of the button.

7. Switch to editing the scene and, with the button on the stage selected,
   open the Actions panel.

8. In the Action panel's Expert mode, enter the following code:

```
on (release) {
    getURL ("{Button URL}", "{Button Target}");
}
```

This modification allows Dreamweaver to set a link and target within the Flash movie.

9. Save the movie as an .fla file so that you can adjust it later.

10. Choose File > Export Movie and select Generator Template as the file type. Save the template in your Dreamweaver user Configuration/Flash Objects/Flash Buttons folder.

If no other custom buttons have been installed on your system, you need to create the Flash Objects and Flash Buttons folder. If that's the case, go ahead and make another subfolder within Flash Objects: Flash Buttons Preview.

Now let's switch to Dreamweaver to complete the custom Flash Button. Choose Insert > Interactive Images > Flash Button, or select the Flash Button symbol from the Insert bar's Media category to open the Flash Button dialog box. As shown in Figure 8.2, the button is blank and displays no sample text.

8.2

The Flash Button dialog box is used to create its own previews.

To create an accurate preview that includes the sample text, follow these steps:

1. Open Dreamweaver and save a blank page.

2. Choose the Insert Flash Button object.

3. Select your newly inserted button from the Style list.

4. Enter desired default values in the Text, Font, and Size fields.

    These values will be preset whenever this particular Flash Button is chosen.

5. In the Save As field, store the file under the same name as your style in the Dreamweaver user Configuration/Flash Objects/Flash Buttons Preview folder and click OK when you're finished.

The next time the Flash Button object is accessed—Dreamweaver does not need to be restarted—the custom template will display a full preview, with text and preset values.

Working with Flash MX

Macromedia's decision to discontinue support of Generator in Flash MX is a significant blow to the further exploitation of the Flash Object architecture in Dreamweaver. However, communication between Dreamweaver and Flash is by no means dead. In fact, with Dreamweaver MX and Flash MX, a more robust data exchange is now possible.

In addition to the basic functionality that permits round-trip editing of Flash movies from Dreamweaver, there are numerous ways to pass information between the two programs. Three of these methods will be examined in the remainder of this chapter:

- **FlashVars**—Passes variables and values from Dreamweaver to Flash.

- **LoadVariables**—Brings Dreamweaver-structured data into Flash.

- **Flash Remoting**—Sends dynamic objects—including entire recordsets—from Dreamweaver to Flash.

Communication between HTML and other web pages and Flash movies is a particularly vibrant field. Given Macromedia's recent emphasis on developing rich Internet applications, it's a safe bet that techniques for cross-application communication between Dreamweaver and Flash will continue to grow.

Passing *FlashVars*

Although the `FlashVars` syntax was introduced in Flash MX, the concept has been available for several versions of the program. Basically, a `FlashVars` parameter passes a name/value pair to a corresponding variable in Flash. In earlier versions of Flash, this was done by appending an argument string to the `src` attribute, like this:

```
<embed src="navbtn.swf?name=BigCo">
```

Although this technique still works in Flash MX, the preferred syntax is to use the `FlashVars` parameter:

```
<embed src="navbtn.swf" flashvars="name=BigCo">
```

To be available on the widest range of browsers, the Flash movie should be inserted into the Web page using both the `<object>` and `<embed>` tags. In the `<object>` tag, the `FlashVars` attribute is enclosed in a `<param>` statement. A more complete version of our example would read like this:

```
<object classid="clsid:D27CDB6E-AE6D-11cf-96B8-444553540000"
codebase="http://download.macromedia.com/pub/shockwave/cabs/flash/
swflash.cab#version=6,0,29,0" width="106" height="23">
   <param name="movie" value="navbtn.swf">
   <param name="quality" value="high">
   <param name="FlashVars" value="name=BigCo">
   <embed src="buttontest.swf" width="106" height="23" quality="high"
   pluginspage="http://www.macromedia.com/go/getflashplayer" type=
   "application/x-shockwave-flash" flashvars="vartext=BigCo"></embed>
</object>
```

For `<object>` tag

For `<embed>` tag

You can pass multiple name/value pairs to Flash by joining each pair with an ampersand:

```
<param name="FlashVars" value="name=BigCo&onSale=yes">
```

TIP: Dreamweaver's Property inspector is a handy tool for URL encoding complex text strings. However, you must be sure that your Preferences are set correctly. In the Code Rewriting category of Preferences, you'll see two entries under Special Characters. For this technique, you want to select the first one (Encode Special Characters in URLs Using %) and deselect the second one (Encode <, >, &, and " in Attribute Values Using %).

With your Preferences set correctly, enter the string to be encoded in the Link field of the Text Property inspector while you're in Design view. Doing so creates a dummy link that you can remove later. Then switch to Code view and copy the URL encoded value from the `href` attribute of the `<a>` tag and paste it into the proper `<param>` statement. Be sure to delete the dummy link.

To include special characters, the name/value pairs must be URL encoded. For example, my name in quotes would read `%22Joseph%20Lowery%22` because `%22` is the URL encoded value for a quotation mark and `%20` is the encoded value for a space. The plus sign also can represent single spaces.

On the Flash side, the implementation of `FlashVars` has a few restrictions. First, all variables affected by the `FlashVars` statement must be in the root timeline. Variables used in symbols, including buttons, are loaded before the Flash movie begins playing; therefore, they fall comfortably into this category. Second, the amount of data that can be passed is limited to 64K.

Let's walk through the creation and implementation of a navigation button using the `FlashVars` technique that emulates Dreamweaver's Flash Buttons. The initial phase begins in Flash:

1. After you design the background of the button, insert the button label as dynamic text.

2. Give the text string a unique variable name in the Var field of the Property inspector, as shown in Figure 8.3.

    I've chosen `vartext` for my variable name.

3. Note the variable name to be used later in the `FlashVars` statement.

    As it stands, the button just created—once published as a .swf file—replicates the core functionality of the Flash Button object, customizing the label. Let's take it a step further and introduce a graphic element in our button that can be conditionally shown or hidden with the `FlashVars` statement.

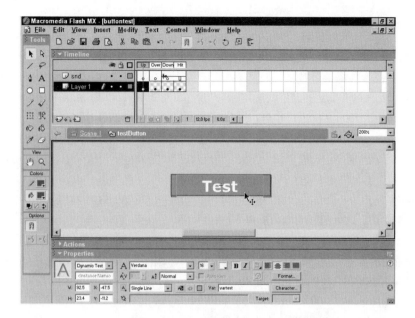

8.3

Dynamic text fields are a common method for taking advantage of the FlashVars capability.

4. Create a new symbol, either as a movie clip or a graphic.

   For this example, I've made a star-shaped symbol.

5. Add an instance of the new symbol to the button and give it a unique name, such as theStar.

6. In the first frame of the movie, add the following code through the Actions panel:

```
var showSymbol;
if (showSymbol == "yes") {
    theStar._visible = true;
} else {
    theStar._visible = false;
}
```

   Here, showSymbol is the variable to be passed by FlashVars.

7. Publish and save your button movie in a Dreamweaver site.

In Dreamweaver, insert the newly created Flash movie by dragging the movie from the Flash category of the Assets panel onto the page. The bulk of the code is entered automatically for you—all that's left are the FlashVar statements.

The easiest way to enter the `FlashVar` statements is to select the Flash movie and choose Parameters from the Property inspector. Then, under the Parameter column, enter `FlashVars`. Press Tab and then, under the Value column, enter the name/value pairs corresponding to the label variable and the conditional variable. Be sure to URL encode your entry. In my example, the `FlashVars` values are `vartext=BigCo&showSymbol=yes`. Entering values through the Parameter dialog box both creates `<param>` statements for the `<object>` tag and inserts the `FlashVars` attribute and its value into the `<embed>` tag.

Using *LoadVariables* in Flash

The `FlashVars` technique is a decent small-scale solution, but for larger data transfers, there is a better way: the `LoadVars` object, which is new in Flash MX but a direct descendent of the `LoadVariables` action. `LoadVars` is similar to `FlashVars` in that they both rely on URL encoded name/value pairs, but the similarity between the two ends there.

With `LoadVars`, variables no longer need to be in the root timeline. Furthermore, the restrictive 64K limit on data does not apply. The most important difference, however, is that unlike `FlashVars`, the `LoadVars` object can both receive and send data from a web application. With the advantage of two-way communication, designers can couple a Flash-designed front end with a Dreamweaver-coded backend.

After a `LoadVars` object is created in Flash, a variety of methods are available for it. To create an instance of a `LoadVars` object, use this ActionScript syntax:

```
formData = new LoadVars();
```

After an object is created, you can attach properties to it. The properties can either be strings or values from Flash input fields:

```
formData.theNumber = "1";
formData.theName = namefield.text;
```

If the variables are empty, it's a good idea to initialize the variables, like this:

```
formData.theGuess = "";
```

Although the `LoadVars` object opens the lanes of communication, it's not instantaneous; the data transfer of name/value pairs takes time. To ensure that the transfer is complete before the data is used, the `onLoad` event handler invokes a separate function—known generally as a *callback function*—if the data is handled successfully:

```
replyData.onLoad = playAnswer;
```

In this example, the `playAnswer()` function is executed as soon as the `onLoad` event for the `LoadVars` object, `replyData`, is successful. The function called by the `onLoad` event accepts a Boolean argument, so make sure that the data transfer was successful. Test for a successful transfer like this:

```
function playAnswer(success) {
    if(success) {
        //play mp3
    } else {
        //alert user to error
    }
}
```

As noted earlier, data can either be loaded into or sent from Flash. In fact, there is single method that combines both types of communication:

```
formData.sendAndLoad(submitURL,replyData,"POST");
```

In this code snippet, one instance of the `LoadVar` object—`formData`—is being sent while another—`replyData`—acts as a receptacle for data being received. The `sendAndLoad` method (as well as the corresponding single-operation `send` and `load` methods) takes three arguments:

- **URL**—The URL of the application to be processed

- **Target**—The `LoadVars` object to receive the data

- **Method**—Either "GET" or "POST"

To illustrate the use of the LoadVars object, I've created a pseudo-quiz that tests the player's knowledge of Elvis Costello trivia. If the player gets the answer right (sending the guess from a Flash user interface to the Dreamweaver-coded application), an MP3 clip filename is sent from the application to Flash to be played. In the Flash user interface (see Figure 8.4), one dynamic text field is used with the variable name of theChoice.

8.4

This Flash application uses two instances of the LoadVars object: one for sending data and one for receiving it.

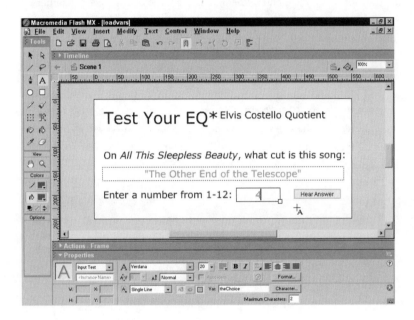

The ActionScript code is fairly succinct and is shown in Listing 8-1 in its entirety:

Listing 8-1   **LoadVars_ex.fla** (08_loadvars_ex.fla)

Application location

```
submitURL = "http://localhost/loadvars_ex.asp"
```

Executed after data loaded

```
function playAnswer(success) {
    if(success) {
        snd = new Sound();
        snd.loadSound(replyData.mpfilename,true);
        snd.start();
    } else {
        //alert user to error
        errorbox._visible = true;
```

Data from application

```
      }
}

function checkAnswer() {
    formData = new LoadVars();
    formData.theGuess = "";
    formData.theCut = "1";
    formData.theGuess = theChoice;
    replyData = new LoadVars();
    replayData.theAnswer = "";
    replyData.theGuess = "";
    replyData.mpfilename = "";
    replyData.songtitle = "";
    replyData.onLoad = playAnswer;
    formData.sendAndLoad(submitURL,replyData,"POST");
}

stop();
```

Data to application

With the Flash side of our `LoadVars` application complete, it's time to move over to Dreamweaver. The dynamic page called by the `LoadVars` object—in our example, it was `http://localhost/loadvars_ex.asp`—is all server-side code and not a bit of HTML. You can, if you prefer, completely hand-code this page. In the following description, I'm going to use Dreamweaver to handle the connection and recordset basics.

The basic responsibility of a server-side page used in a `LoadVars` technique is to receive any variables passed by Flash, use those variables to process a server-side function, and then pass the results back to Flash.

In the example, my server-side page gets the value entered by the user representing the guess made in the trivia game, compares that value to a retrieved recordset, and then returns a corresponding filename, which is used to play an MP3 tune in Flash. Let's see how it works.

NOTE: To view the completed code, see Listing 8-2 at the end of this section.

If you'd like to use Dreamweaver to create the basic page and recordset for you, do this:

1. Select File > New. Then, under Category, choose Dynamic Page and, under Dynamic Page, select the server model you're working with. Click Create when you're ready.

   In this example, I use an ASP VBScript page.

2. Switch to Code view and delete all the code from the opening <html> to the closing </html>, inclusive.

   Be sure to leave any server-side directives that might be placed above the <html> tag.

3. From the Bindings panel in the Application panel group, follow any remaining steps listed on the checklist. If all but the final one are checked off, select Add (+) and choose Recordset (Query).

4. Use either the Simple or Advanced Recordset dialog box to create the desired recordset.

   In my example, I used a connection called connCostello and named the recordset rsBeauty; all the fields in the small data source were requested, and I sorted the recordset by the field cutnumber.

5. Save the page. As a matter of personal preference, I save both the Flash movie and the server-side page in the same folder.

When you're finished, you'll have a page with only server-side code, ready for Flash connectivity. In my example application, all the code necessary to receive the variable from Flash, process it, and return it is contained in one code block. I'm using ASP VBScript. To get the Flash-passed variable, I use a Request object:

```
theGuess = Request("theGuess")
```

Then I loop through an array of information from my recordset looking for a match. When a corresponding entry is found, the loop is broken and I have an index value, stored in pos, to use:

```
For i = 0 to UBound(theArray,2)
    If cStr(theArray(1,i)) = theGuess Then
        pos = i
        Exit For
    End If
Next
```

Finally, we're ready to send the URL-encoded name/value pairs back to
Flash. Again, the exact code will vary according to your server model, but
here is how it's done in ASP VBScript:

```
returnToFlash = "mpfilename=" & Server.URLEncode(theArray(2,pos)) &
"&songtitle=" & Server.URLEncode(theArray(0,pos))
Response.Write(returnToFlash)
```

In this example, I'm sending back two name value pairs: mpfilename and
songtitle. The first will be used to play the MP3 file, whereas the second
will display the name of the song.

Here's the entire custom ASP code block:

```
<%
Dim theArray, i, theAnswer, theGuess
theArray = rsBeauty.GetRows
theGuess = Request("theGuess")                                          Variable from Flash
For i = 0 to UBound(theArray,2)
    If cStr(theArray(1,i)) = theGuess Then
        pos = i
        Exit For
    End If
Next
returnToFlash = "mpfilename=" & Server.URLEncode(theArray(2,pos)) &     Variables to Flash
"&songtitle=" & Server.URLEncode(theArray(0,pos))
Response.Write(returnToFlash)
%>
```

Listing 8-2 **LoadVars_ex.asp** (08_loadvars_ex.asp)

NOTE: If you're passing more than just a couple of strings from the server to Flash or if the processing is fairly time intensive, consider adding a Now processing type message to the Flash movie to be displayed when the LoadVars object functions are working.

```asp
<%@LANGUAGE="VBSCRIPT" CODEPAGE="1252"%>
<!--#include file="../Connections/connCostello.asp" -->
<%
Dim rsBeauty
Dim rsBeauty_numRows

Set rsBeauty = Server.CreateObject("ADODB.Recordset")
rsBeauty.ActiveConnection = MM_connCostello_STRING
rsBeauty.Source = "SELECT *  FROM cds ORDER BY cutnumber ASC"
rsBeauty.CursorType = 0
rsBeauty.CursorLocation = 2
rsBeauty.LockType = 1
rsBeauty.Open()

rsBeauty_numRows = 0
%>
<%
Dim theArray, i, theAnswer, theGuess
theArray = rsBeauty.GetRows
theGuess = Request.Form("theGuess")
For i = 0 to UBound(theArray,2)
    If cStr(theArray(1,i)) = theGuess Then
        pos = i
        Exit For
    End If
Next
returnToFlash = "mpfilename=" & Server.URLEncode(theArray(2,pos)) &
"&songtitle=" & Server.URLEncode(theArray(0,pos))
Response.Write(returnToFlash)
%>

<%
rsBeauty.Close()
Set rsBeauty = Nothing
%>
```

Flash Remoting

When Macromedia introduced Studio MX, it unleashed a powerhouse of connectivity with a tool called Flash Remoting. Flash Remoting enables direct connection between a rich client—Flash—and a server-side component. Instead of being restricted to passing URL-encoded strings as with `FlashVars` and `LoadVars`, Flash Remoting permits virtually any kind of data object to be transferred: booleans, dates, arrays, and many more, including recordsets and queries.

Flash Remoting is built into ColdFusion MX and JRun 4 and is available as an add-on for .NET and Java servers; to use it fully, you also need to install the Macromedia Flash Remoting Components, which add several APIs to Flash MX. The Macromedia Flash Remoting Components are available from the Macromedia site at www.macromedia.com/software/flash/flashremoting/.

The ColdFusion configuration for Flash Remoting, used throughout this section, is extremely robust and, remarkably, it's fairly straightforward to implement. Here's an overview of the process:

- The server-side functions are stored as a ColdFusion Component (CFC), which allows the routines to be called as a web service.

- The Flash movie is constructed and includes the Flash Remoting-specific code, available as separate files.

- A connection is made from the Flash movie to the Flash Remoting gateway, which simplifies the connection while preserving security.

- One or more of the functions contained in the CFC is called from within Flash, passing any necessary arguments.

- The CFC processes the request and returns the requested data object(s).

- Flash receives the data and, if necessary, manipulates it further with ActionScript.

- Flash displays the transformed data in the movie. Flash MX includes special Flash Remoting APIs called DataGlue for binding the data to Flash components—special built-in, reusable user interface elements, such as combo boxes and list boxes.

In the example that follows—a Flash movie that displays details about specific songs found on user-selected CDs—you'll see how to actualize each of these steps.

Coding a ColdFusion Component

One of the key factors contributing to the ease of use is the reliance on ColdFusion Components (CFCs). A CFC is a separate file stored on the ColdFusion server that contains processing functions. The functions in a CFC can be called either from a local ColdFusion application or a remote one. If the CFC is set to act as a remote type, it becomes a web service and is accessible to other applications, including Flash. A web service is a function or application that other applications can use. Dreamweaver provides an interface and structure for coding and implementing ColdFusion Components.

Here's the basic CFC format for a local function:

```
<cfcomponent>
    <cffunction name="myFunction" access="public"
    returntype="string">
        <cfargument name="myArgument" type="string" required="true">
        <cfset myResult="foo">
        <cfreturn myResult>
    </cffunction>
</cfcomponent>
```

Set local or remote access ——— (points to `access="public"`)

Specifies arguments into CFC ——— (points to `<cfargument ...>`)

Code processed here ——— (points to `<cfset myResult="foo">`)

Specifies results from CFC ——— (points to `<cfreturn myResult>`)

The structure is fairly straightforward. The `<cfcomponent>` tags surround one or more `<cffunction>` blocks. Within each uniquely named `<cffunction>`, the type of access is specified—generally public or remote, although a `<cffunction>` can be private as well—and the type of data to be returned. The `<cfargument>` is used to detail parameters that are passed to the function; a function can have as many `<cfargument>` tags as necessary. After the arguments are specified, the code representing the actual work of the function is presented. In my simple example, a single tag is used, `<cfset myResult="foo">`. However, in real applications, the coding is much more involved. The CFC function is completed with the `<cfreturn>` tag, which passes a data object back to the calling application.

To illustrate how ColdFusion Components work with Flash Remoting, I constructed a small application to display details about specific Elvis Costello songs, shown in Figure 8.5.

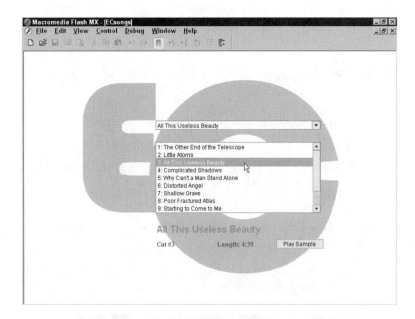

8.5

Flash Remoting is used in this application to retrieve data objects from a ColdFusion data source.

In the Flash movie, a list of albums is given in a drop-down list; the list is pulled from a data source query, which is contained in my CFC. After an album has been selected, the full list of songs on that album is displayed. Again, the song list is supplied by a CFC query. When a song title is chosen, details about that song, retrieved from a final CFC query, are displayed. In total, the CFC used for this application has three different functions, each triggered by different Flash events.

As noted earlier, there are two basic routes to creating CFC: completely by hand or by combining the output of a Dreamweaver command, Create Component, with hand-coding. If you'd prefer to do it all by scratch, choose File > New and select Dynamic > ColdFusion Component as the page type. Dreamweaver creates a page with the basic code given in the beginning of this section. It's up to you to modify the page to build the specific functions needed. When you're ready, save the file in the ColdFusion web root. Dreamweaver automatically appends the .cfc extension.

NOTE: To view the completed code, see listings 8-3 and 8-4 at the end of this section.

The disadvantage of the hand-coding approach is that you end up replacing much of the placeholder code—in essence, doing twice the work. When you start with code generated by Dreamweaver's Create Component dialog box, although a few more steps are involved, your precise structure—complete with function names, arguments, and return statements—is prepared. Here's how it is done:

1. From the Components panel, choose Add (+) to open the Create Components dialog box.

   Create Components makes an entirely new document, and you don't need to have a blank document open.

2. In the Component category of the dialog box, enter the name for the component in the Display Name field. This name is also used to invoke the component.

3. In the Name field, enter the filename for the component without the .cfc extension.

   For the example, I used `costellosongs` for both the Display Name and the Name field, as shown in Figure 8.6.

8.6

In the first category of the Create Component dialog box, you specify the names of the component.

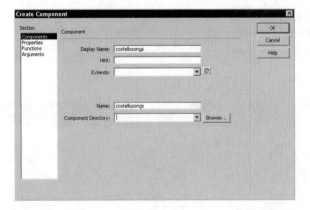

4. Locate the Component Directory (where the CFC is to be stored) by selecting the Browse button.

   Most frequently, the directory will be a folder within the ColdFusion web root.

5. Switch to the Functions category and select Add (+) to make the first function.

6. In the Function field, replace the word *Function* in the Name field with a unique name for your function.

   The first function in the example is called `getAlbums`.

7. Change the Access from Public to Remote.

8. Select the data object to output from the Return Type list, as shown in Figure 8.7.

   All the functions in my example use the Query type.

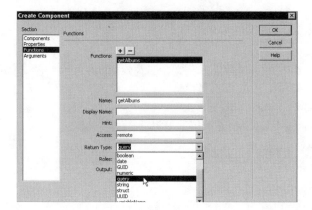

8.7

Specify all the necessary functions at once in the Create Component dialog box.

9. Repeat steps 5–8 for all the functions in the CFC.

10. Select Arguments from the Category list.

11. In the Arguments category, select a function from the Available Functions list that takes a parameter.

12. Chose Add (+) to create the first argument.

13. Enter the name of the argument in the Name field.

14. Choose the Type from the drop-down list.

15. If desired, select the Required option for this argument.

16. Repeat steps 12–15 for additional arguments for the specified function.

17. Repeat steps 11–16 for all other functions that require arguments. Click OK when you're finished to create the CFC.

NOTE: To simplify the creation of the CFC, I intentionally skipped over many of the available features of the Create Component dialog box. For details on all the options, choose Help > Using ColdFusion and then select the Building ColdFusion Components section.

For the example, I created three functions, two of which used arguments, and all of which returned queries. The code generated by Dreamweaver looked like this:

```
<!--- Generated by Dreamweaver MX 6.0.1722   (Win32) - Thu Jun 27
08:19:46 GMT-0400 (Eastern Daylight Time) 2002 --->


<cfcomponent displayName="costellosongs">
  <cffunction name="getAlbums" access="remote" returnType="query"
  output="false">
    <!--- getAlbums body --->
    <cfreturn >
  </cffunction>
  <cffunction name="getSongTitles" access="remote"
  returnType="query" output="false">
    <cfargument name="album" type="string">
    <!--- getSongTitles body --->
    <cfreturn >
  </cffunction>
  <cffunction name="getSongDetails" access="remote"
  returnType="query" output="false">
    <cfargument name="songtitle" type="string">
    <!--- getSongDetails body --->
    <cfreturn >
  </cffunction>
</cfcomponent>
```

First function code goes here

No variable is included

There are two key items to note: First, Dreamweaver inserts a comment where the code functionality needs to go for each function. Second, although the `<cfreturn>` statement is included, no value or variable is specified.

The first function in the CFC example is called `getAlbums`, and its purpose is to gather a distinct list of albums from a data source and return them to Flash. To accomplish this, a `<cfquery>` statement is added and the results are returned, like the bold portion of the following code:

```
<cffunction name="getAlbums" access="remote" returnType="query"
output="false">
  <cfquery name="q_albums" datasource="costello">
     SELECT Distinct(album) FROM cds WHERE album is not NULL
     Order by album
  </cfquery>
  <cfreturn q_albums>
</cffunction>
```

The second function, `getSongTitles`, uses the passed argument, album, to
control the SQL statement in a `<cfquery>`:

```
<cffunction name="getSongTitles" displayName="getSongTitles"
access="remote" returnType="query">
  <cfargument name="thisAlbum" type="string" required="true">
  <cfquery name="q_songs" datasource="costello">
     SELECT songtitle,album,cutnumber FROM cds
     WHERE album = '#TRIM(thisAlbum)#'
     ORDER by cutnumber
  </cfquery>
  <cfreturn q_songs>
</cffunction>
```

The final function, `getSongDetails`, works in a similar fashion to
`getSongTitles`, although rather than the value representing the album, a
similar value representing the song title (based on a user selection in Flash)
is passed to the function:

```
<cffunction name="getSongDetails" access="remote"
returnType="query" output="false">
  <cfargument name="thisSong" type="string" required="true">
  <cfquery name="q_songdetails" datasource="costello">
     SELECT * FROM cds
     WHERE songtitle = '#thisSong#'
  </cfquery>
  <cfreturn q_songDetails>
</cffunction>
```

The Component panel represents one of the coolest features of Dreamweaver integration of CFCs. After the CFC is stored, you'll see it listed under its folder in the tree of the Component panel. As you drill down into the component, you'll see that each of the functions is exposed—and even specific arguments—as shown in Figure 8.8; this facility is known as *introspection*. If you were invoking the CFC functions from another Dreamweaver-created page, the introspected functions could be dragged right onto the page. However, because we are connecting through Flash, the process is slightly different, as you'll see in the next section.

8.8

ColdFusion Components are self documenting and can be introspected easily in Dreamweaver.

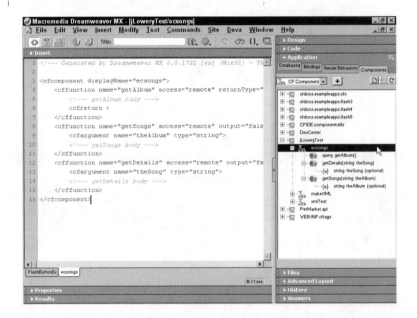

Connecting to the Flash Gateway

With the ColdFusion Component constructed, the server side of a Flash Remoting application is finished and we can turn our attention to crafting the necessary Flash elements. The first step in such an application is generally to construct the user interface. Flash MX simplifies the process through the availability of Flash UI Components. The sample application, shown in Figure 8.9, uses a combo box, a list box, a push button, and numerous dynamic text fields—all created with drag-and-drop ease in Flash.

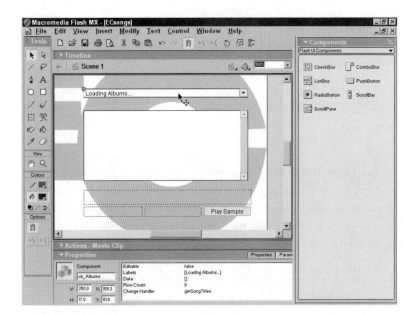

8.9

This Flash Remoting application user interface employs several Flash UI Components and dynamic text fields.

The ActionScript for the application is generally placed on its own layer in the first frame of the movie. To use Flash Remoting functionality, you'll need to include several external ActionScript files:

```
#include "NetServices.as"
#include "NetDebug.as"
#include "DataGlue.as"
```

These three files are installed as part of the Flash Remoting Components. Flash automatically recognizes their location—you don't have to specify additional paths. Only the `NetServices.as` file is required; however, the `NetDebug.as` file is helpful during the initial testing to make sure that all the connections are trouble free. In this case, DataGlue.as simplifies the displaying of recordset data in a list box.

After the files are included, we're ready to open the Flash Remoting Gateway. Regardless of how many times the service is used, the gateway needs to be opened only once. Consequently, this type of code is often used as a container:

```
if (isGatewayOpen == null) {
  isGatewayOpen = true;
}
```

The function is executed only if a flag has not been set. The actual opening of the gateway is handled in code like this:

```
NetServices.setDefaultGatewayUrl(
"http://127.0.0.1:8500/flashservices/gateway");
gatewayConnnection = NetServices.createGatewayConnection();
```

The HTTP address designates a standalone ColdFusion server installed on a localhost; the port number, 8500, is the default ColdFusion port. The `flash-services/gateway` address is a logical path and not a physical one. The actual connection to the Flash Remoting Gateway is handled by the `NetServices.createGatewayConnection()` call.

The next step is to create a Flash service object referring to the ColdFusion Components file, `costellosongs.cfc`:

```
songService =
gatewayConnnection.getService("beyond.fremoting.costellosongs",
this);
```

Note that the path to CFC, which is stored in folders within the ColdFusion web root, is designated with periods instead of slashes.

Calling CFCs and Displaying Responses

The final element in the initialization routine for the example is to call the first function in the service:

```
songService.getAlbums();
```

In this situation, a call to one of the CFC functions is required to populate a form element—a drop-down list—on the interface. The calls to the other functions take place in response to user actions and are contained in separate ActionScript functions:

```
function getSongTitles() {
    if (cb_Albums.getSelectedIndex() > 0) {
        songService.getSongTitles(cb_albums.getSelectedItem());
    }
}
```
——————————— *Passes combo box choice*

```
function getSongDetails() {
    songService.getSongDetails(lb_Songs.getValue());
}
```
——————————— *Passes list box choice*

As you can see, the second and third functions pass a user selection as an argument. In the case of the `getSongTitles()` function, the argument passes the album selected by the user, and with `getSongDetails`, the argument indicates the specific song that is selected. You'll recall that, in all cases in the example, the CFC returns query objects. Let's look now at how Flash receives data from the CFC.

Corresponding to each Flash function that calls a CFC function is another function to gather the result, known as a *responder*. These responders use the same function name as the calling function with a `_Result` appended and an argument specified; therefore, the responder for `getAlbums()` is `getAlbums_Result(result)`. Generally, the responder function is also responsible for displaying the data in the Flash movie in some fashion, like this:

```
function getAlbums_Result(result) {
    cb_Albums.setDataProvider(result);
    cb_Albums.addItemAt(0, "Select an album", "NONE");
    cb_Albums.setSelectedIndex(0);
}
```
——————————— *Puts data in combo box*

The query object returned from the CFC `getAlbums` function is used by a method of Flash's combo box component, `setDataProvider()`, to populate the specified combo box instance. The other two lines in the function dynamically add a generic entry and set the selection to that entry.

The getSongTitles_Result() function illustrates another technique to integrate returned data:

```
function getSongTitles_Result(result) {
  DataGlue.bindFormatStrings(lb_Songs, result, "#cutnumber#:
  #songtitle#", "#songtitle#");
}
```

The DataGlue.bindFormatStrings() function takes four arguments in this syntax:

```
DataGlue.bindFormatStrings(dataConsumer, dataProvider,
labelString, dataString)
```

TIP: The DataGlue API includes one other useful method, bindFormatFunction, which formats the data through a user-defined function. The syntax for the function is this:

```
DataGlue.bindFormat
Function(dataConsumer,
dataProvider,
formatFunction)
```

The formatFunction referenced should return the results in this format:

```
return {label:
theLabel,data:theData};
```

where:

- The dataConsumer is the target UI element in Flash, typically either a combo box or a list box instance.

- The dataProvider is the data object.

- The labelString is the formatted string, with fieldnames surrounded by hash marks (such as #songtitle#), which is set in a label attribute of the UI element and displayed.

- The dataString is the formatted string—again using the #fieldname# format—set to the data attribute of the UI element.

The final method for displaying data results in our Flash Remoting example populates dynamic text fields rather than list or combo boxes. This flexible approach allows you to combine data with static text as well as data from separate fields. Here is how it is used in the example:

```
function getSongDetails_Result(result) {
    _root.theSong=result.items[0].songtitle;
    _root.theCut="Cut #" + result.items[0].cutnumber;
    _root.theLength="Length: " + result.items[0].cutlength;
}
```

Data source field name

Combines static text with dynamic text

To set a dynamic text field—or any other variable—to data returned via Flash Remoting, use this syntax:

```
theVariable = dataProvider.items[0].fieldname;
```

where:

- The *dataProvider* is the data object.

- The *items[0]* function is a static reference to the base element of the array.

- The *fieldName* is the data source field name.

In our example, the variables used were all assigned to dynamic text fields on the first frame, and the text fields were formatted with different font sizes, colors, and styles. This powerful type of data manipulation is really only possible because the ColdFusion Component, built in Dreamweaver, is able to pass entire recordsets to the Flash movie.

Listing 8-3   **costellosongs.cfc** (08_costellosongs.cfc)

```
<!--- Generated by Dreamweaver MX 6.0.1722    (Win32) - Wed Jun 26
17:16:26 GMT-0400 (Eastern Daylight Time) 2002 --->


<cfcomponent displayName="costellosongs" hint="Elvis Costello
Songs">

    //gets a list of all the albums in data source
    <cffunction name="getAlbums" access="remote"
    returnType="query">
        <cfquery name="q_albums" datasource="costello"
        username="margot">
```

continues

```
                          SELECT Distinct(album) FROM cds WHERE album is not NULL
                          Order by album
                      </cfquery>
                      <cfreturn q_albums>
                  </cffunction>



                  //gets a list of all the song titles given a particular album
                  <cffunction name="getSongTitles" displayName="getSongTitles"
                  access="remote" returnType="query">
                      <cfargument name="album" type="string" required="true">
                      <cfquery name="q_songs" datasource="costello"
                      username="margot">
                          SELECT songtitle,album,cutnumber FROM cds
                          WHERE album = '#TRIM(album)#'
                          ORDER by cutnumber
                      </cfquery>
                      <cfreturn q_songs>
                  </cffunction>



                  //gets details for the selected song
                  <cffunction name="getSongDetails" access="remote"
                  returnType="query" output="false">
                      <cfargument name="thisSong" type="string" required="true">
                      <cfquery name="q_songdetails" datasource="costello"
                      username="margot">
                          SELECT * FROM cds
                          WHERE songtitle = '#thisSong#'
                      </cfquery>
                      <cfreturn q_songDetails>
                  </cffunction>



</cfcomponent>
```

Listing 8-4   **ecsongs.fla** (08_ecsongs.fla)

```
#include "NetServices.as"
#include "NetDebug.as"
#include "DataGlue.as"
if (isGatewayOpen == null) {
  // do this code only once
  isGatewayOpen = true;
  NetServices.setDefaultGatewayUrl(
  "http://127.0.0.1:8500/flashservices/gateway");
  gatewayConnnection = NetServices.createGatewayConnection();
  songService = gatewayConnnection.getService
  ("beyond.fremoting.costellosongs", this);
  songService.getAlbums();
  trace
}


function getSongTitles() {
   if (cb_Albums.getSelectedIndex() > 0) {
      songService.getSongTitles(cb_albums.getSelectedItem());
   }
}


function getSongDetails() {
   songService.getSongDetails(lb_Songs.getValue());
}


//Responders

function getAlbums_Result(result) {
   // This function will be invoked by the server when it has
      finished processing
   cb_Albums.setDataProvider(result);
   cb_Albums.addItemAt(0, "Select an album", "NONE");
   cb_Albums.setSelectedIndex(0);
    }
```

continues

```
function getSongTitles_Result(result) {
    DataGlue.BindFormatStrings(lb_Songs, result, "#cutnumber#:
    #songtitle#", "#songtitle#");
}

function getSongDetails_Result(result) {
    _root.theSong=result.items[0].songtitle;
    _root.theCut="Cut #" + result.items[0].cutnumber;
    _root.theLength="Length: " + result.items[0].cutlength;
}
```

✳ _____

Chapter 9

Coding with Classes and Libraries

Dreamweaver ships with a standard set of JavaScript classes and libraries of code that you can take advantage of in your extensions or adapt for use in your web pages. The benefits of using these prewritten code snippets are many—they've been pretested by Macromedia, and are used in much of Dreamweaver's own code base. Chances are good that a problem you are struggling with has already been solved in one of these libraries, and even if it hasn't, it's likely that you can use this code as a starting point for solving your specific issue. Either way, Dreamweaver's JavaScript libraries are sure to save you development time and effort compared to creating everything from scratch.

In this chapter, we'll take a look at the standard classes and libraries that ship with Dreamweaver and how you can use them in your own extensions. We'll also discuss object-oriented programming techniques in JavaScript and show you how to create your own classes. Finally, we'll create a working example of a high-level JavaScript class that implements an Include/Exclude list of items, like the ones you see on Yahoo!'s preferences screens and many other places on the web.

Coding with Standard Classes and Libraries

Take a look inside the Configuration folder, which is in the same folder as the Dreamweaver application, and you'll see two important folders: one named JSExtensions, and one named Shared. Inside these folders are a treasure trove of JavaScript and C++ code and other resources that you can employ in your own extensions. Indeed, much of this code is already in use by many of the standard extensions that ship with Dreamweaver. In this section, we'll examine some of these prebuilt libraries and classes and how they can be used by your own projects.

The Dreamweaver Standard Libraries

Inside the Shared folder of the Dreamweaver MX Configuration folder, you will find a couple of folders named Common and MM. This is where Macromedia stores the JavaScript libraries and other resources that are shared among the Macromedia extensions and provided for use by third parties. The general convention is that, if you create your own code libraries and want to make them available to other developers, you should create your own folder inside the Shared folder with the name of your company or other identifying name and store the code in there.

NOTE: DO NOT store your shared code in the MM folder. It is reserved for use by Macromedia.

Inside the Common folder are two other folders: Cache and Scripts. The Cache folder won't be of use to you, but the Scripts folder contains a tremendous number of resources that other extensions can use, such as functions, objects, and classes. You'll also find a Script folder within the MM folder, but this contains versions of some of the same JavaScript files in the Common\Scripts folder and is included for backwards-compatibility with Dreamweaver 4 and its extensions. The MM\Script folder, however, also contains numerous useful scripts not duplicated in the Common\Scripts folder.

Shared Images

There is one resource within the MM folder that could prove useful—the Images folder. The Images folder contains several images that represent common user interface-related icons and pictures. To use these in your extensions, simply include an image in your extension's HTML user interface and define the src attribute as a folder-relative path to the image you want to use. For example, to use the "confirm" icon in one of your extensions, you would use an image tag like this:

```
<img src="../Shared/MM/Images/confirmIcon.gif">
```

Using the shared images provided in the Shared/MM/Images folder ensures that your user interface is consistent with that of Dreamweaver's, and that your extension will automatically pick up any changes that are made to those images.

Shared Scripts in the MM folder

The Scripts folder contains two subfolders: Class and CMN. The Class folder contains several JavaScript object class definitions for common objects such as check boxes, files, and list controls. The Class folder contains JavaScript source files that provide object prototypes for several useful classes (more on what prototypes are later). These classes provide functionality that encapsulates the behavior of check boxes, files, tree controls, list controls, radio buttons, and even tabbed dialogs. You can use these classes in your own Dreamweaver extensions just like you would use the regular JavaScript source files in the CMN folder.

The following table lists the files in the Class folder and the functionality they provide. Those files marked with an asterisk (*) have parallel files in the Shared\Common\Scripts folder.

File	Description
classCheckbox.js	Provides methods for working with check boxes and sets of check boxes.
FileClass.js	Provides methods for working with files as objects.
GridClass.js	Contains methods for working with tree control user interface objects.
GridControlClass.js*	Offers methods for working with parameter dialogs.
ImageButtonClass.js*	Provides support for image buttons.
ListControlClass.js*	Contains methods for working with list boxes.
NameValuePairClass.js	Provides a general mechanism for working with lists of name/value pairs.
PreferencesClass.js	Provides an object-based interface for working with sets of preferences for an extension. Uses the MMNotes extension, discussed later.

continues

File	Description
PageControlClass.js	Provides support for a page of controls, as seen in Windows-style property sheets.
RadioGroupClass.js*	Provides methods for working with radio button groups.
TabControlClass.js	Provides support for a tab control, like those seen in tabbed dialog boxes.

The CMN folder contains common JavaScript source files that are organized by area of functionality. In addition to scripts created specifically for use by Macromedia, general-purpose scripts are available for working with documents, user interface controls, files, forms, strings, and more. This table lists the more useful script files in the CMN folder and what they contain.

File	Contents
docInfo.js	Contains methods for getting information about a given document, such as extracting lists of tags, getting the selected object, and creating unique object names for a document.
DOM.js	Implements several useful methods for working with a document's DOM structure, such as traversing all document tags, determining if a tag has a certain parent, and creating lists of tags.
file.js	Provides methods for working with documents and files, such as getting a file's full path, determining whether a given file is open in Dreamweaver, and extracting a file's name from its path.
form.js	Contains methods for working with forms, such as determining if a FORM tag encloses the current selection.
string.js	Provides several string-manipulation functions.
UI.js	Provides methods for working with user interface elements in extension dialogs.

Although not officially documented anywhere, the code provided in these files is reasonably well commented, and examples of its usage can almost always be found in the standard Dreamweaver extensions that ship with the application ships. You can use Dreamweaver's Find feature to search through the Configuration folder for examples of each script's usage patterns.

Shared Code Highlights

The following functions and objects are among the more useful provided by the Dreamweaver Standard Libraries and shouldn't be overlooked:

File	Function	Description
docInfo.js	selectionInsideTag	Checks to see whether the current selection is contained within a given tag name.
	createUniqueName	Creates a name attribute for an object that is unique throughout the document.
DOM.js	getRootNode	Returns the root node of the document. Equivalent to dw.getDocumentDOM ('document').documentElement.
	findTag	Searches the document for a tag with the same name as the given one. If also given a node to start searching from, it will only search below that tag.
	traverse	Traverses the entire document structure, calling handler functions for each type of node encountered.
	isInsideTag	Checks to see whether a given tag is inside another tag.
file.js	getFullPath	Converts relative paths into full paths that start with "file://".
	fileIsCurrentlyOpen	Returns true if the file specified by the given path is open in Dreamweaver.
form.js	checkForFormTag	Checks to see whether the selection is currently enclosed by a form tag, and returns the input string wrapped by a form tag if not. Useful when inserting form controls into a document.
	IPIsInsideOfForm	Returns true if the selection is inside a form.
string.js	escQuotes/unescQuotes	Finds quote characters such as ', ", and \ in a string and escapes them by placing a backslash (\) character in front of them; unescQuotes performs the opposite function.

continues

File	Function	Description
	reformat	Reformats a string by inserting substrings after a given number of source characters—for example, `reformat("7604346267", 0, "(", 3, ")", 3, "-")` returns `"(760)434-6267"`.
	Trim	Removes whitespace from the front and back of a string.
	entityNameEncode/ entityNameDecode	Encodes and decodes a string of characters that has high-ASCII characters or other special characters in it.
UI.js	findObject	Locates a named object and returns a reference to it. For example, instead of using `document.forms[0].elementName` to refer to an element, you can just use `findObject("elementName")` to obtain its reference. Then, if you move the element elsewhere in the document, the references to it won't break.
	loadSelectList	Takes a select list object reference and an array of strings and populates the list with the contents of the array.

The Dreamweaver Standard JavaScript Extensions

In addition to the standard JavaScript classes and libraries, Dreamweaver ships with a standard set C++ shared libraries that live inside the Configuration\JSExtensions folder. These JSExtensions provide JavaScript programmers with access to such things as native platform files, Fireworks scripting, HTTP connectivity, and Design Notes. Chapter 10, "Beyond JavaScript: Interfacing with Dreamweaver Through C++," contains more information about creating your own JSExtensions, but in this section, we'll concentrate on how to best take advantage of all the work that the Dreamweaver development team has already done for you.

The Standard JSExtensions

Every copy of Dreamweaver comes with these standard JSExtensions:

- DWfile, which provides access to platform-native files. You can create, delete, read data from, write data to, and otherwise manipulate files and directories on the user's system.

- MMNotes, which exposes Dreamweaver's Design Notes functionality to extensions. Using MMNotes, you can manipulate Design Note information for files directly.

- MMHttp*, a set of methods that provides HTTP connectivity to extensions. Using MMHttp, your extension can communicate with any web server in the world.

- FWLaunch, which provides access to Fireworks scripting from within Dreamweaver.

    *MMHttp is not technically an actual JSExtension file—its functionality is built directly into Dreamweaver. It is, however, a useful extension to the JavaScript language, so we elected to include it in this chapter.

You may notice that the JSExtensions folder has many more JSExtensions than the four listed here; most of them are used internally to the Dreamweaver application or have specialized uses. These four JSExtensions are the most commonly used by developers and will be the focus of this section.

Manipulating Files and Directories with DWfile

The DWfile JSExtension allows JavaScript extension developers to manipulate files and directories on the user's system directly. DWfile provides methods for reading, writing, copying, deleting, and displaying the attributes of files. In addition, you can create folders and retrieve the contents of a folder as a list.

The following table lists the file-related methods available in DWfile.

Method	Description
exists	Tests for the existence of a file at a given path.
read	Reads the entire contents of a file as a single text string.
write	Writes the contents of a file. Can either replace the existing content or append it to the end of the file.

continues

Method	Description
copy	Copies a file from one location to another.
remove	Deletes a file by placing it in the operating system's trash bin.
getAttributes	Retrieves the attributes of a file.
getModificationDate	Retrieves the date a file was last modified.
getCreationDate	Retrieves the date a file was created.

The following table lists the folder-related methods available in DWfile.

Method	Description
createFolder	Creates a new empty folder at a specified path.
listFolder	Retrieves the contents of a folder. You can specify files only, folders only, or both.

The following table lists the utility methods available in DWfile.

Method	Description
getPlatform	Returns the platform that Dreamweaver is currently running on. This method has been deprecated in favor of navigator.platform, now a part of the core Dreamweaver API.
runCommandLine	Unsupported (and undocumented), available on Windows systems only. Executes a DOS command line.

Creating and Working with Files

No explicit method is available to create a file in Dreamweaver; you simply use the write() method to write data out to a given file path, and the file is created automatically. You can use the exists() method to first see if the file exists before it is written out. When writing data to a file, you have the choice of either writing the entire contents of the file, or appending data to the end of an existing file.

The following function prompts the user for a place to save a file and then writes out some sample data:

```
function writeDataFile()
{
    // get the path to save the file to
    var pathToFile = dw.browseForFileURL("save", "Save Data File",
    false, true);

    // if the user cancels the save dialog, the length
    // of the returned path will be 0.
    if (pathToFile.length > 0)
    {
        if (DWfile.exists(pathToFile))
            alert("File exists already!");
        else
        {
            DWfile.write(pathToFile,"This is a test.");
            DWfile.write(pathToFile,"more text","append");
        }
    }
}
```

Checks to see if chosen file exists

Creates a new text file and adds two lines

The data is written out using two forms of the write() method. In the first case, the last argument is omitted, which causes DWfile to replace the contents of the file with the string being written. In the second case, the last argument is "append", which tells DWfile to add the data to the end of the file. No method is provided to randomly access the file stream.

Reading files with DWfile is straightforward: The read() method reads the entire contents of the file. It's impossible to read individual chunks of a file.

The following function prompts the user for a file to read and then reads the contents of the file:

```
function readDataFile()
{
    var pathToFile = dw.browseForFileURL("open","Select File");
    if (pathToFile.length > 0)
    {
```

```
        var str = DWfile.read(pathToFile);
        alert(str);
    }
}
```

Working with Folders

DWfile includes two methods for working with folders: createFolder() and
listFolder(). The createFolder() function creates a new folder at the location
given by a file:// URL that you supply as the only argument to the function.
The listFolder() function lists the entire contents of a folder, optionally
including in the list only files or only other folder names.

Example: Using DWfile to Process an Entire Folder

The following example demonstrates how to use DWfile to process all of the files
in a particular folder.

```
var folderURL = "file:///c¦/temp/";
processFiles(folderURL);


processFiles(strFolderPath)
{
    var i=0;
    var filesArray = DWfile.listFolder(strFolderPath + "*.*",
    "files");
    for (i=0; i<filesArray.length; i++)
    {
        processOneFile(filesArray[i]);
    }
}


function processOneFile(strFilePath)
{
    // do whatever single file processing logic you
    // need to do in this function. Just replace the
    // call to alert() below with your code.
    alert(strFilePath);
}
```

Loops through all files ——————

An Undocumented Function

The DWfile JSExtension contains one undocumented (and unsupported) function that can be particularly useful, although it only works on Windows: runCommandLine(). This function takes one argument, a string that contains the DOS commands that you want to execute in the Windows command shell. Using this function, you can start up other applications with arguments. For example, in a Windows copy of Dreamweaver, the JavaScript code snippet

```
DWfile.runCommandLine("regsvr32 SomeControlName.ocx")
```

registers an OCX control with the Windows registry. This can be particularly useful if your set of extensions requires complex installation that you want to place inside a Dreamweaver Startup command.

Working with Design Notes via MMNotes

The Design Notes feature of Dreamweaver allows you to store notes about files that you work on and have them automatically maintained for a particular site. Other users can then read these notes when they synchronize their local machines with the site, providing a rudimentary form of collaboration. This feature is implemented in Dreamweaver by the MMNotes shared library, which exposes an API for use by extensions. Using the MMNotes JSExtension, your extension can manipulate the design note information for all of the files in a particular site, just as Dreamweaver does.

How Design Notes Are Stored

All design notes are stored in a folder named _notes, which is inside the folder for which a particular file has designed notes attached. For example, if you have a folder named Joe's Documents, and inside that folder is a file named index.html, then any design notes attached to that file will be stored in a folder named _notes inside the Joe's Documents folder.

If you look inside one of these folders, you'll find files that end with the suffix .mno, indicating that this is a design note file. The part of the filename that precedes the .mno is the name of the file to which the design note is attached.

If you open a design note file, you will see that it is essentially an XML file that contains one root tag (`<info>`). That root tag has one or more subtags (`<infoitem>`), each of which has two attributes: `key` and `value`. `key` and `value` hold the name and value of each design note.

For example, this design note file contains two design notes:

```xml
<?xml version="1.0" encoding="iso-8859-1" ?>
<info>
    <infoitem key="status" value="needs attention" />
    <infoitem key="notes" value="This file looks good, but needs
    work." />
</info>
```

One of the nice features of Design Notes is that Dreamweaver's site-management functionality automatically uploads and downloads these notes from the web site that they are defined for (but only, of course, if you are using Macromedia's built-in Site Window—these files are not automatically picked up by other FTP tools). This means that your extensions can add design notes to files for a given site and have them automatically tracked and managed by the Dreamweaver application.

The Design Notes API

The Design Notes interface provides methods for creating, setting, retrieving, and removing design notes for a file, as well as determining which site a file belongs to, getting information about the keys stored in a document, and converting file paths from platform-specific paths into `file://` URLs.

The methods for working with design note information are set forth in the following table.

Method	Description
open	Opens a design note file for a specified file. Optionally creates one if none exists.
set	Creates or updates a design note in the specified design note file.

Method	Description
get	Retrieves a design note for the specified design note file.
remove	Removes a design note from the specified design note file.

The next table details the methods for working with file paths.

Method	Description
filePathToLocalURL	Converts a platform-specific file path into a local `file://` URL.
localURLToFilePath	Converts a `file://` URL into a platform-specific file path.
getSiteRootForFile	Retrieves the local `file://` URL for the site root folder for the site that contains the specified file.

The following table shows the methods for working with design note keys.

Method	Description
getKeys	Returns an array of all of the key names in the specified design note file.
getKeyCount	Returns the number of key/value pairs in the specified design note file.

The miscellaneous methods can be found in the next table.

Method	Description
getVersionName	Returns the version of the MMNotes JSExtension as a string indicating the name of the application that implemented it.
getVersionNum	Returns a string containing the version number of the MMNotes JSExtension in the form of "majorVer.minorVer". Currently, this is 2.0.

Example: Using Design Notes to Store Extension Preferences

In addition to storing design-related information about a particular file in a site (which is what Design Notes were intended for), they can store just about any information about any file. After all, Design Note files are simply XML files, and they store key/value pairs that can correspond to any set of information an extension wants to store.

You can use these characteristics of Design Notes to store preference information for your extensions. For example, the following are three functions that can create a preferences file and read and write preference settings to the file:

```
var prefsFile = 0;
function createPrefsFile()
{
   // document.URL is a file URL path to your extension
   // force the prefs to be created if they aren't already there
   prefsFile = MMNotes.open(document.URL, true);
}


// given an array of objects that contain preference data, write
// each one out to the preference file.
// Assume each object has two properties: prefName and prefData.
function writePreferences(prefObjArray)
{
   var numPrefs = prefObjArray.length;
   var c=0;

   for (c=0; c<numPrefs;c++)
   {
      MMNotes.set(prefsFile,prefObjArray[c].prefName,
prefObjArray[c].prefData);
   }
}


// read in all the preferences from the file and pass them back
// as an array of Objects, each with two properties: prefName
// and prefData.
function readPreferences()
```

```
{
    var prefObjArray = new Array();
    var keysList = MMNotes.getKeys();
    var c=0;
    var prefData;

    for (c=0; c<keysList.length; c++)
    {
        prefData = MMNotes.get(prefsFile, keysList[c]);
        prefObjArray[c] = new Object();
        prefObjArray[c].prefName = keysList[c];
        prefObjArray[c].prefData = prefData;
    }
    return prefObjArray;
}
```

To use these routines, you would just store your preferences as an array of
objects that had prefName and prefData properties, and call these routines
to read them from and write them to the preferences file.

Connecting to the Internet via MMHttp

If you've ever found yourself thinking, "Gosh, my extension would be so
much more useful if it could connect directly to the Internet!," then the
MMHttp object is just what you've been looking for. With this JSExtension,
your Dreamweaver extensions can communicate directly with any web server
anywhere in the world.

NOTE: MMHttp does not
currently support the
secure HTTPS method of
communication.

The MMHttp API is deceptively simple because Dreamweaver takes care
of most of the work your extension needs to do when communicating with
the Internet. MMHttp exposes the methods listed in the following table in
its API.

Method	Description
getFile()	Retrieves a file from a given web address and saves it inside the Configuration/Temp folder. This method automatically creates the necessary folder structure that mirrors the server address of the file. For example, if you retrieve a file index.html from the address www.somedomain.com/ documents, then the index.html file is saved inside the documents folder, which will be inside the www.somedomain.com folder. You can also prompt the user for the location to save the file.
getText()	Retrieves the contents of the document at the specified web address.
GetFileCallback()	Performs the same function as the getFile() method, but allows you to specify a function that should be called when the HTTP request is completed.
GetTextCallback()	Performs the same function as the getText() method, but allows you to specify a function that should be called when the HTTP request is completed.
PostText()	Sends a given string of text to the server at the specified web address.
PostTextCallback()	Performs the same function as postText(), but allows you to specify a function to call when the HTTP request is complete.
ClearTemp()	Deletes the contents of the Configuration/Temp folder.

All of the MMHttp methods return an object as the function result, except for the clearTemp() method. This object has two properties: statusCode and data. The statusCode property contains the status code that is returned by the web server. The following table lists the codes that might be returned.

Code	Meaning
200	Okay. Everything was fine, and request processed normally.
400	Unintelligible request. The server could not understand the HTTP request.
404	File not found. The requested URL could not be found.

Code	Meaning
405	Server doesn't understand the requested method (GET or POST). Try using a different request method.
500	Unknown server error.
503	Server capacity reached.

Using these methods, your extensions can post and retrieve text to and from any web server right from within Dreamweaver. For example, your extensions could retrieve Help text or examples from your web site, allow users to post registration information to your site, or even download updated versions of themselves automatically.

NOTE: Posting information via the postXXX() methods assumes that you've encoded the text string using HTTP form encoding. Dreamweaver does not do this for you.

Example: Creating a New Document Based on a Web Page

This example shows how to create a new document based on an existing web page. The function uses the MMHttp object to download the text for the web page and then creates a new document in Dreamweaver and sets its content to the text returned from the MMHttp object.

```
function newPageFromWeb(strWebPageAddr)
{
    // get the page contents from the server
    var objHTTPResult = MMHttp.getText(strWebPageAddr);
```
Must be full URL
```
    // always check the result to make sure things are OK
    if (objHTTPResult.statusCode == 200)
    {
        // create the new empty document
        var newDOM = dw.createDocument();
        // set its contents to the returned HTML text
        newDOM.documentElement.outerHTML =
        objHTTPResult.data;
    }
    else
        alert("Couldn't get the text from " + strWebPageAddr + "
        because an error occurred:" + objHTTPResult.statusCode);
}
```

Scripting Fireworks with FWLaunch

One of the most useful features of Dreamweaver is its ability to communicate and work directly with Fireworks, Macromedia's web graphics editing application. Like Dreamweaver, Fireworks has a JavaScript interpreter built in and has an extensibility API. To get Fireworks to perform a function, you send it some JavaScript code, which it executes and then returns a result. This communication is provided by the FWLaunch JSExtension and can be used by extension developers who want to use Fireworks to manipulate web graphics. In fact, Macromedia's own Create Web Photo Album extension uses the FWLaunch object to implement all of its features.

The following table lists the functions that make up the FWLaunch API.

Method	Description
ValidateFireworks	Ensures that a particular version of Fireworks is installed on the user's computer.
MayLaunchFireworks	Determines whether a Fireworks optimization session can be launched.
OptimizeInFireworks	Optimizes a given image in Fireworks and optionally resizes it.
BringDWToFront	Brings the Dreamweaver application to the front.
BringFWToFront	Brings the Fireworks application to the front.
ExecJSInFireworks	Executes the given JavaScript code in Fireworks. This can either be a string of actual JavaScript code or a `file://` URL reference to a `.jsf` file on the user's computer.
GetJSResponse	Gets the result of the JavaScript call to Fireworks.

To execute JavaScript code in Fireworks, your extension follows these general steps:

1. Determine that the proper version of Fireworks is installed. Each version of Fireworks has greater capabilities than the previous version, so you must make sure that the features your extension needs are present in the Fireworks version that the user has installed on his system.

2. If the correct version of Fireworks is installed, launch it and give it some JavaScript code to execute, either in the form of a string or a `file://` URL to a `.jsf` file.

3. Periodically check to see if Fireworks is finished running the script. If it is, the script will either have executed correctly or generated an error.

4. Report any errors to the user, or take action based upon the successful execution of the JavaScript code.

The `validateFireworks()` function is used to make sure that the proper version of Fireworks is installed. It accepts a floating-point number that corresponds to the version of Fireworks you want to test against. For example, to make sure that the user has at least Fireworks 3 installed, you would write this:

```
var isFW3 = FWLaunch.validateFireworks(3.0);
```

Example: Executing JavaScript in Fireworks

This example shows how to pass a string of JavaScript code to Fireworks for execution and check for a response. Because the `getJsResponse()` function returns immediately and doesn't wait for Fireworks to finish, we use the `setTimeout()` method on the window object to repeatedly check the Fireworks response until we either get a number (indicating an error code) or a string (indicating success).

```
var gFWJSResult = null;

function FireworksAlert() {
    var isFireworks3 = FWLaunch.validateFireworks(3.0);
    if (!isFireworks3)
        return;

    // Tell Fireworks to execute the alert() method.
    gFWJSResult = FWLaunch.execJsInFireworks
        ("alert('Dreamweaver told me to alert!')");

    // A null result means FW wasn't launched,
    // a number result means an error code
    if (gFWJSResult == null ||
        typeof(gFWJSResult) == "number")
    {
```

```
            alert("an error occurred");
            gFWJSResult = null;
    } else {
        // bring Fireworks to the front
        FWLaunch.bringFWToFront();
        // Check to see if Fireworks is done yet
        checkIfFinished();

    }

}


function checkIfFinished () {
    // Call checkJsResponse() every 1/2 second to see
    // if Fireworks is done yet
    window.setTimeout("checkFWResponse();", 500);
}


function checkFWResponse() {
    var response = null;

    // We're still going; ask Fireworks how it's doing
    if (gFWJSResult!= null)
    {
        response = FWLaunch.getJsResponse(gFWJSResult);

        if (response == null) {
            // still waiting for a response, reset timer
            checkIfFinished();
        } else if (typeof(response) == "number") {
            // if the response was a number, an error
            // occurred
            // the user cancelled in Fireworks
            window.close();
            alert("an error occurred:" + response);

        } else {
            // Valid response
```

```
        window.close();
        // bring Dreamweaver to the front
        FWLaunch.bringDWToFront();
        alert("Got a valid response!");
      }
   }
}
```

Creating Your Own JavaScript Objects

You can go only so far using other people's code—the real power of
JavaScript isn't apparent until you begin creating your own JavaScript objects.
The following section—after a brief discussion of object-oriented programming—describes defining objects, passing arguments, and creating properties
and methods.

Object-Oriented Programming Concepts

Most JavaScript programs written today are created using a style of programming called *procedural programming*, in which you write a set of related but
independent functions that take arguments and perform some useful work to
return a result. However, JavaScript is capable of much more than just plain-
old functions and variables. It is a complete object-oriented programming
language, much like Java or C++. You can create classes of functionality that
are reusable across your development work and share them with friends and
colleagues.

This section provides a brief introduction to object-oriented programming
principles, but it is beyond the scope of this section to cover the entire subject
of object-oriented programming and its advanced topics such as inheritance
and polymorphism. Several good resources are available on the Internet and
at your local bookstore that focus on these subjects.

Defining Classes

Generally speaking, object-oriented programming is a style of programming
in which you create and use objects in your programs to represent collections
of related functions and data. Instead of writing separate functions to work
with a specific piece of data, you define an object that *encapsulates* data and

NOTE: Traditional
object-oriented
programming
languages, such as
C++ or Java, have a
concept called a *class*.
Classes define the
information that an
object contains using
member variables,
which hold data, and
the behavior of how
the object works using
functions called
member methods.
JavaScript, however,
does not contain the
formal notion of a
class, but approxi-
mates its functionality
through the use of
what are called
prototypes. A prototype
defines a JavaScript
object's initial methods
and properties when
the object is first
created by a script.

the functions that manipulate that data all in one place. This way, you can refer to a single object that holds all the relevant information that you need to work with. For example, the JavaScript Date object contains not only the various properties of a date, such as the day and year, but also the various methods needed to work with dates, such as computing the number of days between two dates.

To create a prototype for an object, you begin by writing the object's *constructor* function. This is the function that will be called when the user creates a new object of the type that you are defining—in other words, it "constructs" the object. The constructor function has the same name as the object type. For example, to write a constructor function for an object of type Bottle, use this syntax:

```
function Bottle()
{
}
```

Then, to create a new Bottle object, you would simply use the JavaScript new operator with the object's type:

```
var myBottleObject = new Bottle();
```

The preceding example isn't very useful because the Bottle object has no properties or methods associated with it. To give our object some methods and properties, we define them in one of two ways: either within the object's constructor function, or by using the base JavaScript Object's class property called prototype. This example shows both methods.

First method (within the constructor):

```
function Bottle()
{
    this.bottleSize = 12; // 12 ounce bottle size
    this.amountLeft = 12;
    this.getAmount = Bottle_getAmount();
}
```

Second method (using the `prototype` property):

```
function Bottle()
{
}


Bottle.prototype.bottleSize = 12;
Bottle.prototype.amountLeft = 12;
Bottle.prototype.getAmount = Bottle_getAmount();


function Bottle_getAmount()
{
    return this.amountLeft;
}
```

In each case, you must provide an implementation for any methods that you define in the prototype. Our example defines one method, `getAmount()`, which returns the amount of liquid left in the bottle.

Now, a user of our object can simply instantiate a new `Bottle` object by writing `new Bottle()`, and the object will automatically receive the default properties and methods.

Passing Arguments to the Constructor

You can also pass default arguments to the constructor. For example, to pass a default size and amount to the `Bottle` constructor in our preceding example, you would write the following:

```
function Bottle(size, amount)
{
    this.bottleSize = size;
    this.amountLeft = amount;
}


Bottle.prototype.getAmount = Bottle_getAmount();
```

```
function Bottle_getAmount()
{
    return this.amountLeft;
}
```

Now, users of our `Bottle` object can create `Bottle` objects of different sizes and amounts. In the revised example, we have used a combination of the "within the constructor" and "object prototype" methods. The member variables are defined in the constructor, whereas the methods are defined using the prototype property. This is a common method of defining objects in JavaScript.

Static Properties and Methods

Not all properties and methods are unique to each object. In our previous example, the properties and methods that we defined were attached to each object that was created and had a distinct value for each separate object. For example, the `bottleSize` property could be different for each `Bottle` object that was created.

However, sometimes it is useful to define properties and methods that are common to all objects of a particular type because they won't change from object to object. These types of properties and methods are called *static properties* and *static methods*.

To declare a member of a class that is static, you define it not as part of the constructor or class `prototype` property, but directly as a member of the class. For example, suppose we decided that all of our `Bottle` objects would have the same manufacturer. We could declare a static property for this by writing the following:

```
function Bottle(size, amount)
{
    this.bottleSize = size;
    this.amountLeft = amount;
}

Bottle.manufacturer = "BigBottleCompany, Inc.";
```

This property will now be created whenever a `Bottle` object is created, just like the other properties, but it will be the same for all `Bottle` objects. If someone changes the value of a static property or method, then it changes for all objects of that type. To refer to a static property of an object, you precede it with the name of the class, not the name of the object variable. For example:

```
var b = new Bottle(12,12);
alert(b.bottleSize) // shows "12"
alert(b.manufacturer) // shows "undefined"
alert(Bottle.manufacturer) // shows "BigBottleCompany, Inc."
```

Note that referring to a class property by using the variable that represents an object results in an undefined value.

Example: The Inclusion list

This example shows how to implement an inclusion list, like those seen in 9.1.

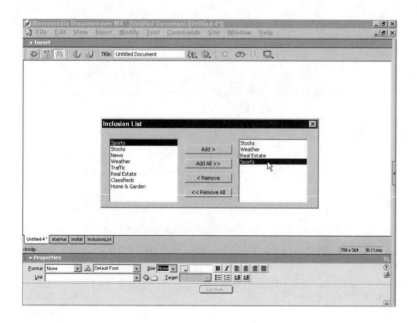

NOTE: To view the completed code, see Listings 9-1 and 9-2 at the end of this section.

9.1

Use an inclusion list to pass values from one select list to another.

This object allows the user to pick values from an "available" list and add or remove them from a "selected" list. Such lists are usually provided to allow a user to choose several entries from a list of available options. This object is actually a compound object; it represents two select lists in a web page as a single object. It also provides the necessary methods for moving items between the two lists.

Start by creating a blank JavaScript page and saving it as `inclist.js`. In the new document, writing the constructor function for the object first:

```
function InclusionList(oFromList, oToList)
{
    this.oSourceList = oFromList;
    this.oDestList = oToList;
}
```

The constructor function takes two arguments, each of which is an object reference to `<select>` lists in the web page: one acts as the source while the other is the destination.

Next, we declare some global variables to use as error messages:

```
var g_sICL_NOSELECTION = "Please select an item to be added."
var g_sICL_NOTHINGTOREMOVE = "Please select an item to be removed."
```

Now we need to define the properties and methods that the list object will use. Our list object defines two static properties and four regular (or *instance*) methods. The two static properties are error codes that are shown to the user when errors are encountered, such as having nothing selected in the "available" list to add to the "selected" list, or nothing selected in the "selected" list to remove. The four regular methods—added using the `prototype` class property—are responsible for the `Add`, `Add All`, `Remove`, and `Remove All` functions.

```
InclusionList.ERRMSG_NOSELECTION = g_sICL_NOSELECTION;
InclusionList.ERRMSG_NOTHINGTOREMOVE = g_sICL_NOTHINGTOREMOVE;
```

Static properties
Static properties

```
InclusionList.prototype.addItem = icl_AddItem;
InclusionList.prototype.addAll = icl_AddAll;
InclusionList.prototype.removeItem = icl_RemoveItem;
InclusionList.prototype.clearItems = icl_ClearItems;
```

Methods
Methods
Methods
Methods

After the properties and methods have been defined, we need to write the implementations for the object's methods. The first method handles the Add method for the object. It detects the selection in the "available" list and copies it over to the "selected" list.

```
function icl_AddItem()
{
    var iItemToAdd = this.oSourceList.selectedIndex;
    var sNewItemText='';
    var sNewItemValue='';

    if (iItemToAdd == -1) {
        alert(InclusionList.ERRMSG_NOSELECTION);
        return;
    }

    sNewItemText = this.oSourceList.options[iItemToAdd].text;
    sNewItemValue = this.oSourceList.options[iItemToAdd].value;
    this.oDestList.options[this.oDestList.options.length] = new
    Option(sNewItemText,sNewItemValue);
    this.oDestList.options.selectedIndex =
    this.oDestList.options.length-1;
}
```

No item selected

The InclusionList object also supports an Add All function, in which all of the entries in the "available" list are copied over to the "selected" list. This is handled by the icl_AddAll function:

```
function icl_AddAll()
{
    var i=0;
    var sNewItemText='';
    var sNewItemValue='';

    for (i=0; i < this.oSourceList.options.length; i++)
    {
        sNewItemText = this.oSourceList.options[i].text;
        sNewItemValue = this.oSourceList.options[i].value;
        this.oDestList.options[this.oDestList.options.length] = new
        Option(sNewItemText,sNewItemValue);
    }
    this.oDestList.options.selectedIndex =
    this.oDestList.options.length-1;
}
```

Removing an item from the "selected" part of the Inclusion list deletes the selected entry from the list.

```
function icl_RemoveItem()
{
    var iItemToRemove = this.oDestList.selectedIndex;
    if (iItemToRemove == -1) {
        alert(InclusionList.ERRMSG_NOTHINGTOREMOVE);
        return;
    }
    this.oDestList.options[iItemToRemove]=null;
    if (this.oDestList.options.length > 0)
        this.oDestList.options.selectedIndex = (iItemToRemove > 0)
        ? --iItemToRemove:iItemToRemove;
}
```

Nothing selected ⎯⎯⎯

The last method handles the `Remove All` functionality. Using a `while` loop, each of the items is, in turn, set to `null`.

```
function icl_ClearItems()
{
    while (this.oDestList.options.length) this.oDestList.options[0]
    = null;}
}
```

Using the Inclusion List

To use the Inclusion list object, you include the JavaScript code in your HTML page using a `<script>` tag with an `src` attribute that points to the JavaScript file for the object. Then, you declare a global variable that holds a new instance of the Inclusion list object. The two arguments to the constructor are the two select lists that implement the object.

```
<script language="JavaScript" src="inclist.js"></script>

<script>
var g_oICList;
function initialize()
{
    g_oICList = new
InclusionList(document.forms["form1"].source,document.forms
["form1"].dest);
}
</script>
```

Could also use findObject()

In the web page, you include a form that contains the two select lists, along with the controls that trigger the Add/Add All/Remove/Remove All functions. The Inclusion list object has been designed to be flexible in that the page elements that control the functionality of the list can be anything that responds to events and can call JavaScript code. In this example, regular form buttons are used to provide the adding and removing functionality, but it could also have been done using image buttons, link text, or anything else that can respond to user events.

```
            <form name="form1" method="post" action="">
              <table border="0">
                <tr>
                  <td align="center">
                    <select name="source" size="10" style="width:150px">
                      <option value="sports">Sports</option>
                      <option value="stocks">Stocks</option>
                      <option value="news">News</option>
                      <option value="weather">Weather</option>
                      <option value="traffic">Traffic</option>
                      <option value="realestate">Real Estate</option>
                      <option value="classifieds">Classifieds</option>
                      <option value="homegarden">Home &amp; Garden</option>
                    </select>
                  </td>
                  <td align="center">
                    <p>
                      <input type="button" name="add" value="Add &gt;"
                      onClick="g_oICList.addItem()" style="width:100px">
                      <br>
                      <input type="button" name="Button" value="Add All &gt;
                      &gt;" onClick="g_oICList.addAll()" style="width:100px">
                      <br>
                      <input type="button" name="remove" value="&lt; Remove"
                      onClick="g_oICList.removeItem()" style="width:100px">
                      <br>
                      <input type="button" name="clear" value="&lt;&lt; Remove
                      All" onClick="g_oICList.clearItems()" style="width:100px">
                    </p>
                  </td>
                  <td align="center">
                    <select name="dest" size="10" style="width:100px">
                    </select>
                  </td>
                </tr>
              </table>
            </form>
```

Could be dynamically populated — (annotation pointing to the `<select name="source" size="10" style="width:150px">` line)

Character entity for > — (annotation pointing to the `value="Add &gt;"` line)

That's all there is to it. This example could be improved a bit; for example, there's no error checking to make sure that the same two items in the "available" list aren't included more than once, but this is a functioning example that you can use in your own web pages or extensions.

Listing 9-1   **Inclusion List JavaScript File** (09_inclist.mxp)

```
// JavaScript Document
function InclusionList(oFromList, oToList)
{
    this.oSourceList = oFromList;
    this.oDestList = oToList;
}
// some global variables used for error messages.
var g_sICL_NOSELECTION = "Please select an item to be added."
var g_sICL_NOTHINGTOREMOVE = "Please select an item to be removed."

InclusionList.ERRMSG_NOSELECTION = g_sICL_NOSELECTION;
InclusionList.ERRMSG_NOTHINGTOREMOVE = g_sICL_NOTHINGTOREMOVE;

InclusionList.prototype.addItem = icl_AddItem;
InclusionList.prototype.addAll = icl_AddAll;
InclusionList.prototype.removeItem = icl_RemoveItem;
InclusionList.prototype.clearItems = icl_ClearItems;

function icl_AddItem()
{
    var iItemToAdd = this.oSourceList.selectedIndex;
    var sNewItemText='';
    var sNewItemValue='';

    if (iItemToAdd == -1) {
        alert(InclusionList.ERRMSG_NOSELECTION);
        return;
    }

    sNewItemText = this.oSourceList.options[iItemToAdd].text;
```

continues

```
         sNewItemValue = this.oSourceList.options[iItemToAdd].value;
         this.oDestList.options[this.oDestList.options.length] = new
         Option(sNewItemText,sNewItemValue);
         this.oDestList.options.selectedIndex =
         this.oDestList.options.length-1;
}


function icl_AddAll()
{
    var i=0;
    var sNewItemText='';
    var sNewItemValue='';

    for (i=0; i < this.oSourceList.options.length; i++)
    {
        sNewItemText = this.oSourceList.options[i].text;
        sNewItemValue = this.oSourceList.options[i].value;
        this.oDestList.options[this.oDestList.options.length] = new
        Option(sNewItemText,sNewItemValue);
    }
        this.oDestList.options.selectedIndex =
        this.oDestList.options.length-1;
}


function icl_RemoveItem()
{
    var iItemToRemove = this.oDestList.selectedIndex;
    if (iItemToRemove == -1) {
        alert(InclusionList.ERRMSG_NOTHINGTOREMOVE);
        return;
    }
    this.oDestList.options[iItemToRemove]=null;
    if (this.oDestList.options.length > 0)
        this.oDestList.options.selectedIndex = (iItemToRemove > 0)
        ? --iItemToRemove:iItemToRemove;
}
```

```
function icl_ClearItems()
{
    while (this.oDestList.options.length) this.oDestList.options[0]
    = null;
}
```

Listing 9-2   **Inclusion List HTML File** (09_inclist.mxp)

```
<html>
<head>
<title>Inclusion List</title>
<meta http-equiv="Content-Type" content="text/html; charset=
iso-8859-1">
<script language="JavaScript" src="inclist.js"></script>
<script>
var g_oICList;
function initialize()
{
    g_oICList = new InclusionList(document.forms
    ["form1"].source,document.forms["form1"].dest);
}
</script>

</head>

<body onLoad="initialize()">
<form name="form1" method="post" action="">
  <table border="0">
    <tr>
      <td align="center">
        <select name="source" size="10" style="width:150px">
          <option value="sports">Sports</option>
          <option value="stocks">Stocks</option>
          <option value="news">News</option>
          <option value="weather">Weather</option>
          <option value="traffic">Traffic</option>
```

continues

```html
                        <option value="realestate">Real Estate</option>
                        <option value="classifieds">Classifieds</option>
                        <option value="homegarden">Home &amp; Garden</option>
                </select>
            </td>
            <td align="center">
                <p>
                    <input type="button" name="add" value="Add &gt;"
                    onClick="g_oICList.addItem()" style="width:100px">
                    <br>
                    <input type="button" name="Button" value="Add All
                    &gt;&gt;" onClick="g_oICList.addAll()"
                    style="width:100px">
                    <br>
                    <input type="button" name="remove" value="&lt; Remove"
                    onClick="g_oICList.removeItem()" style="width:100px">
                    <br>
                    <input type="button" name="clear" value="&lt;&lt;
                    Remove All" onClick="g_oICList.clearItems()"
                    style="width:100px">
                </p>
            </td>
        <td align="center">
            <select name="dest" size="10" style="width:150px">
            </select>
        </td>
    </tr>
  </table>
</form>

</body>
</html>
```

Chapter 10

Beyond JavaScript: Interfacing with Dreamweaver Through C++

Around the time of the Beta release of Dreamweaver 2, Macromedia had begun to realize that the JavaScript extensibility architecture built into Dreamweaver was bumping up against its limits. Developers were asking for features that standard JavaScript simply didn't support, such as access to the local file system on a user's computer or the Windows Registry. Some developers also had code that they wanted to protect from prying eyes due to trade secrets or other confidentiality needs. Macromedia's development partners, such as Apple and Nokia, needed ways to integrate Dreamweaver with existing proprietary systems, which was out of the reach of the native capabilities of the JavaScript language.

Macromedia could have solved these problems by adding proprietary extensions to the JavaScript language to handle things such as file access, HTTP networking, Design Notes, and so on. Instead, true to form, the Dreamweaver team took the extensible approach—allowing developers to create their own extensions to JavaScript (called JSExtensions) by writing directly in native C++ code. These new features became natural extensions to JavaScript by manifesting themselves as objects within the JavaScript namespace. For example, if a developer creates a C++ library for file access and calls it DWfile, then a new object named DWfile is suddenly available to all JavaScript developers and Dreamweaver users who install that library in their copy of Dreamweaver.

Using this mechanism opens up entirely new possibilities for Dreamweaver extensions. By creating JavaScript extensions in C++, you can create much more complex user interfaces in modal dialogs, communicate with network-based server machines, read foreign file formats, and even create a C++-based bridge to Java, allowing you to call directly into Java code or JavaBean components. The upside to all of this is tremendous; you are no longer confined to the restrictions that the JavaScript language imposes on extensions. The downside, however, is that because you are using C++, you have to implement your extensions twice if you want to support both Macintosh and Windows versions.

WARNING: This chapter assumes that you have a working knowledge of C/C++ and is not intended as a primer for those languages.

In this chapter, we'll introduce Dreamweaver's C++ extensibility layer and examine some of the standard DLLs that ship with the application. Next, we'll show how to build extensions to Dreamweaver's JavaScript layer by writing C++ DLLs, and how to convert data between the JavaScript and C environments. Finally, we'll build a practical example: a C++ library that provides direct access to the operating system's Clipboard on both Macintosh and Windows.

Calling C++ Code from JavaScript

In general, calling C++ code from within JavaScript is just like calling a method on any other JavaScript object. You simply use standard JavaScript `object.method()` notation to call a given method. For example, to create an object of type `Date` and then call a method on the object, in regular JavaScript code, you would write something like this:

```
var theDate = new Date();
var theDay = theDate.getDay();
```

To do the same thing with a C++ object in Dreamweaver, you would simply call the method on a prenamed object. You don't need to create the C++ objects the way you do with built-in classes; you simply give the name of the class and method you want to call. For example, if a JSExtension named `MyExt.dll` exists in the JSExtensions folder and one of the methods it exposes to the JavaScript namespace is `myMethod`, then the syntax for calling the method would be as follows:

```
MyExt.myMethod();
```

Making Sure a JSExtension Is Present Before Using It

Because JSExtensions are not built into the Dreamweaver application and not all Dreamweaver users might have a particular JSExtension installed, it is necessary to first make sure that a given JSExtension is actually present and loaded into memory before attempting to use it. This is accomplished by using the `typeof()` JavaScript function to retrieve the type of a JSExtension object. For example, to make sure that a JSExtension named `MyExt` is installed properly, you would use the following code:

```
if (typeof(MyExt) != "undefined")
    // go ahead and call object's methods -- it is installed
else
    alert("The MyExt Extension is not installed.");
```

The expression `typeof(MyExt)` attempts to retrieve the type of the given argument. If the extension is not present, or is present but fails to load properly, then the `typeof` function will return the string `"undefined"`. At this point, you might show an error message to the user or avoid calling methods on the JSExtension object.

The Standard JavaScript Extensions

Dreamweaver MX ships with a standard set of JSExtensions that developers can take advantage of right out of the box. The extensions include these:

- DWfile—Provides access to platform-native files. You can create, delete, read data from, write data to, and otherwise manipulate files and directories on the user's system.

- FWLaunch—Provides access to Fireworks scripting from within Dreamweaver.

- MMNotes—Exposes Dreamweaver's Design Notes functionality to extensions. Using MMNotes, you can manipulate Design Note information for files directly.

- SWFFile—Allows developers to build Flash objects that create simple Flash content.

These JavaScript extensions are stored inside the JSExtensions folder, which is inside Dreamweaver's Configuration folder. Several other extensions are also stored in this directory that are for the internal use of the Dreamweaver application, such as MM.dll and MMSiteSettings.dll.

When Dreamweaver starts up, it scans the JSExtensions folder looking for these C++ extension DLLs and adds each one of them to the built-in JavaScript namespace, as illustrated in Figure 10.1. Each JSExtension tells Dreamweaver what methods it makes available to JavaScript developers and what arguments are necessary for each method. JavaScript developers can then call those methods just like they do any other JavaScript method.

10.1

During the bootup process, Dreamweaver scans the Configuration/JSExtensions folder to include any DLLs found there.

TIP: Dreamweaver maintains a link to these DLLs while running, so you'll need to quit the program if you ever need to uninstall or remove one of the DLLs.

Extending Dreamweaver with C++

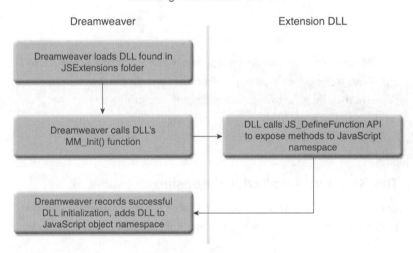

Example: Using the DWfile JSExtension

One of the more useful JSExtensions that ship with Dreamweaver is the DWfile extension, which provides methods for creating and manipulating files on the user's local machine, a capability not supported by standard JavaScript. This functionality can be used to create and store preference files, read data files that are stored in a format that Dreamweaver does not understand, create or list the contents of directories, and generally perform many other types of file access that a JavaScript extension needs to do.

The following code uses the DWfile extension to create a new text file:

```
function testDWfile()
{
    var theFile = "file:///D¦/temp/myTestFile.txt"
if (typeof(DWfile) != "undefined")
    DWfile.write(theFile, "This is some text", false);
}
```

When the preceding function is executed in Dreamweaver, a new file named `myTestFile.txt` will be created with `"This is some text"` as its contents. The first argument specifies a file to write information to, written as a standard `file://` URL string. The second argument is the string to write to the file. The third argument is a Boolean value indicating whether the data should be appended to the existing file (true) or should replace the existing content (false).

TIP: If the `file://` portion of the file URL specifier string is left out, then the file is created in the same directory as the Dreamweaver application.

Creating JavaScript Extensions for Dreamweaver

To create JavaScript Extensions for Dreamweaver, you will need an understanding of at least the C programming language (C++ is optional) and a development environment that can create shared libraries for your target platforms, such as Microsoft Visual C++ or Metrowerks CodeWarrior. You can use other development environments to build JSExtensions; however, Visual C++ and CodeWarrior are the most common. Consult the documentation for your particular development environment for information on how to build shared libraries (usually called Dynamic Link Libraries, or DLLs, on Windows).

To create JavaScript extensions for Dreamweaver, you generally follow these steps:

1. Create the project file for the extension to build a shared library.

2. Create the main source file and write some common initialization code that all JSExtensions use.

3. Define the methods that will make up the internal logic of the extension.

4. Expose these internal methods to the JavaScript layer.

5. Test and debug the extension.

In addition to these steps, it will be necessary to convert data types from the JavaScript environment to the C environment, report errors that occur within your extension to the user, and sometimes even call back into the JavaScript environment from within the extension's C code, as seen in Figure 10.2. The Dreamweaver C extensibility API provides methods for doing all of these things.

10.2

Calls to the DLL from within a Dreamweaver begin and end in the JavaScript-based extension.

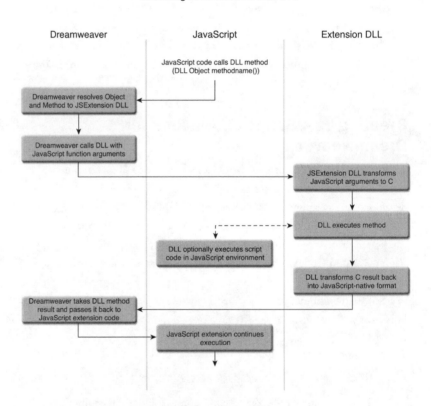

Extending Dreamweaver with C++

Setting Up the Project

JSExtension projects must be created as shared libraries (DLLs on Windows). Your particular development environment will have all the necessary information on how to do this; information presented in this book is intended for users of Microsoft Visual C++ 6.0 and Metrowerks CodeWarrior Pro 5.

Building a Shared Library in Windows

If you are using Visual C++ 6.0, building a DLL is easy.

1. From the File menu, select New, and then select the Projects tab in the dialog box that appears.

   You can choose to create a plain C++ DLL or use the MFC AppWizard to create an MFC DLL (see the next section about this process).

2. Select the type of DLL you want to create in the list of project types.

3. Use the Location field to type or browse to a path to the directory where you want the project to be created.

4. Supply a name for the project in the Project Name field and click OK.

5. Select the type of DLL you want to create from the next dialog box. Click Finish.

   Usually, you'll select either An Empty DLL Project or A Simple DLL Project. Select A DLL That Exports Some Symbols if your DLL will export more than just the Dreamweaver C extensibility symbols.

You are now ready to add source files to your Windows extension project.

> **NOTE:** The standard header file mm_jsapi.h automatically exports the necessary functions to call your extension's initialization code. You do not need to add a .DEF file to your DLL unless you plan to export functions other than the Dreamweaver initialization entry point.

Building JSExtensions as MFC DLLs

You can use the MFC AppWizard to create extensions that use the Microsoft Foundation Classes, but you will need to do some extra work in your methods that you expose to the JavaScript environment.

Specifically, any of your exported methods that call into the MFC class library must include the macro `AFX_MANAGE_STATE` as the first line of the method. This ensures that MFC can correctly load any resources that MFC uses from the MFC resources instead of your extension's resources. MFC manages an internal state context that keeps track of where to load resources from, and this macro makes sure that the contexts don't get mixed up. More information on this topic is available in Microsoft Tech Notes 58 and 35, available at the MSDN Library (`msdn.microsoft.com/library`).

Building a Shared Library in Macintosh

NOTE: These instructions are provided for users of CodeWarrior Pro 5, although most recent CodeWarrior versions are similar. See your version's documentation for more details.

Building shared libraries on the Macintosh using CodeWarrior is rather straightforward. All of the settings that need to be changed can be accessed under the Project Settings dialog box, accessed via the "{Project Name} Settings" item in the Edit menu (where the {Project Name} is replaced by the name of your project).

1. In CodeWarrior, choose New from the File menu.

2. In the Project tab, select MacOS C/C++ Project Stationery. Enter a name for the project in the Project Name edit field, and select a folder to store your project in. (If you type the name of a nonexistent folder, the folder will be created for you.) Click OK.

   A new project will be created and opened for you, containing some sample source code and link libraries that you will need to link your extension to the Mac system. The project will be divided into Debug and Release build sections.

3. In the new project window, remove any files from the Sources and Resources sections that CodeWarrior automatically added.

4. Under the Edit menu, select the menu item named {Project Name} Settings, where {Project Name} is the name of your project.

5. In the Target Settings tab, set the Linker selection to MacOS PPC Linker.

6. Set the Output Directory to point to the folder where you want the finished shared library to be placed when it's built.

TIP: You can set this path to point directly to the JSExtensions directory of your Dreamweaver installation; this will save you the step of having to copy it there manually after each build.

7. Under the Runtime Settings tab, set the Host Application for Libraries and Code Resources to point to the Dreamweaver executable.

8. Under the PPC Target tab, set the Project setting to Shared Library. Name the shared library the same name as your project. Set the Creator setting to ???? and the Type field to shlb. This will provide a default icon for your library in the Finder. If you want to use a custom icon, you can set the Creator field to your Apple Developer Creator ID.

9. In the PPC PEF tab, set the Export menu to use #pragma. This will automatically export the Dreamweaver initialization point for you.

You are now ready to add source files to your Macintosh extension project.

Basic Structure of the Extension

Consider Listing 10-1, a code listing for a JSExtension that adds two
numbers and returns a result:

Listing 10-1   **AddNumbers.cpp** (10_addnumbers.cpp)

```
1:   // AddNumbers.cpp : Takes two numbers and adds them together, then
2:   // returns the result back to the JavaScript world.
3:
4:   #ifdef _WIN32    // Windows
5:   #include "windows.h"
6:   #else            // Mac
7:   #include <MacHeaders.h>
8:   #endif
9:
10:  #ifdef __cplusplus
11:  extern "C" {
12:  #endif
13:  #include "mm_jsapi.h"
14:  #ifdef __cplusplus
15:  }
16:  #endif
17:
18:  MM_STATE
19:
20:  void
21:  MM_Init( void )
22:  {
23:    JS_DefineFunction( "addTwoNumbers", addTwoNumbers, 2);
24:  }
25:
26:  JSBool addTwoNumbers ( JSContext* cx, JSObject* obj, unsigned
int argc, jsval* jsArgv, jsval* rval )
27:  {
28:    int firstNumber;
29:    int secondNumber;
30:    int result;
```

continues

```
31:
32:    // Get the arguments from JavaScript and convert them to C
33:    // data types.
34:    JS_ValueToInteger(cx, jsArgv[0], &firstNumber);
35:    JS_ValueToInteger(cx, jsArgv[1], &secondNumber);
36:
37:    // Add them together
38:    result = firstNumber + secondNumber;
39:
40:    // Convert the result to a JavaScript value and return it
41:    *rval = JS_IntegerToValue( result );
42:
43:    return JS_TRUE;
44: }
```

This C extension is divided into three distinct sections: including the necessary header files, writing the initialization code, and implementing the extension's functionality.

Including Platform-Specific Headers

Lines 4–8 of Listing 10-1 include some platform-specific header files depending on the platform the extension is being compiled for:

```
4:    #ifdef _WIN32    // Windows
5:    #include "windows.h"
6:    #else            // Mac
7:    #include <MacHeaders.h>
8:    #endif
```

These header files contain all the necessary definitions needed to call the built-in functions for the Mac and Windows operating systems.

Including mm_jsapi.h

Line 13 is the core of the next stage as it includes the file "`mm_jsapi.h`". All JSExtensions must include this header file. The `mm_jsapi.h` file includes definitions that are needed for your JSExtension code to communicate with Dreamweaver and perform other tasks related to converting data types and initializing your extension.

```
10: #ifdef __cplusplus
11: extern "C" {
12: #endif
13: #include "mm_jsapi.h"
14: #ifdef __cplusplus
15: }
16: #endif
```

Macromedia header

It is surrounded by an `extern "C"` declaration block to prevent the C++ compiler from mangling the object code names of the included functions. You must do this if you write your initialization code in a C++ file instead of a plain C file.

NOTE: You can find the latest version of mm_jsapi.h on the Dreamweaver Exchange.

Writing the Initialization Code

Lines 18–24 show the common initialization code that all JSExtensions must call. First, on line 18, the macro `MM_STATE` is declared, which expands into a function that sets up some initialization parameters used by the extension. The `MM_STATE` macro must be explicitly declared exactly once by each JSExtension.

```
18: MM_STATE
19:
20: void
21: MM_Init( void )
22: {
23:   JS_DefineFunction( "addTwoNumbers", addTwoNumbers, 2);
24: }
```

This macro calls the extension's `MM_Init()` function (lines 20–24), which is where the extension declares the functions that will be exposed to the JavaScript environment and associates them with the internal C functions that will perform the necessary work with `JS_DefineFunction()`. In this example, the function name—`JS_DefineFunction()`'s first argument—as seen by the JavaScript developer has the same name as the internal C function, but that is not required. We could have named the C function anything we wanted to, as long as it was a valid C function name.

The second argument is the C function within the extension that actually implements the logic for the function that the JavaScript programmer will call. The last argument is the number of arguments that the JavaScript function expects to receive.

Exposing Functions to the JavaScript Environment

In the final code block, lines 26–44 declare the C implementation of the function that the JavaScript code will call.

```
26: JSBool addTwoNumbers ( JSContext* cx, JSObject* obj, unsigned
int argc, jsval* jsArgv, jsval* rval )
27: {
28:   int firstNumber;
29:   int secondNumber;
30:   int result;
31:
32:   // Get the arguments from JavaScript and convert them to C
33:   // data types.
34:   JS_ValueToInteger(cx, jsArgv[0], &firstNumber);
35:   JS_ValueToInteger(cx, jsArgv[1], &secondNumber);
36:
37:   // Add them together
38:   result = firstNumber + secondNumber;
39:
40:   // Convert the result to a JavaScript value and return it
41:   *rval = JS_IntegerToValue( result );
42:
43:   return JS_TRUE;
44: }
```

Every C implementation function of a JavaScript method has the same function header and accepts the same arguments. Its basic format is this:

```
JSBool function(JSContext *cx, JSObject *obj, unsigned int argc,
jsval *argv, jsval *rval)
```

The first argument is a pointer to a JSContext. This is an opaque data type that is passed to all JSExtension methods that are called from the JavaScript environment, and you will need to pass it along to all of the functions that Dreamweaver exposes to your extension to operate on JavaScript objects. The second argument, a pointer to a JSObject, is the object within whose scope the extension function will execute. In the JavaScript namespace, this object corresponds to the object referenced by the "this" keyword. The third argument is the number of arguments that your function was called with in the JavaScript environment in Dreamweaver. The fourth argument is an array of jsval values, which represent the actual arguments that your extension function was called with. The last argument, rval, is a pointer to a jsval that your extension sets as the return value of the function in the JavaScript environment. For example, our extension will be called from the JavaScript environment with this code:

```
var result = 0;
result = SampleExt.addTwoNumbers(5,6);
```

The result that the JavaScript developer gets back from the function call is passed back from the C layer in the rval parameter.

All of your JSExtension methods that are called from the JavaScript environment must return a Boolean value of either JS_TRUE or JS_FALSE. This return value indicates to Dreamweaver whether your extension function executed without errors. If everything executes normally, then you should return JS_TRUE. A return value of JS_FALSE results in an error message being shown to the user. Unless you supply your own error message, a default message alert box will be displayed to the user. (The section entitled "Handling and Reporting Errors" provides details on supplying your own error messages.)

Converting JavaScript Data Types to C

When Dreamweaver passes arguments to your C extension, they are passed in JavaScript format. Before you can operate on these arguments, you must first convert them from JavaScript format into C data types. Similarly, when you're passing data back to the JavaScript environment from your extension, you must convert the data to JavaScript format before JavaScript-based extensions can use it.

The arguments that are passed to your extension from Dreamweaver are in a special JavaScript format represented by a data type called a "jsval". JavaScript is a "loosely typed" language; in other words, JavaScript does not enforce restrictions on what types of data can be stored in a variable. For example, a JavaScript variable can contain a string, a number, an Object, and so on, and all of these types are stored in a jsval. The C language, however, is "strongly typed"; it expects programmers to explicitly declare what type of data a variable will contain before the program can use it. It is for this reason that you must convert all JavaScript arguments to C data types before attempting to operate on them.

Dreamweaver provides a set of functions that JSExtensions can use to convert JavaScript variables to C types. The following table lists the conversion functions and their purpose.

Function	Purpose
JS_ValueToString()	Convert a JavaScript value to a C-style string. Returns a character pointer (char *).
JS_ValueToInteger()	Convert a JavaScript value to a long integer.
JS_ValueToDouble()	Convert a JavaScript value to an 8-byte floating-point number.
JS_ValueToBoolean()	Convert a JavaScript value to a Boolean value.
JS_ValueToObject()	Convert a JavaScript value to a JSObject pointer.

All of these methods, with the exception of JS_ValueToString(), return a JSBool indicating whether the supplied jsval could be successfully converted to the requested data type. In the case of JS_ValueToString(), a return value of null indicates failure.

In lines 34 and 35 of the example, the extension method addTwoNumbers()
calls JS_ValueToInteger() on the two arguments passed to the extension
to convert them to C-style integers to add them together:

```
34:    JS_ValueToInteger(cx, jsArgv[0], &firstNumber);
35:    JS_ValueToInteger(cx, jsArgv[1], &secondNumber);
```

Converting C Data Types to JavaScript

Just as you must first convert JavaScript variables to C data types before your
extension can operate on them, you must convert all C data types to
JavaScript values before sending them back to the JavaScript environment.
Each function that Dreamweaver provides for converting JavaScript values to
C data types has a counterpart that performs the opposite function: converting C data types to JavaScript values. The following table lists those functions
and their purpose.

Function	Purpose
JS_StringToValue()	Convert a C-style string to a JavaScript value.
JS_IntegerToValue()	Convert a long integer to a JavaScript value.
JS_DoubleToValue()	Convert an 8-byte floating point number to a JavaScript value.
JS_BooleanToValue()	Convert a Boolean value to a JavaScript value.
JS_ObjectToValue()	Convert a JSObject pointer to a JavaScript value.

In our example extension, line 41 converts the C-style integer result to a
JavaScript value and stores the result in rval, which will pass the result back
to the JavaScript caller:

```
41:    *rval = JS_IntegerToValue( result );
```

Handling Complex Data Types

The preceding methods are intended for dealing with basic data types, such
as integers and strings. Dealing with more complex data types, such as arrays,
is more complicated and requires a few additional utility functions.

Accessing data within arrays that have been passed to your extension as arguments requires converting the jsval that represents the Array to a JSObject, checking its type to make sure that it is an Array object, and retrieving each element from the array. Passing an array back to the JavaScript environment requires creating a new object to represent the array and adding each element to the array object.

The methods used to accomplish these tasks are described in the following table.

Function	Purpose
JS_ObjectType()	Return a description of a given JSObject.
JS_GetArrayLength()	Return the number of elements in an array.
JS_GetElement()	Retrieve an element from an array.
JS_SetElement()	Convert a Boolean value to a JavaScript value.
JS_NewArrayObject()	Create a new array object.

Retrieving Data from an Array

The steps required to retrieve elements from an array are relatively straight-forward. Typically, they follow this general order:

1. Convert the jsval that represents the array to a JSObject.

2. Ensure that the resulting JSObject is an array by checking its type.

3. Get the length of the array to determine how many elements are in it.

4. Iterate over the array using a loop, retrieving one element at a time.

5. Convert the element from a jsval to a C data type for processing.

The following code snippet shows how to retrieve data from an array:

```
void workWithArray(JSContext*cx, jsval arrayVal)
{
    JSObject *arrObj;
```

```
    // first convert the jsval to a JSObject
JS_ValueToObject(cx, arrayVal, &arrObj);

// now make sure that we have an Object of type "Array"
if (!strcmp(JS_ObjectType(arrObj),"Array"))
{
    // once we're sure we have an array, we can extract data
    // get the length of the array
    int length = JS_GetArrayLength(cx, arrObj);
    for (int k=0; k < length; k++)
    {
        // get the next element from the array
        jsval theVal;
        JS_GetElement(cx, arrObj, k, &theVal);

        // Do whatever you want with it...
    }
}
}
```

Adding Data to an Array

Adding data elements to an array for return to the JavaScript environment is
only marginally more difficult than retrieving elements from an array. The
general steps for adding elements to an array are as follows:

1. Create a new array object.

2. Convert each element you want to add to the array from a C data type
   to a jsval.

3. Add the element to the array.

4. Convert the array object to a jsval from a JSObject.

The following code snippet demonstrates how to add elements to a newly
created array and return the array to the calling function as a jsval:

```
jsval createNewArrayOfIntegers()
{
    JSObject arrObj;
    arrObj = JS_NewArrayObject(cx, 10, NULL);
    for (int k=0; k<10; k++)
    {
        // add each new element
        jsval theVal;
        theVal = JS_IntegerToValue(i);
        JS_SetElement(cx, arrObj, i, &theVal);
    }
    // convert the array to a jsval and return it
    return JS_ObjectToValue(arrObj);
}
```

TIP: There are two
ways to call
JS_NewArrayObject.
You can either pass an
array of jsval values
as the third parameter
to populate the array,
or you can pass NULL
as the third argument,
and manually place the
elements in the array
as we did in the
example. The first
method works well if
you already have an
array of jsvals built;
the second is better if
you create each new
jsval on the fly. Note
that the length of the
array must be specified
when it is created.

Executing JavaScript Code from within C

Sometimes it can be useful to execute JavaScript code from within your
C extensions. This is useful for several reasons; perhaps you have some
JavaScript code that you want to hide from the public, or you want to take
advantage of some built-in JavaScript functionality rather than rewrite it
yourself. A good example of this is using regular expressions. JavaScript
already has a good RegExp evaluation engine, so it's not necessary to try to
build your own. The only problem is that your C code can't directly take
advantage of this functionality; it is, after all, part of the JavaScript engine.
Fortunately, Dreamweaver provides a way to call JavaScript code from within
your C code just as if it were executing as a regular JavaScript extension.

The method you use to run JavaScript code from within your C extension is
called JS_ExecuteScript, which has this prototype:

```
JS_ExecuteScript(JSContext *cx, JSObject *obj, char *script,
unsigned int sz, jsval *rval);
```

The JSContext argument is the same one that is passed to your extension.
The JSObject argument represents the object whose scope the JavaScript
code will execute in. This object is equal to the value of the "this" keyword
while the script is running. It is usually the same as the one passed to your

extension, but as we'll see shortly it can be an object of your own creation. The `script` argument is a string representing the actual JavaScript code that you want to execute, and the `sz` argument is the length of the script string. The last argument, `rval`, is a pointer to a `jsval`. If the JavaScript code you are executing returns a value, it will be returned to your C code in this argument.

To use a practical example, take the scenario outlined earlier: You want to use a regular expression from within your C code, but you don't have a RegExp library that you can use. One possible solution would be to write your own RegExp implementation, but that would consume precious development time and would become a maintenance headache. It would also detract from the focus of your extension and make your code larger than it has to be. A far better solution would be to use the RegExp engine that is already built into JavaScript.

The following code snippet demonstrates how to do this:

```
function testRegExp(JSContext *cx, JSObject *obj, unsigned int
argc, jsval *argv, jsval *rval)
{
    // Define the JS code we want to execute. This is a simple
    // pattern replacement operation, which will replace the
    // word "name" with "moniker" in theStr.
    char *pTheJS = "var theStr=\"My name is Joe. Nice to meet
    you.\"; theStr.replace(/name/i,\"moniker\");";
    jsval retVal;
    unsigned int length;

    JS_ExecuteScript(cx, obj, pTheJS, strlen(pTheJS),&retVal);

    // Since the return value is a jsval, we can convert it
    // into a C data type that we can use ourselves.
    char *resultStr = JS_ValueToString(cx, retVal,&length);

    // Continue on processing the string. . .

    return JS_TRUE;
}
```

Executes JavaScript and returns jsval

Here, we are performing a simple string search-and-replace pattern using a regular expression. First, we build a string of JavaScript code to execute in Dreamweaver and store it in the variable `pTheJS`. In this example, the string is hard coded, but we could have built up a regular C string from any arguments that we were given as part of the function. The part of the JavaScript code string that reads `theStr.replace(/name/i,\"moniker\")` is a regular expression that basically means "Replace the first instance of 'name' with 'moniker', and don't worry about whether the word 'name' is uppercase or lowercase." The result of the call to the RegExp `replace()` function is a string that contains the results of the pattern substitution.

The call to `JS_ExecuteScript()` will run this JavaScript snippet inside Dreamweaver and return a result in the `retVal` argument. Because this argument is a `jsval` just like any other, we can convert it from a `jsval` to a string using `JS_ValueToString()`, and then continue processing it just as any other C string.

Working with Complex Objects

Another good example of executing JavaScript code in C is demonstrated by assigning arbitrary properties to generic JavaScript objects. For example, consider the following JavaScript code snippet:

```
function createNameObject()
{
    var theObject = new Object();
    theObject.firstName = "Joe";
    theObject.lastName = "Marini";
    return theObject;
}
```

This function creates a JavaScript object and assigns two properties to it: `firstName` and `lastName`. Unfortunately, you can't do this using the provided Dreamweaver C functions; you can only create arrays and insert elements by index.

To accomplish the same thing in C as shown in the preceding JavaScript code, you could write the following function:

```
function createNameObject(JSContext *cx, JSObject *obj, unsigned int
argc, jsval* jsArgv, jsval* rval)
{
char *pNewObject = "new Object();";
    char *pFirstName = "this.firstName = \"Joe\";";
    char *pLastName = "this.lastName = \"Marini\";";
    JSObject *jsObj;
    jsval objVal;

    // Call the JavaScript code to create a new object
    JS_ExecuteScript(cx,obj,pNewObject,strlen(pNewObject),&objVal);

    JS_ValueToObject(cx, objVal, &jsObj);                          Convert return value to
                                                                          JSObject

    // Now use the new JSObject pointer to set the firstName
    // and lastName properties
    JS_ExecuteScript(cx,jsObj, pFirstName,strlen(pFirstName),&objVal);
    JS_ExecuteScript(cx,jsObj, pLastName,strlen(pLastName),&objVal);

    *rval = JS_ObjectToValue(jsObj);                              Convert JSObject to jsval

    return JS_TRUE;
}
```

The first three lines are the JavaScript code that will create and set the properties of our new JavaScript object. They are hard-coded here for convenience of the example, but they could be built up from parameters just like any other C string.

The first call to JS_ExecuteScript() runs the code that actually creates a new object in the JavaScript environment and returns the created object to our C code.

Here's where we get tricky. We convert the return value to a JSObject, and then we use that JSObject as the subsequent JSObject parameter to the remaining JS_ExecuteScript() calls. This switches the scope of the current object to the one we just created, which means that all references to the "this" keyword in the JavaScript environment will operate on our new object. The next two calls to JS_ExecuteScript() call the JavaScript code that sets the properties of our newly created object using the "this" keyword.

Now all we need to do is convert the JSObject that we've been using back into a jsval, and we can return it to the JavaScript environment. There, the JavaScript developer can operate on it just like any other custom object. This is what the final call to JS_ObjectToValue() does.

Handling and Reporting Errors

At some point, it will be necessary to display one or more error messages to users of your extension. You could just return error codes from your extension and hope that developers will check for errors, but as we all know from experience, that rarely happens. Even if developers do in fact check for errors that come back from your extension, the chances that they will all coordinate among each other and display the same consistent error messages to the end user are slim to none.

To avoid this problem, Dreamweaver provides a way for C extensions to report execution errors that occur inside the C code to the end user in the same way that internal JavaScript engine errors are reported. This is accomplished by using the JS_ReportError() function, which has the following prototype:

```
JS_ReportError(JSContext *cx, char *error, size_t sz);
```

The first argument is the ubiquitous JSContext that is passed to all JSExtension methods that the JavaScript developer can call from JavaScript. The second argument is the error message to display. The third argument is the length of the string passed in the second argument. If you pass 0 for this argument, then the length of the null-terminated string in argument two is computed for you.

You don't have to worry about reporting what line number the error occurred on. Dreamweaver takes care of this for you automatically.

How would you use this function? Let's take a fresh look at our original example code listing for addTwoNumbers(), the function that takes two numbers and adds them together:

```
JSBool addTwoNumbers ( JSContext* cx, JSObject* obj, unsigned int
argc, jsval* jsArgv, jsval* rval )
{
int firstNumber;
int secondNumber;
int result;

// Get the arguments from JavaScript and convert them to C
// data types.
firstNumber = JS_ValueToInteger(cx, jsArgv[0]);
secondNumber = JS_ValueToInteger(cx, jsArgv[1]);

// Add them together
result = firstNumber + secondNumber;

    // Convert the result to a JavaScript value and return it
    *rval = JS_IntegerToValue( result );

    return JS_TRUE;
}
```

This code is making a couple of rather startling assumptions, starting with
the fact that it assumes two numbers are actually being passed to the
function. Because JavaScript is a loosely typed language, the interpreter
doesn't check to make sure that the function is actually receiving the same
number of arguments that it expects. In addition, the two arguments passed
might not even be numbers; they could be strings or objects.

To make this code more useful to JavaScript developers, we need to return
some customized error messages instead of just the generic "A JavaScript
error occurred" that you get for free with Dreamweaver. We need to let
developers know specifically what went wrong and what to do to fix it.
Consider the revised listing that follows:

```
JSBool addTwoNumbers ( JSContext* cx, JSObject* obj, unsigned int
argc, jsval* jsArgv, jsval* rval )
{
```

```
int firstNumber;
int secondNumber;
int result;

    // Check to see if two arguments were actually passed!
    if (argc < 2)
    {
        JS_ReportError(cx, "Wrong number of arguments passed to
        addTwoNumbers!", 0);
        return JS_FALSE; // return false in case of error
    }


// Get the arguments from JavaScript and convert them to C
// data types.
if (!JS_ValueToInteger(cx, jsArgv[0], &firstNumber))
{
        JS_ReportError(cx, "First argument isn't a number!", 0);
        return JS_FALSE; // return false in case of error
}
if (!JS_ValueToInteger(cx, jsArgv[1], &secondNumber))
{
        JS_ReportError(cx, "Second argument isn't a number!", 0);
        return JS_FALSE; // return false in case of error
}


// Add them together
result = firstNumber + secondNumber;

    // Convert the result to a JavaScript value and return it
    *rval = JS_IntegerToValue( result );

    return JS_TRUE;
}
```

In this improved version of the function, we alert the JavaScript developer to two different types of problems. The first is that the function doesn't have enough arguments to work correctly. This error is handled by the code that checks the value of `argc` to see how many arguments were passed in. If fewer than two arguments were supplied, the function reports the error and returns. (Note: The function doesn't check for exactly two arguments because in the case that more than two were supplied, the function just uses the first two.)

The second type of error is handled by the code that checks the return values of the calls to `JS_ValueToInteger`, which returns false when the given argument cannot be converted to a number (that is, the user passed "abc").

Now, our function proceeds to add two numbers only if it was in fact given at least two valid numbers to add together, and reports accurate and descriptive errors if not.

TIP: When creating your own error messages, it's a good idea to store them in string resources so they are easily localizable.

Example: The DWClipboard JSExtension

In this section, we will create a working JSExtension that can place text onto and receive text from the system Clipboard. This allows JavaScript developers direct access to the Clipboard to see what kind of information is available.

Our extension will have three functions that JavaScript developers can call: `setClipboardContent`, `getClipboardContent`, and `getClipboardContentSize`.

- `setClipboardContent()`
  - Inserts a string of text into the Clipboard

- `getClipboardContent()`
  - Retrieves the contents of the Clipboard

- `getClipboardContentSize()`
  - Returns the number of characters on the Clipboard

NOTE: The following example uses the Windows and Macintosh API functions to access each system's Clipboard. For more information on these functions, you should consult the documentation for your particular development environment.

In addition, both the Mac and Windows source code will be in the same file. We will make sure that the correct code is compiled for the correct platform by using standard C conditional compilation directives.

Setting Up the Project

Create a new extension project for your particular platform by following the directions at the start of the chapter. Name your extension project DWClipboard. Create a new text file named DWClipboard.cpp and add it to your extension project.

After this is done, you can begin writing the extension code.

NOTE: To view the completed code, see Listing 10-2 at the end of this section.

Including the Header Files and Definitions

First, we need to include the necessary header files and define the function prototypes that will be used in the extension:

```
#ifdef _WIN32    // Windows
#include "windows.h"
#else              // Mac
#define _MAC 1
#define HANDLE Handle
#include <Memory.h>
#include <Scrap.h>
#endif

#ifdef __cplusplus
extern "C" {
#endif
#include "mm_jsapi.h"
#ifdef __cplusplus
}
#endif

// Define the forward function prototypes
JSBool
setClipboardContent( JSContext* cx, JSObject* obj, unsigned int
argc, jsval* jsArgv, jsval* rval );

JSBool
getClipboardContent( JSContext* cx, JSObject* obj, unsigned int
argc, jsval* jsArgv, jsval* rval );

JSBool
getClipboardContentSize( JSContext* cx, JSObject* obj, unsigned
int  argc, jsval* jsArgv, jsval* rval );

void MM_Init( void );
```

The first few lines include any necessary platform-specific header files needed by the extension to call the OS API functions to access the Clipboard. In addition, for coding convenience, we define a HANDLE macro on the Macintosh to represent the Mac-specific Handle type. This simplifies things later on in the code for OS functions that accept handles to memory blocks; we don't need to write specific code for each platform just to define two different memory handle variables.

We also define forward function prototypes for the functions that the extension will use. These are not absolutely required by most compilers, but it is usually a good idea to include them.

Writing the Initialization Code

The next step is to write the initialization code for the extension. Here is where the MM_STATE declaration can be found, as well as the code for the MM_Init() function that will define the three functions that are available in the JavaScript environment:

```
MM_STATE

void
MM_Init( void )
{
    JS_DefineFunction("setClipboardContent", setClipboardContent, 1 );
    JS_DefineFunction("getClipboardContent", getClipboardContent, 0 );
    JS_DefineFunction("getClipboardContentSize",
getClipboardContentSize, 0);
}
```

Setting the Clipboard Content

The JavaScript developer calls the setClipboardContent() function to place a string of text onto the Clipboard.

```
JSBool setClipboardContent( JSContext* cx, JSObject* obj, unsigned
int  argc, jsval* jsArgv, jsval* rval )
{
```

```
            char *clipText;
            unsigned int clipTextLen;
            HANDLE hMem;

            // Get the first argument
            clipText = JS_ValueToString(cx, jsArgv[0], &clipTextLen);
    if ( clipText == NULL) {
            *rval = JS_IntegerToValue( 0 );
            return JS_TRUE;
        }

#ifdef _WIN32
    LPVOID pText;

        if (::OpenClipboard(NULL))
        {
            ::EmptyClipboard();

            // Create the memory handle
            hMem = ::GlobalAlloc( GMEM_MOVEABLE + GMEM_DDESHARE +
            GMEM_ZEROINIT, clipTextLen);
            pText = ::GlobalLock(hMem);

            memcpy(pText,clipText,(size_t)clipTextLen);
            ::GlobalUnlock(hMem);

            // Set the clipboard contents
            ::SetClipboardData(CF_TEXT, hMem);

            ::CloseClipboard();
            *rval = JS_IntegerToValue( 1 );
        }
        *rval = JS_IntegerToValue( 0 );
#else
    ::ZeroScrap();
    ::PutScrap(clipTextLen,'TEXT',clipText);
```

```
    *rval = JS_IntegerToValue( 1 );
#endif
    return JS_TRUE;
}
```

The function first attempts to convert the first argument to a string. If it fails and `clipText` is equal to `NULL`, the function returns a result of `0` to the JavaScript environment but does not report an error.

The next line, `#ifdef _WIN32`, uses a "conditional compiler" flag to compile code only if the symbol `_WIN32` is defined. Most compilers define these kinds of symbols automatically for you so that your code can compile differently under different platforms and compilers. Here, the Microsoft Visual C++ compiler defines this symbol if compiling on Windows. If this symbol is not defined, the code that is contained in the `#else` section of the conditional block is compiled instead. This is how you can compile code for more than one platform in your extensions.

The Windows code calls the `OpenClipboard()` function to gain access to the Clipboard. If the function returns `TRUE`, then the `EmptyClipboard()` function is called to clear the Clipboard of its current contents.

Next, a Windows construct called a "memory handle" is allocated from the system to hold the text that will be placed on the Clipboard. (The Windows Clipboard API expects the contents to be stored in a `memory handle`.)

The extension places the text on the Clipboard by calling `SetClipboardData()` and then cleans up by calling `CloseClipboard()`. The function then returns a non-zero value to the JavaScript environment to indicate that the function completed successfully.

The Mac code is much simpler in this case. First, the function `ZeroScrap()` is called to clear the current Clipboard contents, and then `PutScrap()` is called to set the Clipboard to the supplied text string. (The Mac uses the term "Scrap" because the original name for the Clipboard was the ScrapBook.)

Getting the Clipboard Content

Getting the Clipboard content is essentially the reverse of setting the Clipboard content.

```
JSBool getClipboardContent( JSContext* cx, JSObject* obj, unsigned
int  argc, jsval* jsArgv, jsval* rval )
{
    HANDLE hMem;
    char *pText = NULL;
    unsigned int iTextSize = 0;

#ifdef _WIN32
    // get the clipboard text if there is any
    if (::OpenClipboard(NULL))
    {
        if (::IsClipboardFormatAvailable(CF_TEXT))
        {
            // get the string data
            hMem = ::GetClipboardData(CF_TEXT);
            pText = (char *)::GlobalLock(hMem);
            iTextSize = strlen((const char *)pText);
            JS_StringToValue(cx,pText,iTextSize,rval);
            ::GlobalUnlock(hMem);
        }
        else
            *rval = (jsval)NULL;

        ::CloseClipboard();
    }
    else
        *rval = (jsval)NULL;
#else
    long offset;

    iTextSize = ::GetScrap(NULL, 'TEXT', &offset);
    hMem = NewHandleClear(iTextSize);
```

```
    ::GetScrap(hMem, 'TEXT', &offset);
    HLock(hMem);
    JS_StringToValue( cx, *hMem, iTextSize, rval );
    HUnlock(hMem);
    DisposeHandle(hMem);
#endif
    return JS_TRUE;
}
```

The Windows part of the code starts by calling OpenClipboard(), and then checks to see if the Clipboard contains any text by calling IsClipboardFormatAvailable(). This is an important check because the system Clipboard can contain text, images, or other custom data that applications store there.

If the Clipboard contains text, then it is retrieved by a call to GetClipboardData(). This returns a Windows memory handle, which stores the string. The string is then converted to a JavaScript value by calling JS_StringToValue().

The Mac part of the code is more complex than the previous function, although simpler than the Windows code. The steps of determining whether text data is available and what its length is are combined in the call to GetScrap().

The first call to GetScrap() passes a NULL value for the first argument, which essentially means "Just tell me the length of whatever is there, but don't retrieve it yet." After the length has been retrieved, a Mac memory handle is created to hold the returned text. This time, the call to GetScrap() passes this memory handle as the first argument, which causes the Mac to store the string that represents the Clipboard contents in the handle.

The resulting string is then converted to a JavaScript value via JS_StringToValue() and returned to the caller.

Getting the Clipboard Content Length

In our last function, we retrieve the length of the text on the Clipboard.

```
JSBool getClipboardContentSize( JSContext* cx, JSObject* obj,
unsigned int  argc, jsval* jsArgv, jsval* rval )
{
    HANDLE hMem;
    char *pText;
    unsigned int iTextSize = -1;


#ifdef _WIN32
    if (::OpenClipboard(NULL))
    {
        if (::IsClipboardFormatAvailable(CF_TEXT))
        {
            // get the string data
            hMem = ::GetClipboardData(CF_TEXT);
            pText = (char *)::GlobalLock(hMem);
            iTextSize = strlen((const char *)pText);
            ::GlobalUnlock(hMem);
        }

        ::CloseClipboard();
    }
#else
    long offset;

    iTextSize = ::GetScrap(NULL, 'TEXT', &offset);
#endif

    *rval = JS_IntegerToValue(iTextSize);


    return JS_TRUE;
}
```

The Windows code opens the Clipboard by calling `OpenClipboard()` and then checks to see if text data is available. This check is necessary because the system Clipboard can contain text, pictures, and other custom data types that applications store there.

If textual data is on the Clipboard, it is retrieved by calling `GetClipboardData()`, which returns a memory handle that references the text string. The length of the string is calculated using the standard C function `strlen()`, and the result is converted to a JavaScript value before being returned to the caller.

Again, the Mac code is much simpler because the steps of determining whether text data is available and, if so, its length are combined by the call to `GetScrap()`.

Testing the Extension

The following is a simple command that can be used to test the DWClipboard extension. The command exercises the three API functions that have been exposed to the JavaScript environment by setting and retrieving the contents of the Clipboard. To use this command, save it in the Commands folder and restart Dreamweaver.

The command first retrieves the current contents of the Clipboard and displays it in an alert box. Next, the command copies a new string to the Clipboard, retrieves the size of the new string, and displays it in an alert box. Finally, the command retrieves the new string from the Clipboard and displays it.

```
<html>
<head>
<title>Test DWClipboard</title>
<script>
function test()
{
    alert("Current Clip Content");
    alert(DWClipboard.getClipboardContent());
    alert("Copying 'Hello World' to clipboard...");
    DWClipboard.setClipboardContent("Hello World");
```

```
        alert("Getting the clip size...");
        alert(DWClipboard.getClipboardContentSize());
        alert("Getting the clip content...");
        alert(DWClipboard.getClipboardContent());
    }
</script>

</head>
<body onLoad="test()">
</body>
</html>
```

Listing 10-2   **DWClipboard.cpp** (10_dwclipboard.cpp)

```
#ifdef _WIN32    // Windows
#include "windows.h"
#else             // Mac
#define _MAC 1
#define HANDLE Handle
#include <Memory.h>
#include <Scrap.h>
#endif

#ifdef __cplusplus
extern "C" {
#endif
#include "mm_jsapi.h"
#ifdef __cplusplus
}
#endif

// Define the forward function prototypes
JSBool
setClipboardContent( JSContext* cx, JSObject* obj, unsigned int
argc, jsval* jsArgv, jsval* rval );
```

```
JSBool
getClipboardContent( JSContext* cx, JSObject* obj, unsigned int
argc, jsval* jsArgv, jsval* rval );

JSBool
getClipboardContentSize( JSContext* cx, JSObject* obj, unsigned int
argc, jsval* jsArgv, jsval* rval );

void MM_Init( void );

MM_STATE

void
MM_Init( void )
{
    JS_DefineFunction("setClipboardContent", setClipboardContent, 1 );
    JS_DefineFunction("getClipboardContent", getClipboardContent, 0 );
    JS_DefineFunction("getClipboardContentSize", getClipboardContentSize, 0);
}

JSBool setClipboardContent( JSContext* cx, JSObject* obj, unsigned
int  argc, jsval* jsArgv, jsval* rval )
{
    char *clipText;
    unsigned int clipTextLen;
    HANDLE hMem;

    // Get the first argument
    clipText = JS_ValueToString(cx, jsArgv[0], &clipTextLen);
if ( clipText == NULL) {
        *rval = JS_IntegerToValue( 0 );
        return JS_TRUE;
    }
```

continues

```
#ifdef _WIN32
    LPVOID pText;

    if (::OpenClipboard(NULL))
    {
        ::EmptyClipboard();

        // Create the memory handle
        hMem = ::GlobalAlloc( GMEM_MOVEABLE + GMEM_DDESHARE +
        GMEM_ZEROINIT, clipTextLen);
        pText = ::GlobalLock(hMem);

        memcpy(pText,clipText,(size_t)clipTextLen);
        ::GlobalUnlock(hMem);

        // Set the clipboard contents
        ::SetClipboardData(CF_TEXT, hMem);

        ::CloseClipboard();
        *rval = JS_IntegerToValue( 1 );
    }
    *rval = JS_IntegerToValue( 0 );
#else
    ::ZeroScrap();
    ::PutScrap(clipTextLen,'TEXT',clipText);

    *rval = JS_IntegerToValue( 1 );
#endif
    return JS_TRUE;
}


JSBool getClipboardContent( JSContext* cx, JSObject* obj, unsigned
int  argc, jsval* jsArgv, jsval* rval )
{
    HANDLE hMem;
    char *pText = NULL;
    unsigned int iTextSize = 0;
```

```
#ifdef _WIN32
    // get the clipboard text if there is any
    if (::OpenClipboard(NULL))
    {
        if (::IsClipboardFormatAvailable(CF_TEXT))
        {
            // get the string data
            hMem = ::GetClipboardData(CF_TEXT);
            pText = (char *)::GlobalLock(hMem);
            iTextSize = strlen((const char *)pText);
            JS_StringToValue(cx,pText,iTextSize,rval);
            ::GlobalUnlock(hMem);
        }
        else
            *rval = (jsval)NULL;

        ::CloseClipboard();
    }
    else
        *rval = (jsval)NULL;
#else
    long offset;

    iTextSize = ::GetScrap(NULL, 'TEXT', &offset);
    hMem = NewHandleClear(iTextSize);
    ::GetScrap(hMem, 'TEXT', &offset);
    HLock(hMem);
    JS_StringToValue( cx, *hMem, iTextSize, rval );
    HUnlock(hMem);
    DisposeHandle(hMem);
#endif
    return JS_TRUE;
}


JSBool getClipboardContentSize( JSContext* cx, JSObject* obj,
unsigned int  argc, jsval* jsArgv, jsval* rval )
```

continues

```
    {
        HANDLE hMem;
        char *pText;
        unsigned int iTextSize = -1;

#ifdef _WIN32
        if (::OpenClipboard(NULL))
        {
            if (::IsClipboardFormatAvailable(CF_TEXT))
            {
                // get the string data
                hMem = ::GetClipboardData(CF_TEXT);
                pText = (char *)::GlobalLock(hMem);
                iTextSize = strlen((const char *)pText);
                ::GlobalUnlock(hMem);
            }

            ::CloseClipboard();
        }
#else
        long offset;

        iTextSize = ::GetScrap(NULL, 'TEXT', &offset);
#endif

        *rval = JS_IntegerToValue(iTextSize);

        return JS_TRUE;
    }
```

Index

U-V

W

VOICES THAT MATTER

HOW TO CONTACT US

VISIT OUR WEB SITE

WWW.NEWRIDERS.COM

On our web site, you'll find information about our other books, authors, tables of contents, and book errata. You will also find information about book registration and how to purchase our books, both domestically and internationally.

EMAIL US

Contact us at: **nrfeedback@newriders.com**

- If you have comments or questions about this book
- To report errors that you have found in this book
- If you have a book proposal to submit or are interested in writing for New Riders
- If you are an expert in a computer topic or technology and are interested in being a technical editor who reviews manuscripts for technical accuracy

Contact us at: **nreducation@newriders.com**

- If you are an instructor from an educational institution who wants to preview New Riders books for classroom use. Email should include your name, title, school, department, address, phone number, office days/hours, text in use, and enrollment, along with your request for desk/examination copies and/or additional information.

Contact us at: **nrmedia@newriders.com**

- If you are a member of the media who is interested in reviewing copies of New Riders books. Send your name, mailing address, and email address, along with the name of the publication or web site you work for.

BULK PURCHASES/CORPORATE SALES

The publisher offers discounts on this book when ordered in quantity for bulk purchases and special sales. For sales within the U.S., please contact: Corporate and Government Sales (800) 382-3419 or **corpsales@pearsontechgroup.com**. Outside of the U.S., please contact: International Sales (317) 581-3793 or **international@pearsontechgroup.com**.

WRITE TO US

New Riders Publishing
201 W. 103rd St.
Indianapolis, IN 46290-1097

CALL/FAX US

Toll-free (800) 571-5840
If outside U.S. (317) 581-3500
Ask for New Riders
FAX: (317) 581-4663

New Riders

WWW.NEWRIDERS.COM

VIEW CART

search ⊙

› Registration already a member? Log in. › Book Registration

Publishing
the Voices
that Matter

OUR AUTHORS

PRESS ROOM

| web development | design | photoshop | new media | 3-D | server technologies |

EDUCATORS

ABOUT US

CONTACT US

You already know that New Riders brings you the **Voices That Matter**.

But what does that mean? It means that New Riders brings you the

Voices that challenge your assumptions, take your talents to the next

level, or simply help you better understand the complex technical world

we're all navigating.

Visit **www.newriders.com** to find:

▶ **10% discount** and **free shipping** on all book purchases

▶ Never before published chapters

▶ Sample chapters and excerpts

▶ Author bios and interviews

▶ Contests and enter-to-wins

▶ Up-to-date industry event information

▶ Book reviews

▶ Special offers from our friends and partners

▶ Info on how to join our User Group program

▶ Ways to have your Voice heard

New
Riders

WWW.NEWRIDERS.COM

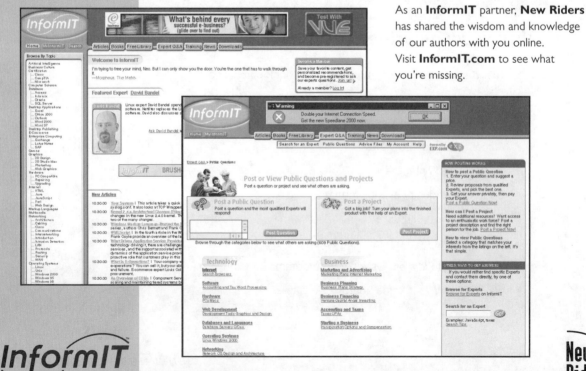

Colophon

This book was written and edited in Microsoft Word, and laid out in Quark XPress. The font used for the body text is Caslon and Mono. It was printed on 50# Husky Offset Smooth paper at Von Hoffmann Inc. in Owensville, Missouri. Prepress consisted of PostScript computer-to-plate technology (filmless process). The cover was printed at Moore Langen Printing in Terre Haute, Indiana, on 12 pt., coated on one side.